Veronika Bernard, Hatice Övgü Tüzün (Eds.)

IMAGES (III)
Images of the City

ETHNOLOGIE
ANTHROPOLOGY

Band / Volume 57

LIT

I M A G E S (III)
Images of the City

The Conference Proceedings

edited by

Veronika Bernard and Hatice Övgü Tüzün

LIT

Veronika Bernard | Department for German Language and Literature, University of Innsbruck; Innsbruck, Austria | Research Platform CEnT ("Cultural Encounters and Transfers") | Research Centre "KiK / Cultures in Contact"

Hatice Övgü Tüzün | Department of American Culture and Literature, Bahçeşehir University, Istanbul, Turkey

This publication is supported by: Federal Government of Tyrol; University of Innsbruck, Vice-Rectorate for Research; University of Innsbruck, Research Area Cultural Encounters – Cultural Conflicts

Gefördert von

Bibliographic information published by the Deutsche Nationalbibliothek
The Deutsche Nationalbibliothek lists this publication in the Deutsche Nationalbibliografie; detailed bibliographic data are available in the Internet at http://dnb.d-nb.de.

ISBN 978-3-643-90511-6

A catalogue record for this book is available from the British Library

©LIT VERLAG GmbH & Co. KG Wien,
Zweigniederlassung Zürich 2014
Klosbachstr. 107
CH-8032 Zürich
Tel. +41 (0) 44-251 75 05
Fax +41 (0) 44-251 75 06
E-Mail: zuerich@lit-verlag.ch
http://www.lit-verlag.ch

LIT VERLAG Dr. W. Hopf
Berlin 2014
Fresnostr. 2
D-48159 Münster
Tel. +49 (0) 2 51-62 03 20
Fax +49 (0) 2 51-23 19 72
E-Mail: lit@lit-verlag.de
http://www.lit-verlag.de

Distribution:

In the UK: Global Book Marketing, e-mail: mo@centralbooks.com
In North America: International Specialized Book Services, e-mail: orders@isbs.com
In Germany: LIT Verlag Fresnostr. 2, D-48159 Münster
Tel. +49 (0) 2 51-620 32 22, Fax +49 (0) 2 51-922 60 99, E-mail: vertrieb@lit-verlag.de

In Austria: Medienlogistik Pichler-ÖBZ, e-mail: mlo@medien-logistik.at
e-books are available at www.litwebshop.de

EDITORS' NOTE

When we closed our conference "IMAGES (III) – Images of the City" at the Austrian Cultural Forum in Istanbul on November 1, 2013, we were at the end of two highly intense days of plenary sessions in which we had been able to bring together thirty speakers from Canada, the UK, Portugal, Belgium, France, Algeria, Switzerland, Italy, The Netherlands, the Czech Republic, Poland, Turkey, Iran, and Austria. Their presentations made a well-balanced programme, which was very much appreciated by the audience and motivated lively discussions and so made our conference a success. Another ten speakers, unfortunately, had cancelled within the last month before the conference; we regretted this very much.

What added to the positive and fruitful atmosphere at the conference even more was the fact that Vienna based LIT Verlag, like with the previous IMAGES conference (Images of the Poor, Istanbul 2012), had already shown thorough interest in publishing the conference proceedings in advance of the conference.

Finally, a high percentage of speakers decided to submit articles to this volume of conference proceedings. The jury selected nineteen of these articles to be included. We would like to take the opportunity to thank all who submitted articles for their discipline and cooperation in producing this book.

We would further like to take the opportunity to thank Doris Danler and Peter Waas, director and deputy director of the Austrian Cultural Forum Istanbul, for their assistance in organizing and implementing our conference, and LIT Verlag's Richard Kisling and Corinna Ladurner for their kind support of our publication project.

Veronika Bernard and Hatice Övgü Tüzün

INHALT

Editors' Note 5

Introductory Section 11

Veronika Bernard (Innsbruck and Kufstein/ Austria): The IMAGES project 13

Veronika Bernard (Innsbruck and Kufstein/ Austria): Introduction 17

The Relativity of Urbanity 23

Nicolas Marqué (Toulouse/ France): "Putting the Town outside the Town" – Redefining Urbanity 25

Nerma Cridge (London/ UK): Else Where :: Every Where 37

Veronika Bernard (Innsbruck and Kufstein/ Austria): Thinking Society – Fictional Cities as Products and Generating Forces in Shaping Society 49

Cityscapes as Statements 61

Peter Volgger (Innsbruck/ Austria): The Sleeping Beauty – Imaging the City in the Context of Neo-Colonialism 63

Mladen Stilinovic (Brussels/ Belgium): The Militarised Images of the City 73

Shaida Ghomashchi (Tehran/ Iran)/ Farzaneh Bahrami (Lausanne/ Switzerland): Horror Vacui 83

The Psychology of the City/ Urbanity as an Issue of a Developed Civil Society 91

Nilüfer Nahya (Kayseri/ Turkey)/ Fulya Anılır (Istanbul/ Turkey): The Nature and the City – The Picture of Nature in Istanbul 93

Magdalena Łukasiuk (Warsaw/ Poland): The Image of Contemporary Warsaw in the Context of Architecture and Local Discourse 103

Giovanni Comoglio (Turin/ Italy): Metamorphosis and Multiplication of an *Imaginaire* 113

Sandra C. S. Marques (Lisbon/ Portugal): Kolkatascapes: Images of an Indian City 125

Images of the City/ Urbanity in Literature 137

Hatice Övgü Tüzün (Istanbul/ Turkey): Celebrating Multiculturalism: London in Zadie Smith's *White Teeth* 139

Gönül Bakay (Istanbul/ Turkey): The Industrial City in Charles Dickens' *Hard Times* and Elizabeth Gaskell's *Mary Barton* 147

Burcu Alkan (Istanbul/ Turkey): Writing Istanbul: A Diachronic Narrative 157

Lisa Maria Teichmann (Leiden/ The Netherlands): Reflecting on Istanbul in Turkish Literature – A Comparative Approach to the Issue of Urban Change 167

Souad Baghli Berbar (Tlemcen/ Algeria): From Reality to Myth – the City of Alexandria in Lawrence Durrell's *Justine* (1957) 175

Images of the City/ Urbanity in Feature Films 185

Massimiliano Gaudiosi (Naples/ Italy): Film as a Map: Cinema, City and Spatial Practices 187

The Impact of the Arts and the Media on the Perception of Urbanity 195

Anna Notaro (Dundee/ UK): The Magic Line in Matteo Pericoli's *Unfurled Cities* 197

Daniele Campobenedetto (Paris/ France and Turin/ Italy): The Satirical Line. The Image of the City in the *New Yorker's* Cartoon 1968 – 1978 209

Jakub Machek (Prague/ Czech Republic): New Metropolitans and their Popular Press in *Fin de siècle* Prague 219

Nicole De Togni (Turin, Turin/ Italy): When Architecture Was the World 229

Rear Matter 237

The Editors 239

The Contributors 241

Introductory Section

THE IMAGES PROJECT (WWW.IMAGES-1.OVER-BLOG.ORG)

The IMAGES project (www.images-1.over-blog.org) has been planned and scheduled as a series of conferences, publications, exhibitions and online photo contests for the years 2011-2014. It has been initiated by the research centre Cultures in Contact (Kulturen im Kontakt/ KiK), which is part of the humanities research platform CEnT (Cultural Encounters and Transfers) and the research area Cultural Encounters – Cultural Conflicts (Kulturelle Begegnungen – Kulturelle Konflikte), all based at Leopold-Franzens-University in Innsbruck/ Austria. Throughout the years 2011-2013 the senior project partner was Kadir Has University in Istanbul/ Turkey. The idea for the project has been developed by Associate Professor (Privatdozent) Dr. Veronika Bernard (University of Innsbruck) and Associate Professor Dr. Serhan Oksay (Kadir Has University until January 31, 2013).

IMAGES is an interdisciplinary project, and it strongly relies on the cooperation with international academic and non-academic partners.

IMAGES deals with the discourse of cultural encounters within the context of social co-existence. The project defines “discourse of cultural encounters” as the discourse within the context of cultural encounters, and as the discourse on cultural encounters. Within this scope, the project deals with both verbal and non-verbal communication and focuses on the thematic fields of cultural encounter, poverty, and migration.

IMAGES adopts a cultural studies definition of the term “culture”. Cultural studies define culture by the concept of the group, seeing culture as the sum of all features and ways of behaviour people show and adopt deliberately in order to become distinct from others and to form their specific identities.[1]

IMAGES further includes perspectives on cultural phenomena taken by communication studies. The project starts from the idea that the images you form (of you and of others) essentially determine relations and communication between both individuals and communities and at the same time are their results. Contemporary communication studies see images (as the images an individual holds of his or her own self and the images others form of you) as part of a communicative system formed of values, evaluation and selective perception. No matter which our values are, as a whole they build the very system by which we evaluate and judge the ways others act, look and speak in order to decide whether they fit in with our values. In case they do, there is the realistic chance of a positive and fruitful communicational process; in case they do not, communication may go wrong and end soon – in a comparatively unspectacular way by cutting communicational ties or in a rather dramatic way by leading into conflict.

Intercultural communication studies analyse these mechanisms with individuals from different cultures. From an intercultural perspective (intercultural) communication means that you open your own culture to ideas rooting in the other's culture by dropping own cultural ideas and including ideas rooting in the communication partner's culture. This is possible only, however, if cultures have a minimum amount of ideas in common. Intercultural communication aims at increasing the number of ideas cultures have in common; increasing their number makes the difference between success and failure in terms of intercultural communication. In case there are no ideas in common, intercultural communication will be impossible and the cultures involved will not be able to reach a better mutual understanding.[2]

Considering the communicative mechanism of selective perception, IMAGES understands cultural encounters and the ways they may take as circular patterns, and it sees itself as part of these circular patterns: the academic discourse on cultural encounters, poverty and migration, which is dealt with in the conference and publication series, is contrasted to the results originating from the scheduled online photo contests and being presented to the public in the exhibition series documenting the non-verbal everyday-life discourse. In this way IMAGES adds to the critical discussion on definitions of cultural encounters.

The IMAGES project opened with the online photo contest "Cultural Encounters" and "Images of the Poor" in January 2011. The IMAGES project exhibition series started with the joint exhibitions "Cultural Encounters" and "Images of the Poor" in April 2011; the exhibition opening taking place at Kadir Has University's Cibali Campus on 27 April 2011. The IMAGES project conference series opened with the IMAGES 2011 conference IMAGES – *Films as Spaces of Cultural Encounters* (Istanbul, Kadir Has University, 1-4 June 2011), which unfortunately had to be cancelled in short term.

However, the project directors have been able to offer registered participants the chance to publish their papers; the resulting volume of conference proceedings IMAGES (I) – *Films as Spaces of Cultural Encounters. The 2011 IMAGES Project Publication* opening the IMAGES publication series and being available online (http://cinej.pitt.edu) as a CINEJ special issue and as a select-articles print edition. Having applied the IMAGES project context to the conference topic, the CINEJ 2011 special issue IMAGES (I) – *Films as Spaces of Cultural Encounters* and the select-articles print edition include articles analysing films as spaces of cultural encounters from a cultural studies perspective in general, as well as from inter-cultural, multi-cultural, trans-cultural, semiotic, communication centred, historical, political, and all related perspectives.

The IMAGES project 2012 conference IMAGES (II) - *Images of the Poor* (5-7 September 2012, Austrian Cultural Forum Istanbul) continued the IMAGES conference series; its conference proceedings IMAGES (II) – *Images of the Poor. The Conference Proceedings* being the 2012 IMAGES project publication.

Co-edited by Veronika Bernard and Serhan Oksay and published by LIT Verlag, IMAGES (II) – *Images of the Poor* offers readers a cross-section of current research both on the perception of poverty and on contemporary and historical representations of poverty coming from a variety of fields in people's daily lives all of which are of vital relevancy in shaping the individual's view on the existence, the implications, the consequences, and the possible roots and causes of poverty.

The IMAGES project 2013 conference IMAGES (III) - *Images of the City* (31 October – 01 November 2013, Austrian Cultural Forum Istanbul) takes the IMAGES conference series another step further; its conference proceedings IMAGES (III) – *Images of the City. The Conference Proceedings* being the 2013 IMAGES project publication.

Veronika Bernard

NOTES

[1] For a critical discussion concerning definitions of the term "culture" in cultural studies see Klaus P. Hansen: Kultur und Kulturwissenschaft. Eine Einführung. Tübingen und Basel: A. Francke/ UTB ³2003.

[2] For theory and methodology of intercultural communication see Jean-René Ladmiral, Edmond Marc Lipiansky: Interkulturelle Kommunikation. Zur Dynamik mehrsprachiger Gruppen. Frankfurt a. Main: Campus 2000.

INTRODUCTION

After the conferences IMAGES (I) – *Films as Spaces of Cultural Encounters* (2011) and IMAGES (II) – *Images of the Poor* (2012), the IMAGES project focused on images of the city in its 2013 conference IMAGES (III) – *Images of the City*.

According to recent statistics, the world population reached the approximate number of 7.1 billion (milliard) people by the turn of 2013, and the United Nations estimate that by 2025 this number will have climbed to 8.17 billion (milliard). According to the Germany based *Stiftung Weltbevölkerung* presently about every second world citizen lives in an urban environment; this number is estimated to climb to a third of population worldwide by the year 2050.

On the other hand, statistics point out that the increase in urban population is mainly due to migration movements leading people from very diverse backgrounds into urban environments; most of them seeing the city as kind of a "safe haven" of any sort. As a consequence of these processes the urban environment is undergoing a constant development and change.

Within this context, the IMAGES project has decided to discuss the (historically) changing shaping, representation and perceptions of the city as a cultural concept (i. e. the changing images of the city) in its 2013 conference IMAGES (III) – *Images of the City*; the urban concept creating an unlimited number of potential cases of cultural encounters ranging from architectonical realisations of ideologically motivated views of the world to the development of certain representation practices of cityscapes in photography and the arts, and the (virtual) discussions of concepts and strategies conveyed through urban concepts in fiction; all providing the public with realisations of political, and related ideas of all sorts and thus linking the concept of urbanity to a whole range of socially relevant fields like politics, communication, culture, and migration.

Following this idea, the IMAGES (III) – *Images of the City* conference organisers and editors of this volume of conference proceedings opened several fields of research and interest for paper proposals when launching their Call for Papers in early 2014. In order to discuss issues like the above they invited scholars – both senior scholars and PhD students – in their Call for Papers, but also architects, photographers, writers, artists, and filmmakers to participate in a two days interdisciplinary international conference in order to present their research findings in 20 minutes (paper) presentations in the following fields of research and interest: the relative definition of urbanity; the psychology of feeling urban or/ and rural; cityscapes as statements; the impact of the media (news, internet, daily soaps) on the perception of urbanity/ urban life style; images of the city/ urbanity in feature films (present and past); images of the city/ urbanity in the arts (present and past); the city/ urbanity as seen by photographers (present and past); images of the city/ urbanity in literature (present and past); and images of the city/ urbanity as an issue of a developed civil society (including aspects like migration, social marginalization).

Finally, the conference organisers found the majority of paper proposals reaching them focusing on images of the city seen as statements. They also received a high number of proposals discussing urbanity as a developed society issue as well as proposals dealing with images of the city as represented in literature, feature films, the media, and the arts. Surprisingly enough, however, very similar to the 2012 IMAGES project conference IMAGES (II) – *Images of the Poor* also with the IMAGES (III) – *Images of the City* paper proposals almost completely neglected photography.

The paper proposals selected have finally enabled the conference organisers to put together a well-balanced conference programme, and consequently, the editors of this publication to present a well-balanced volume of conference proceedings; the thematic focuses of the articles setting the following six chapters structuring this volume: The Relativity of Urbanity; Cityscapes as Statements; The Psychology of the City/ Urbanity as an Issue of a Developed Civil Society; Images of the City/ Urbanity in Literature; Images of the City/ Urbanity in Feature Films; The Impact of the Arts and the Media on the Perception of Urbanity.

Like the conference IMAGES (III) – *Images of the City,* this volume of conference proceedings also follows the principle of bringing together works by senior scholars with those by PhD students and postdoctoral academics in an attempt to provide a genuinely democratic academic exchange of ideas.

The order of the chapters in this volume aims at enabling readers first to be introduced to the discussion focusing on the relativity of the urban concept; next, to (critically) evaluate cities' visual appearances as being formed in an attempt to represent (political and architectonical) statements; further, to understand the psychology of urbanity as an issue of a developed civil society; and finally, to (critically) follow recent research on the representation of the city as documented by the written word of literature, by the visual means applied in the current trends in the movie industry, and, last but not least, by the arts and the contemporary media.

The articles of chapter one (The Relativity of Urbanity) provide readers with different perspectives on the issue, introducing them to the realms of a universal discussion on the urban concept. Within this scope, the articles by Nicolas Marque ("'Putting the Town Outside the Town': Redefining Urbanity"), Nerma Cridge ("Else Where :: Every Where"), and Veronika Bernard ("Thinking Society – Fictional Cities as Products and Generating Forces in Shaping Society) discuss images of urbanity from the perspective of (historical) geography, urban architectural design, and the mutual impact of literature and society on each other. Nicolas Marqué takes readers to the (urban) history of Toulouse in his attempt to illustrate the historical change in the understanding of the term 'urbanity'. Nerma Cridges's article reflects on "the creation of images 'borrowed' from somewhere else or else where" and on "the production of images of grey concrete housing blocks, seemingly appearing everywhere"; placing both processes in the context of image production by copying, and discussing the issue primarily with reference to China and Australia. Veronika Bernard, finally, shows how thoroughly linked the concept of urbanity and the promotion of religious, social and political ideologies and ideas have been throughout European history when it comes to works of German, Austrian and Swiss fiction.

Chapter two (Cityscapes as Statements) includes articles by Peter Volgger ("The Sleeping Beauty – Imaging the City in the Context of Neo-Colonialism"), Mladen Stilinovic ("The Militarised Images of the City") and Shaida Ghomashchi and Farzaneh Bahrami ("Horror Vacui"); their articles all dealing with case studies of urban imagery shaped by ideology. While Peter Volgger reports on the findings of his WFW funded project dealing with the Italian style architectural heritage in the Eritrean 'World Heritage' candidate city of Asmara and puts the focus on the political use of this heritage; Mladen Stilinovic presents his research on "the spatial interactions between the military and civil society" in the cities of Skopje and Bitola, showing how "army-related images" have become "elements of the local palimpsests of urban and territorial narratives" and how "the current 'absence' of the military leads to new forms of (violent) spatial contest". Shaida Ghomashchi and Farzaneh Bahrami focus on the crane in their articles on Tehran cityscape and skyline, They understand the crane as a symbol both of an urban "over-densification" and as a "visual element" of a "multiple-faceted presence in the social-urban fabric of Tehran today", pointing out that "the article will take the 'Horror Vacui' [concept] beyond its conventional implication (in visual art) and exploit variant meanings of horror in this context".

Chapter three (The Psychology of the City/ Urbanity as an Issue of a Developed Civil Society) consists of Nilüfer Nahya's and Fulya Anılır's article

"The Nature and the City – The Picture of Nature in Istanbul", Magdalena Łukasiuk's article "The Image of Contemporary Warsaw in the Context of Architecture and Local Discourse", Giovanni Comoglio's article "Metamorphosis and Multiplication of an *Imaginaire*", and Sandra C. S. Marques' article "Kolkatascapes – Images of an Indian City". Nilüfer Nahya and Fulya Anılır present photography based observations on the relation between nature and city dwellers in some Istanbul districts, focusing on the "impact of industrialization and modernity in natural places". Magdalena Łukasiuk presents a "theoretical approach to analyzing the image of the city" based on a research conducted by her among migrants living in Warsaw. Giovanni Comoglio discusses "the shaping of an image for mutations in the urban habitat and the town-countryside distinction in contemporary Shanghai". Last but not least, Sandra C. S. Marques uses the findings of her FCT funded field study to reflect on tourist representations of Kolkata, arguing that the "ambiguity in Kolkata's public spaces is the causal factor of the great anxiety shown by foreigners in the appropriation and representation of this city".

Chapter four (Images of the City/ Urbanity in Literature) offers readers of this volume studies on the representation of urbanity and city life in works of literature coming from the Anglo-Saxon and Turkish world, stretching the scope from works of fiction to pieces of poetry. Hatice Övgü Tüzün ("Celebrating Multiculturalism – London in Zadie Smith's *White Teeth*") examines the portrayal of a polyphonic and multiethnic London in Zadie Smith's first novel, in which "identities are presented as hybrid and fluid and space(s) as continuously negotiated by those who inhabit them". Gönül Bakay ("The Industrial City in Charles Dickens' *Hard Times* and Elizabeth Gaskell's *Mary Barton*") aims at discussing the "function and scope of industrial novels" set in 19th century England. Burcu Alkan ("Writing Istanbul – A Diachronic Narrative") states and shows that Istanbul "transcends being a mere setting and pervades both the imaginations of the writers and their narratives" and has become "manifest as a construct of Romantic imagination" in both works of Ottoman poetry and in pieces of contemporary fiction. Lisa Maria Teichmann ("Reflecting on Istanbul in Turkish Literature – A Comparative Approach to the Issue of Urban Change") focuses on "representations of Turkish [urban] society in fiction". In doing so she compares a work written and published during the early Republican period (*Kiralık Konak* by Yakup Kadri Karaosmanoğlu) with a more recent piece of Turkish fiction (*Ayaşlı ile Kiracılar* by Memduh Şevket Esendal). Her special interest centres upon the representation of the apartment, which is understood as a particularly urban environment. Souad Baghli Berbar ("From Reality to Myth – the City of Alexandria in Lawrence Durrell's *Justine*") analyses the image of Alexandria in

Justine by "trying to trace the gradual transfiguration of the city from a convincingly realistic oriental place to a mythical feminine entity merging the eroticism of a Cleopatra with the mysticism of a Jewess".

Chapter five (Images of the City/ Urbanity in Feature Films) consists of Massimiliano Gaudiosi's article "Film as a Map – Cinema, City and Spatial Practices". By analysing several contemporary US movie productions the author shows how "in some contemporary movies the narrative creates a cartography crossing the screen borders", allowing a "reconfiguration of the city".

Chapter six (The Impact of the Arts and the Media on the Perception of Urbanity) again puts the focus on urban images within a both historical and contemporary context, with special reference to arts and media production. It includes articles written by Anna Notaro ("The Magic Line in Matteo Pericoli's *Unfurled Cities*"), Daniele Campobenedetto ("The Satirical Line. The Image of the City in the *New Yorker's* Cartoon 1968 – 1978"), Jakub Machek ("New Metropolitans and their Popular Press in *Fin de siècle* Prague"), and Nicole De Togni ("When Architecture Was the World"). Anna Notaro's article discusses *Manhattan Unfurled* (2001) and *London Unfurled* (2011) by architect/ illustrator Matteo Pericoli. Daniele Campobenedetto explores "how between 1968 and 1978 the *New Yorker's* cartoon was able to influence and at the same time to capture [the] view of the city". Jakub Machek's article is based on his Czech Science Foundation (GAČR) funded study on the influence of the "sensational pictorial press, its readers and their collective memory" in creating a "shared image" of Prague at the turn of the 20th century. Nicole De Togni explores the role of specialized magazines in theoretically and critically shaping the architectural discourse about Milan during the Nineteen-Fifties and -Sixties.

This volume thus offers readers a cross-section of current research both on the perception of urbanity and on contemporary and historical representations of the city coming from a variety of fields in people's daily lives. The fact that the contributors to this volume are from the UK, Portugal, Belgium, France, Algeria, Switzerland, Italy, The Netherlands, The Czech Republic, Poland, Iran, Turkey and Austria, and that they are writing from very different cultural, ideological, scientific and academic perspectives and backgrounds is adding even more to the diversity of thought and ideas documented. It is the editors' hope that the arguments presented in the contributors' articles will add to both academic discussion on and the social awareness of the special aspects of urban life.

Veronika Bernard

The Relativity of Urbanity

"PUTTING THE TOWN OUTSIDE THE TOWN" – REDEFINING URBANITY

Nicolas Lucien Marqué

University of Toulouse II, Toulouse/ France
nmarque@univ-tlse2.fr

ABSTRACT

What does the term 'urbanity' mean? Is it possible to define the term by a town's boundary? These questions are difficult to answer nowadays. Was it easier to find an answer when most European towns were still surrounded by large fortifications? When did the term 'urbanity' become so hard to define? This article aims at answering these questions by using the case study of Toulouse, a town in southern France. Its rich archives enable us to try and answer some of these questions.

Was bedeutet der Begriff 'Urbanität'? Ist es möglich, eine Stadt über ihre (Außen-)Grenzen zu definieren? Diese Fragen lassen sich heutzutage schwer beantworten. War es aber leichter sie zu beantworten, als die meisten europäischen Städte noch umfangreiche Befestigungsanlagen besaßen? Ab welchem Zeitpunkt wurde es so schwierig, den Stadt-Begriff zu definieren? Dieser Artikel versucht diese Fragen anhand der Fallstudie der Stadt Toulouse zu beantworten.

Introduction

During the eighteenth century, town fortifications provided not only physical but also conceptual security. While the material aspect became less relevant because of improvements in artillery, the walls were still the main element by which the dictionaries of the time defined the word 'town'. Giving a definition of the words 'town' or 'urban' was still quite easy: they were delimited by fortifications.

At the beginning of the nineteenth century, the role of fortifications had become less important and they had already been demolished in many towns. However, it also became much more complicated to provide a satisfying definition to the word 'urbanity': the town no longer had any tangible spatial boundaries. The inhabitants of the suburbs claimed that they lived in the city and should benefit from urban services, while the urban authorities thought the opposite, partly to save money.

During this century, the meaning of the word 'urbanity' changed considerably and became harder to define. Why did this happen, and what was the new meaning of 'urbanity' at the middle of the nineteenth century?

To answer these questions, I will focus on the case study of one of the largest French towns of the period, Toulouse. This city is well known today thanks to its archives, especially its land tax registers. I have used these registers to contribute to developing the G.I.S. urban-hist web database (http://www.urban-hist.toulouse.fr/urbanhistdiffusion/).

One of the main functions of this tool is to generate maps which help to study the changes over time in the concept of urbanity (see below). I argue that from a simple definition ("what is inside the fortifications") the concept of urbanity has changed and acquired multiple and overlapping definitions, including:

- A geographical definition based on the landscape.
- The inhabitants' conception of what 'urbanity' entailed: In the middle of the eighteenth century, many of Toulouse's inhabitants refused to live outside the fortifications because this space was "outside the town", according to them. Yet, fifty years later, these same families accepted the same proposition, revealing that the concept of urbanity had changed during the second half of the eighteenth century.
- An administrative definition: Local authorities provided many urban services and public equipment to some quarters and refused to give the same services and equipment to other places that the politicians considered to be outside the town.
- A fiscal definition: Merchants had to pay a special tax when they brought merchandise inside the town. The authorities chose to modify the fiscal boundaries three times between the beginning of the eighteenth century and 1830. How did they manage to explain these redefinitions of the town's fiscal boundaries?
- A learned definition by the Academy (given mainly by dictionaries of the time): The definition of the word 'town' also changed during the same period; fortifications were mentioned less frequently and the urban landscape and activities within it became increasingly important.

When did these multiple definitions replace the previous definition based on walls? What were the consequences for the administrative management of the town? This article answers these questions in three sections, using the example of Toulouse:

- Until the middle of the eighteenth century, the word 'urbanity' was still easy to define thanks to the large number of fortifications.
- From the middle of the eighteenth century to the beginning of the nineteenth century, the meaning of the word 'urbanity' was harder to pin down because the simple presence of fortifications was no longer sufficient to define a town.
- During the first half of the nineteenth century, fortifications were demolished, both as a physical and as a conceptual barrier. The authorities and the inhabitants of the town had to rely on new criteria for defining urbanity.

Material and Conceptual Security: Fortifications as the Main Definition of Urbanity

A Learned Definition of Urbanity Based on Fortifications

Before 1750, fortifications were always the main element mentioned in French dictionaries to define the word "town". In 1679, Richelet writes that the town is a "[p]lace full of houses and closed by walls and moats"[1], while Furetiere speaks about a "[s]um of houses and streets closed by a common fence, which is usually made of walls and moats" in 1690[2]. These definitions exactly follow the dictionary of the French Academy printed in 1694[3]. This shows that, among learned men, the number of buildings and of inhabitants were not yet important for defining a town.

Maps of Toulouse from this period also show the imposing size of the fortifications. Before the nineteenth century, the walls always appear to be very high and difficult to demolish, yet the reality was quite different and the fortifications were already ruined in many places. Moreover, authors of these maps rarely depicted the suburbs. For example, the *Description de la [...] ville de Toulouse [...]*, by Boisseau in 1645 depicts only few houses outside the fortifications, although the suburbs of the town were already quite large at that time.[4] Why did he not draw this part of Toulouse? His purpose was to describe the town, which was the space delimited by the fortifications. The suburbs were not yet part of the city of Toulouse, even though many people lived there.

Map n°1- Description of the [...] town of Toulouse, by Boisseau. Boisseau, I.: Description de la [...] ville de Toulouse [...]/ Town of Toulouse - Local Archives of Toulouse, II 674

Contemporary paintings also insist on the role of the wall. When Antoine Rivals was asked in 1727 to represent the *Expulsion des Huguenots de Toulouse [...] en 1562,*[5] he chose to paint the wall of the town and the Huguenots at the very moment they were forced to flee from inside the fortifications. We know that there were already some suburbs outside this part of the wall; however, this was not important for the painter who only wished to depict the expulsion from the city, which meant the expulsion from the area within its walls.

Although the fortifications were still important in more official representations of the town, we have to ask if this boundary was also important for the town's inhabitants.

Local Definition of the Town

Even though the wall was partially ruined in the eighteenth century, it was still easy to see: nine meters high and built almost entirely of brick (which the inhabitants of the suburbs were stealing in order to build their own houses[6]). The old towers were also still there, but their function was no longer defensive. In 1686, for example, one of them had become a candle workshop.

Although the walls' military function was less important, these fortifications were still one of the main symbols of the city and also served as a fiscal boundary. Merchants had to pay a special tax when they brought goods inside the town. They did not have to pay this tax when they entered the suburbs; it only had to be paid when they wished to cross the perimeter of the fortifications. This situation had two advantages: it was easier to collect the tax, and the fiscal definition of the town was easily visible.

Even though the wall was partly ruined and thus ineffective for providing military security, it still provided a sort of mental barrier, in that people were reluctant to build their houses outside the walls as it was considered beneath their social rank. The landscape of some suburbs was already urban in the middle of the eighteenth century, but they were still not considered part of the city even though 7,500 people were already living there in 1695.[7]

Moreover, these suburbs were very difficult to define. Even at the end of the century, while the dictionaries of the time usually provide precise definitions for other words, the suburbs had such a negative image in Toulouse as elsewhere that they were simply given a short description. Feraud's dictionary merely mentioned some "[h]ouses located outside a town's fortifications"[8], which is quite vague.

The fortifications were still Toulouse's only boundary until the middle of the eighteenth century. They were still the main element in defining 'urbanity' after this period, but other criteria became increasingly important.

Redefining Urbanity: Before the Fall of the Fortifications

Creating a New Quarter outside the Fortifications (1752) and its Failure

In 1752, Louis de Mondran proposed creating a public walkway outside the fortifications and building a new quarter around it. According to him, this would create both a recreational space and would develop the city. This walkway was quickly created, but apparently few people wanted to live near it.

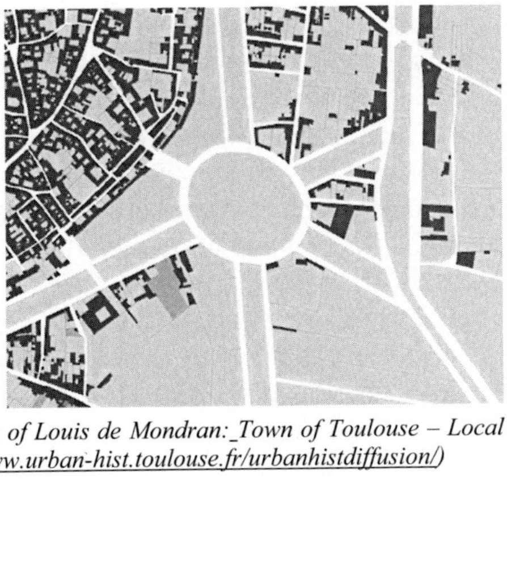

Map n°2 – The alleys of Louis de Mondran: Town of Toulouse – Local Archives of Toulouse, Urban-Hist (http://www.urban-hist.toulouse.fr/urbanhistdiffusion/)

Why did this happen? Even though this walkway was well-known as a recreational area, it was still outside the walls, and therefore considered to be outside the city. Illegal activities and prostitution were common in the areas outside the walls[9], and those who could afford to live in the city much preferred to do so. The military governor even added that the project to create a new quarter there was "a project which put the town outside the town"[10].

During the same period, the suburbs were growing as the less privileged sought housing there. In 1790, 19,000 people were living outside the fortifications of Toulouse. In the suburb Saint-Etienne 400 houses had already been built by 1796. The landscape was urban, but the quarter was still considered "outside the town"[11].

It seems that the inhabitants of these suburbs began to think that they were living in the city, and argued that they should benefit from the public policies, especially concerning drinkable water[12]. Even the local authorities had to admit that these quarters were urban and that their inhabitants were already so numerous that they chose to create a fountain in the suburb Saint-Etienne.

Moreover, the authorities chose to change the city's fiscal boundary in order to include the main suburbs within it. This fact reveals that the definition of urbanity had started to change: the fortifications were still important for defining the word 'urbanity', but the definition in everyday life became a bit more complex.

Dictionaries' Redefinition of Urbanity

The definition of urbanity changed in most of the dictionaries printed at the end of the eighteenth century. The new edition of the *Dictionnaire de l'Académie Française* (1798[13]) was the only one to give the same definition as in 1694, but according to other dictionaries, the meaning of the word 'urbanity' had already changed. Féraud, in his *Dictionnaire critique de la langue française* (1787 – 1788) explains that a town is the "[s]um of a great number of houses and streets and enclosed by a common fence". The fortifications were therefore still important, but the number of houses was now mentioned, and there had to be many of them. In the *Encyclopédie*, Jaucourt was even more accurate and wrote that a town is a "Place enclosed by fortifications which contains many quarters, streets, public places and other buildings"[14].

We can notice the same changes if we look at maps from the end of the eighteenth century.[15] The fortifications are still depicted but are far smaller, while the representations of the houses, and especially of the suburbs, greatly increased in number.

Map n°3 – Map of the town of Toulouse, by Bonifas. Bonifas, M.: Plan de la ville de Toulouse/ Town of Toulouse - Local Archives of Toulouse, II 680

At the end of the eighteenth century, the role of fortifications was still important in defining urban space. However, the definition of urbanity had already changed as new criteria appeared, in particular, the number of houses and streets. What happened to this definition when the fortifications were demolished at the beginning of the nineteenth century?

A Second Step in Redefining Urbanity: After the Demolition of the Fortifications

The Second New Quarter outside the Fortifications (1822) and its Success

In 1822, Toulouse's urban authorities obtained permission from the king to buy many plots in the suburbs to create a new walkway. This project had many things in common with Louis de Mondran's earlier ideas: the walkway was to be a recreational space, it should link the town with the *Canal du Midi*, and a new quarter should be created in the surroundings. The main difference of this project from the previous one was that this time many people chose to build their houses in this area; the fortifications were no longer a mental boundary for the city's inhabitants.

Map n°4 – The new alleys in 1830: Town of Toulouse – Local Archives of Toulouse, Urban-Hist (http://www.urban-hist.toulouse.fr/urbanhistdiffusion/)

In less than ten years, the population of the new quarters had multiplied by a factor of ten and some rich merchants even chose to live there. At the same time, the local authorities tried to demolish the old wall. It had lost its defensive function since the eighteenth century and caused many problems: as the population grew, it became harder and harder to move through the old gates, and the old moats had turned into rubbish dumps.

While the town was an enclosed space with a strongly defensive function, the fortifications were an important element in defining urbanity. Yet at the beginning of the nineteenth century, Toulouse no longer had any real defensive function and the old walls were considered to be a nuisance by the population, who asked for them to be demolished.

The Effect of Demolishing the Walls on the Definition of Urbanity

In Toulouse, the army tried to prevent the destruction of the old walls because the town was located near the Spanish border. However, at the time there was no tension between France and Spain and the local authorities managed to obtain permission from the king to demolish the main part of the old walls at the beginning of the nineteenth century. A few gates had already been demolished, but the real work began in 1826.

This physical demolition was quickly accomplished, but did it change the concept of urbanity? Of course, the walls were no longer an important element of definition, and the suburbs were now considered to be quarters of the city. This is quite easy to see on contemporary maps, for example the *Plan de [...] Toulouse*[16]. Even in the areas where the fortifications had not yet been demolished, the author of the map only drew a small line to portray them. On the contrary, the suburbs were included in the map and drawn with great accuracy.

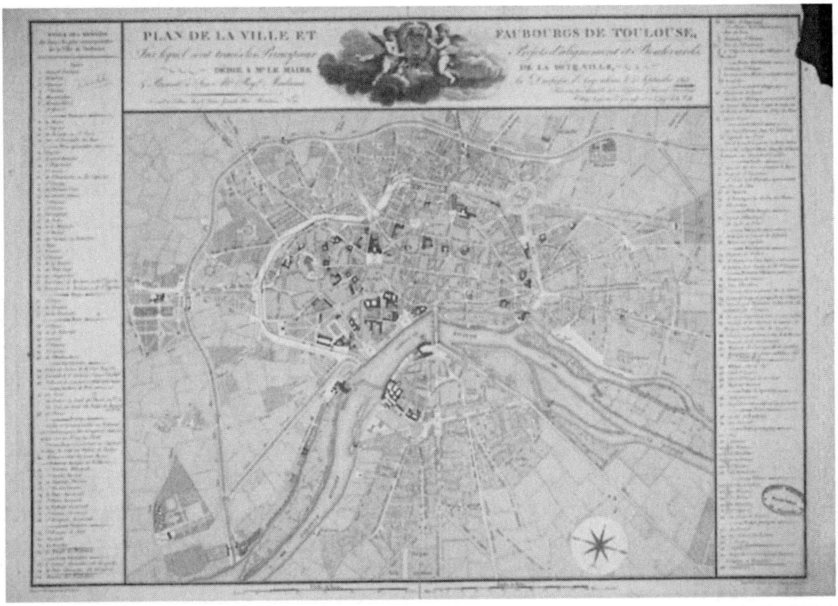

Map n°5 – Map of the town and suburbs of Toulouse, by Vitry. Vitry, U.: Plan de [...] Toulouse, 1815/ Town of Toulouse – Local Archives of Toulouse, 20Fi13

Dictionaries from the early nineteenth century show the same evolution of the definition of urbanity that we can observe concerning the town of Toulouse. The sixth edition of the *Dictionnaire de l'Académie Française*, published in 1835, explains that a town is now a "[s]um of a great number of houses and streets and often surrounded by a common fence[17]". The presence of the fortifications was no longer an obligation for defining the word 'town'. Emile Littre gives exactly the same definition in his famous *Dictionnaire de la langue Française* in 1872[18].

However, as the presence of fortifications was now only an option, and as the suburbs were now part of the town, it became almost impossible to define a new physical boundary to the town of Toulouse. When the authorities tried to redefine the city's fiscal boundaries, they chose to include the suburbs but had a hard time fixing a new physical boundary. When they finally made a decision, the new boundary only had an administrative meaning; it even included many fields.

This reveals that the period of a town's conceptual security had vanished with the old fortifications; the town was now an open space and thus had no obvious limit in space.

According to the dictionaries, at the beginning of the eighteenth century, a town was a sum of buildings limited by a fortification. One hundred years later it was almost impossible to give a simple definition: a town had to contain numerous houses and streets but had no obvious limit in space. The case of Toulouse illustrates this transformation perfectly.

Why had the definition of urbanity changed so much in only one century in Toulouse? First of all, because the functions of the town itself had changed: from a closed place which was supposed to provide a feeling of security for its inhabitants, it became an open space where industry and trade were far more important than defence.

The definition also changed because the shape of the town had changed: from 1680 to 1830, the population of Toulouse increased greatly[19] and many of the new inhabitants chose to live in the suburbs.

Finally, the approach and ideas of the inhabitants also changed: in 1752, the fortification was still a mental obstacle and living outside the walls was considered to be shameful for those who had enough money to live inside the city. This mental boundary disappeared between 1752 and 1830 when the second project to create a new quarter outside the walls was a success. According to the inhabitants of Toulouse, at the beginning of the nineteenth century, the fortifications were no longer a source of security but a source of public nuisance[20].

These changes had consequences. When the definition of urbanity changed, the suburbs became officially urban, yet they never had any physical limit or boundary. The new definition of urbanity inherited this problem, and when the authorities tried to find some new fiscal boundaries, they quickly realized that finding such limits was impossible.

Ever since this period, defining the boundaries of a city and the city itself has been complicated; our geographers have inherited the problems of the nineteenth century.

NOTES

[1] Richelet (P.), *Dictionnaire françois contenant les mots et les choses, plusieurs nouvelles remarques sur la langue françoise: Ses Expressions Propres, Figurées & Burlesques, la Prononciation des Mots les plus difficiles, les genres des Noms, le Regime des Verbes avec Les termes les plus connus des Arts & des Sciences, le tout tiré de l'usage et des bons auteurs de la langue françoise*, 1680. All translations of French sources are by the author.

[2] Furtiere (A.), *Dictionnaire universel, contenant généralement tous les mots françois, tant vieux que modernes et les termes des sciences des arts*, 1690.

[3] *Dictionnaire de l'Académie française*, 1st Edition, 1694.

[4] Boisseau (I.), *Description de la Métropolitaine ville de Toulouse, université et siège du parlement du Languedoc*, Local Archives of Toulouse, II 674.

[5] Rivals (A.), *Expulsion des Huguenots de Toulouse après la Capture de la Ville par les partisans du Prince de Condé en 1562*, painted in 1727, Museum of the Augustins, Toulouse.

[6] Local Archives of Toulouse, 1M 10, *Lettre de Virebent au maire de Toulouse sur l'état des remparts*, 9 floréal an IX (1801).

[7] Departmental Archives of the Haute-Garonne, 2 Mi 905, *Capitation de 1695.*

[8] Feraud (J.-F.), *Dictionnaire critique de la langue française* (1787 - 1788).

[9] Marque (N.), *La marge orientale de Toulouse, des faubourgs au quartier, vers 1680 - vers 1830*, Toulouse, Maîtrise, 2005, p. 54.

[10] Departmental Archives of the Haute-Garonne, 1C 31, *Mémoire abrégé de quelques affaires de la ville de Toulouse*, fol. 1 v°.

[11] Departmental Archives of the Haute-Garonne, 1C 331, "*Mémoire abrégé de quelques affaires de la ville de Toulouse*", fol. 1 v°

[12] Local Archives of Toulouse, DD 329, "*Ordonnance de MM. les capitouls du concernant la place Dauphine*", 15 juin 1782.

[13] *Dictionnaire de l'Académie Française*, 5th Edition, printed in 1798.

[14] Jaucourt (L.), "Ville", in the *Encyclopédie ou Dictionnaire raisonné des sciences, des arts et des métiers, par une Société de Gens de lettres*, between 1751 and 1772.

[15] Bonifas (M.), *Plan de la ville de Toulouse*, created between 1777 and 1789, Local Archives of Toulouse, II 680.

[16] Vitry (U.), *Plan de la ville et faubourgs de Toulouse*, 1815, Local Archives of Toulouse, 20Fi13.

[17] *Dictionnaire de l'Académie Française*, 6th edition, 1835.

[18] Littre (E.), *Dictionnaire de la langue française*, between 1872 and 1877.

[19] Coppolani (J.), *Toulouse, étude de géographie urbaine*, Toulouse, Privat, 1954, pp. 99, 125.

[20] Marque (N.), *La marge orientale de Toulouse, des faubourgs au quartier, vers 1680 - vers 1830*, Toulouse, Maîtrise, 2005, pp. 247-249.

ELSE WHERE :: EVERY WHERE

Nerma Cridge

Architectural Association London, London/UK

nerma@nermacridge.com

ABSTRACT

Two parallel, yet distinct processes are at stake here. The creation of images 'borrowed' from somewhere else or else where is the first one. The other entails the production of images of grey concrete housing blocks, seemingly appearing everywhere. These two processes share one important aspect of image production: they both involve relentless copying. By considering what, in each case, ought to be seen as an 'original', and what may constitute a 'copy', various suggestions such as that one country, namely China, has a fundamentally different understanding of a 'copy' are being questioned. As the example of the black copy of Le Corbusier's Villa Savoye in Canberra (Australia) proves, copying can be and is commonly found everywhere; it just tends to be justified differently.

Zwei parallele, wenn auch von einander zu unterscheidende Prozesse stehen hier zur Diskussion. Das Schaffen von Bildern, die von irgendwo ‚geliehen' sind, stellt den ersten dar. Der zweite zieht die Produktion von Bildern grauer Betonklötze nach sich, die offenbar überall auftreten. Diese beiden Prozesse haben einen wichtigen Aspekt der Schaffung von Bildern gemein: Sie basieren auf dem schier endlosen Kopieren von Vorlagen. Indem man in jedem Fall berücksichtigt, was als ‚Original' zu sehen ist und was als ‚Kopie', werden unterschiedliche Denkansätze diskutiert, wie zum Beispiel der, dass ein Land wie China ein grundlegend anderes Verständnis von ‚Kopie' besitzt. Wie das Beispiel der schwarzen Kopie von Le Corbusiers Villa Savoye in Canberra (Australien) beweist, werden auch anderswo Kopien angefertigt – lediglich mit anderen Begründungen.

As evident from the title, this article was conceived on a simple premise that many urban spaces appear at odds, as though they do not belong to their immediate surroundings. Their visual features connect them to sites separate and distanced from the current ones. On occasion, this visual disassociation is so strong that they actually appear alienated from the cities they are based in and their actual locations. Existing in separation, such fragments of our urban environments arguably belong to not just a different place, but a distinct culture, and even time. Different kinds of images, equally poignant, but operating in an entirely opposite fashion, are again found in any city, and are seemingly everywhere. Images of high-rise modernist concrete housing blocks create repetition, sameness, indifference, and even boredom, saturating our daily lives.

Far from surprising it seems that many inner-city dwellers tend to share more than just an aesthetic appearance of their surroundings with people who live far away. Simultaneously these processes make it possible for many urban inhabitants to have very little, almost no interaction or connection with their physical neighbours.

Crucial to the workings of both types of these images is the notion of copying, making its more precise examination pertinent. Whilst seemingly counter-intuitive, replication is intrinsically at stake here. As not only certain parts of our urban environment are alien from their surroundings, they tend to be, in fact, borrowed or copied from somewhere else. This tends to be usually connected with a neighbourhood's migrant populations, making the case for the proliferation of, for example, so called 'China Towns' that most large cities include.

The most simple and obvious examples of copying, the ones the majority of us have witnessed, consist of "brazen" copies of not just individual but whole groups of buildings and urban areas. This phenomenon seems nowhere so ubiquitously present than in contemporary China. In her recent book *Original Copies* Bianca Bosker[1] discusses the prolific nature and mass scale of copying in China. Bosker argues this to be related to the Chinese understanding of replica which culturally differs from the Western one. In Chinese culture, Bosker suggests, the skillful replica is considered equal, as opposed to less valuable than the original. The results of such attitude to replication are evident in abundance in whole areas of Chinese cities appearing to be 'imported' from their original locations. In some cases, particularly when involving large scale, some might say that the 'new' versions, replicas of an Austrian village, Dutch façades and canals, Venetian gondolas or Parisian cityscapes, for example, have been made more glitzy, even more appealing in the process. However, the difference between themed entertainment parks in the US, for example, is that here mid-class families actually live in the communities replicated from elsewhere, physically inhabit copies on unprecedented scale and detail.

One collection of such artefacts in Shenzen's theme park, entitled aptly 'Window of the World', contains more than 130 replicas of the world's most famous structures including the copy (1/3 of the scale) of the Eiffel Tower. Perhaps the most copied structure in the world is the Eiffel Tower; apart from replicas in China, copies of the tower can be found in places such as Da-lat in Vietnam, Texas (where it has a pink cowboy hat on top), Las Vegas, Tokyo, Mexico and numerous other cities. Buildings like this have such a strong visual identity, and are so instantly recognizable that they promptly take the visitor to their own location of origin. Numbers of whole cities exert a similar effect, for example, it is very hard to take pictures of Venice which do not look like Venice. Yet Venice can be found in the images of St Petersburg, Munich and many other cities. Far from being reserved only for the built architecture, copying is just as, if not more, prolific in the case of the unbuilt or perhaps unbuildable ones. It seems little wonder that Tatlin's Tower, for instance, has been copied and pasted in many places, and reincarnated as a four-star hotel in the post-Communist China.

This process of repetition feeds off and even expands our sightseeing ambitions; for avid tourists amongst us, it is no longer sufficient to visit the one original building, but you also need to include all of its replicas. Not only concerning significant buildings or shopping malls, such repetitions and reiterations transplant even unexpected elements of nature into the city environment, like, for instance, a surfing canal in the centre of Munich. But inhabiting copied-communities in China is furthering this process, as it is seemingly not enough to visit iconic buildings, and to be able to visit many in a single day, or live close to one, but one has to live inside them, literally. However, my argument slightly differs from Bosker's. It seems that the copying is just as prevalent in the West. Only because the tendency to describe and represent such projects is very different, they acquire appearance which seems dissimilar enough; resulting in the fact that some are not even perceived as copying at all. Even if this process may be acknowledged it tends to by enlarge not be perceived as plagiarism. For instance, when an exact copy of Ronchamp was built in China, Le Corbusier's Foundation legally pursued them, and managed to have it destroyed.

Figure 1: Original Villa Savoye, Poissy, France

However, there is another curious replica involving a piece by the same architect; Villa Savoye, which was originally built on the outskirts of Paris. The original building leaked since its inception and was virtually un-inhabitable with the clients threatening legal action. There are a number of copies of this building across the globe, including an odd black version in Switzerland, and of course, in China. However, the most striking example 'copied' by ARM Architects in Canberra, Australia, as part of the National Museum of Australia (more precisely The Institute of Aboriginal Studies), has even received architectural awards including Blueprint public building of the year in 2001. With the original proportions and 1:1 scale, this replica has a stark black façade instead of the famous white one. Somewhat paradoxically, the black colour appears to emphasize the similarity with its predecessor rather than to portray the difference. Also dubbed as its evil twin, or a doppelganger, it embodies colliding even polarizing reactions. For the architect of this building, Howard Raggatt[2], architecture has always been about copying. In a sense, this is a more honest and open way of copying, in fact "direct citation" as opposed to the muted and watered-down versions we are so much more acceptable of. Here we have a 20th century masterpiece from Europe, copied, made black, and pasted into the 21st century on a different continent. The design based on Raggatt's Masters Thesis won this contract through an international competition. The original plan was reversed, making this replica, also back to front. So, the original was made negative in literal sense, through these processes of inversion of opposites: from white to black, back to front, and being literally on the other side of the world – turned upside-down.

Figure 2: Negative Copy, AITSAS Building, Canberra, Australia

One has to question how many users and visitors actually acknowledge the copying at stake in this piece of architecture, and why it was seen by not just the architects, but the clients, the governmental organization, as appropriate to do so. Part of the plan of the adjoining National Museum of Australia, is a copy of Daniel Libeskind's Jewish Museum in Berlin. Apparently, vigorous discussions between the two architectural practices involving the government did take place, but never led to much. In Raggatt's view, this has nothing to do with plagiarism, as they "were not interested in Libeskind's work, but the experience of the building".[3] Raggatt cited his influences included Michael Heizer[4], who created very similar projects in zig-zag form, in land art in 1968 and "suspects Libeskind was probably interested in his work too". Raggatt describes it as an "aggressive response to the way European architecture has been foisted upon the colonies".[5]

In this case, Le Corbusier's Foundation chose not to intervene. Michel MR Richard,[6] director of the Foundation, described it as disrespectful in terms of intellectual property, since no permission to copy was ever requested from them; however, he stopped short of saying whether they would have granted their consent or not. Is the AIATSIS building different enough for them not to be able to pursue a legal case, or is something working here in addition?

Curiously, for Raggatt, Villa Savoye is a theme: “So the theme of villa Savoye suited it quite well, imported architecture, colonial in its form and very strongly occupied and overcome by the occupants. It becomes black architecture instead of white.”[7] The architect also plausibly suggested that rather than knowing anything about the famous French architect the visitors to the AIT-SAS building tend to associate the black face of the building to Ned Kelly’s[8] black mask. When quizzed what the original architect would think of it, Raggatt said that they were not interested in the famous architect, or in this particular building per se, but in the processes and consequences of such iterations taking place, but added that Le Corbusier would probably be pleased.

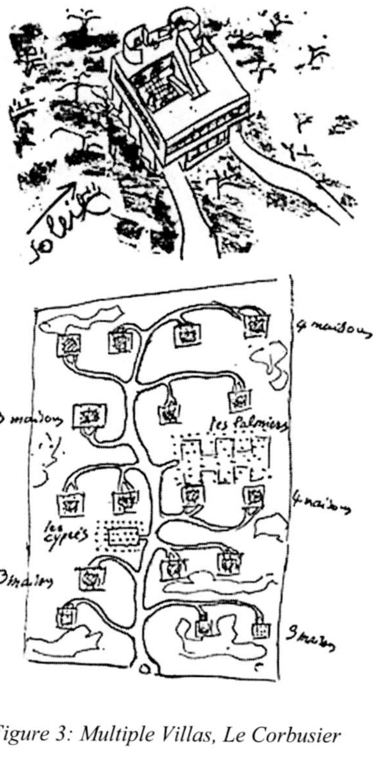

Figure 3: Multiple Villas, Le Corbusier

Le Corbusier’s thinking and designing certainly encouraged mass-production, copying, and repetition. However, if these processes were to take place, it would most likely be in order to maintain his authorship in a very specific way as his sketch of multiple clusters of three and four (seventeen in total) Villas Savoye shows. For Le Corbusier this process is not about copying, but repetition on his, strictly defined terms. In such terms, it becomes about the grid-like domination of the equally spaced out and distributed famous original. The utopian, or I would say, the unbuildable aspect of Le Corbusier's project and one of the powerful motives of his entire oeuvre is not in the scale as maybe the case for some other projects. The scale of an individual villa is perfectly realizable and has indeed been built. The impossible lies in the number of iterations, in the multitude, and in the distribution of identical copies. For Le Corbusier one can never be enough, but numerous copies scattered across the scales, in multiple cities and continents are needed. It seems almost certain, though, that the famous French architect would not approve of not being acknowledged properly, as in addition to not requesting the permission there seems no reference on the building itself or the architect's ARM website of its famous European counterpart.

Even in the case of the built artefact such as Villa Savoye the notion of the missing original seems pertinent here. Perhaps this search is in essence futile as there can never be a built artifact which is enough in itself; it needs to be better, bigger, each time made more modern; as though it can be a re-newed version of itself. With the latest technological developments, the significant shift is in one additional dimension – it is no longer the case of relentless images' duplication. Although pictures, including architectural drawings which blur the distinctions between before and after construction, physical and digital, have never been copied and produced so much, they have arguably never been printed less. In the current age, the search for the missing original results in the mass production of full scale 3-dimensional artefacts which can be experienced in all their physical and material manifestations, accompanied at all stages by images which make it difficult to distinguish between real and image.

Other, more subtle copies occur where people's surroundings appear to belong to time and culture alien from the one they are actually located in. However, this incidence is not about building cheaper, more accessible copies of tourist destinations. Instead, perhaps paradoxically, they demonstrate how cities morph into one another. This is nowhere more the case than in the modernist housing blocks which appear almost inter-changeable – you can easily swap one for another city photograph; even if you just simply change the name, not many people would notice. Another facet of this argument is that where our urban environments seem alien, they do not because they create mini copies of the destinations their inhabitants cannot actually visit, but because they want to re-create environments similar to where they themselves have migrated from. China Towns in many global cities represent another trait of this curious phenomenon of yearning for and always wanting to be elsewhere, other than where you actually are. In this sense, people living in China want to actually inhabit an Austrian village and get close to it if only through the mimicry of their physical surroundings. In parallel, those actually inhabiting a village in Austria may long to visit a mega-polis such as Shanghai.

Here again, the notion of repetition and copying could be at stake. Let us re-examine Walter Benjamin's[9] ideas on reproduction – certainly one of the most referenced and repeated of his citations, seems well placed in this essay about architectural copying. At the first half of the 20th century, long before the digital and computational techniques became available today, Benjamin lamented the loss of "aura" in the works of art, in the age of mechanical reproduction. One needs not to try very hard to imagine how much Benjamin would mourn the loss of "aura" in the prolific copying, not simply of images or even individual buildings, but of whole urban quarters, as it regularly happens today. Unless, of course, we suppose that work of art does not extend to buildings, but is limited to the artistic production excluding architects.

In fact, it seems plausible to claim that there are inherent traits within architectural practice that should allow for copying if not encouraging it. However, it has to be on strictly defined, own terms, like suggested in the multiple Villas Savoye or many grand urban plans schemes by Le Corbusier. How often buildings are being copied without the presence of an architect, by excluding or negating, and without even acknowledging them seems more of an important issue. Compounded to this, we have a culture, which is not based on national or other specific notions of replication, but on a global scale. In this sense, it could be deemed to see buildings and urban quarters as acceptable to copy; and this process as an even democratic one. In political systems different from capitalism, such as briefly the socialism of Soviet Russia or China, you could argue that if nobody copied your work, i. e. if it was reserved for an individual small production, it would be deemed to be a failure. The advantage of a single totalitarian market in such cases, and the complete absence of competition, has precisely to do with total access to large numbers of users on a mass scale. However, I would disagree with the claim that one culture may see it as more appropriate to copy than another, as Bosker suggested. It seems to me to be more of a case of copying by everybody and anybody simply because they can. As evidence show, there are plenty of copies in the US and other western and developing countries and cultures where this process has also been happening on a similar scale. Certainly numerous new and exciting buildings are being built in China, as some of the most currently advanced architectural projects continue to be realized there.

So if we accept copying to be nothing new; and in fact intrinsic to the discipline of architecture, it is also far from being confined to any one culture in particular, but is rather a much more widespread phenomenon. What may be new is that for the first time the experience of being an outsider in one's own city has become also widespread. As opposed to simply creating an experience of a spectacle through a one-off visit to a theme park it is in fact becoming a way of life for many, even the majority, of us. In other words, feelings of being displaced and far from those physically close to you, yet, feeling close to those at considerable geographical distance is no longer unique. No more unusual, this kind of inhabitation is in fact becoming the norm. Experience that used to be reserved for expats or in more extreme cases of refugees/ asylum seekers is becoming much more familiar and common. The feelings of melancholy and nostalgia that this brings should be seen as a necessary part of our urban lives. Make no mistake, this is not nostalgia for a place that actually exists; this is not an urban environment left behind; this 'city' was never there. Built out of yearnings disguised as memories of people who long to be, but never actually do manage to get elsewhere.

Whilst we can reconcile that copies and replicas have always been there, and so have been infinite variants; with the scale and numbers continuously increasing, together with the wide access to the imagery, we are able to collect so many of them in one place and visualize them together in all their similarities, banality and monotony. Ever-increasing ability to copy seems not to necessarily bring about richness in forms, but instead repetition and iterations, producing infinitely changeable components; if ever so slightly.

One comment on the black copy of Villa Savoye, "does this one leak?" would confirm this. A copy of a building almost a century later, in a completely different context with a different purpose, as an Aboriginal Institute; this example shows that not just the acceptance or tolerance of the copying is non-exclusive to one culture or nation; but that global acceptance of copying is rather likely to increase instead of fade. It seems that there is consensus, if they picked a lesser known building to copy, that it would be seen as more acceptable. On the one hand, this may apparently be so, and one suspects that nobody would even remark upon it. On the flipside of the argument, we ought to question if it was not better that 'good' examples are replicated instead of the more mundane architecture. Consequentially, and looking further, it seems to be the case that almost all buildings are a collage of borrowed parts, details and patterns. Some are more subtle or more muddled up to decipher; many are not well-designed or distinct enough to copy, but whether that makes them more or less successful, is highly doubtful.

Finally we get to the visual appearance of our housing blocks, with many of us inhabiting buildings and apartments that would not be deemed good enough to pass in initial stages of architectural schools. Why is there such an in-balance of many attractive signature buildings; with very few of them inhabited or even accessible to the public and our homes? Cramped and clustered together, our urban homes not only are exposed to a very high degree of light and noise pollution, but they also are not spacious.

This is not about lamenting the loss of the original, as we saw how this notion has never actually existed other than in our imagination, but about our inability to turn this prolific copying into our homes, the spaces we inhabit every day. Instead, by being un-homely, and alien to most of us, if not everybody, they also breed the suspicion related to something strange, even evil or simply foreign within our vicinity. Whilst no urban culture should be considered monolithic, isolated solid parts of our urbanity seem to emerge indiscriminately; in the most and the least developed cities alike. This process ought not to be linked with the reproduction of the original, but rather with the multiplication and glorification of the original, by any means possible. The more architects, people, countries want to copy it, the bigger its own value becomes.

The richness of our experience depends on our ability to recognize subtle differences and even improvements. We are all, at all times, building 'better' and richer cities, from their fragments across the globe; not just larger, but otherwise improved or, even paradoxically, an 'older' one than the one we live in.

NOTES

[1] Bianca Bosker, *Original Copies: Architectural Mimicry in Contemporary China,* Spatial Habitus, 2013.

[2] Howard Raggatt, Founding Director, ARM Architects and Adjunct Professor of Architecture at RMIT, Melbourne, Australia.

[3] Howard Raggatt, in conversation with the author, November, 2013.

[4] See Michael Haiser Rift – Nine Nevada Depressions. 1968. Massacre Dry Lake, Nevada, USA.

[5] Howard Raggatt, in conversation with the author, November, 2013.

[6] Michel MR Richard, Director, Le Corbusier Foundation, Paris, 2013 (e-mail correspondence with author).

[7] Howard Raggatt, in conversation with the author, November, 2013.

[8] Ned Kelly, Australian outlaw, Robin-Hood sort of character; was featured with a black mask in a famous series of paintings by Sidney Nolan, 1977, The National Gallery of Australia.

[9] Walter Benjamin, Hannah Arendt, ed., *The Work of Art in the Age of Mechanical Reproduction, Illuminations*. London: Fontana 1936. pp. 214–218.

BIBLIOGRAPHY

Benjamin, Walter. Hannah Arendt (Ed.). *The Work of Art in the Age of Mechanical Reproduction, Illuminations,* London: Fontana 1936. pp. 214-218.

Bosker, Bianca. *Original Copies: Architectural Mimicry in Contemporary China.* Spatial Habitus 2013.

Jenks, Charles. "Constructing Identity", in: *National Museum of Australia Publication.* 2000.

Schaik, Lvan (Ed). Howard Raggatt. "Not Villa Savoye et al", in: *Notness, Findesiecle.* Melbourne 1993.

LIST OF ILLUSTRATIONS

Figure 1: The original Villa Savoye, 1929-3, Le Corbusier, Photograph by Ricardo Ruivo Pereira.

Figure 2: The negative copy, Australian Institute of Aboriginal and Torres Strait Islander Studies (AIATSIS), Canberra, Australia, Copyright: Ashton Raggatt McDougall Architects, 2000.

Figure 3: Multiple Villas, Sketch, Le Corbusier, 1929, Precisions, Le Plan de la Maison Moderne. Copyright: Foundation Le Corbusier/ ADAGP.

Thinking Society – Fictional Cities as Products and Generating Forces in Shaping Society

Veronika Bernard

Leopold-Franzens University of Innsbruck, Innsbruck/Austria
Veronika.Bernard@uibk.ac.at

Abstract

This article offers a survey on the representation of cities in German fiction and poetry based on the author's postdoctoral research findings[1]. The thesis which has been proved in this research states that from medieval times onwards there has been a causal link between political, social, and cultural (including religious) change experienced by people and the appearance of cities in texts of German literature. Within this frame the fictional cities are to be seen as both products and generating forces in shaping German speaking European societies; the city concept conveying the ideological discourse on the cultural ideas relevant in those fields of life affected by change.

Der vorliegende Artikel bietet einen Überblick der Literarisierung von Städten in deutschsprachiger Prosa und Lyrik basierend auf den Ergebnissen der Habilitationsforschung der Autorin zu diesem Thema[2]. Die in dieser Forschung belegte These stellt einen kausalen Zusammenhang her zwischen dem Auftreten der Stadt in deutschsprachiger Literatur und der in zeitlicher Nähe stattfindenden politischen, sozialen und kulturellen Veränderung. Die fiktionalisierte Stadt wird in diesem Kontext als Produkt der Veränderung verstanden und als eine der maßgeblichen gesellschafts-gestaltenden Kräfte. Das städtische Konzept dient hierbei als Vehikel des ideologischen Diskurses über jene kulturellen Ideen, die in den von den Veränderungen betroffenen Bereichen wirksam sind.

Introduction

The author's postdoctoral research on fictionalised cities in German speaking literature started two decades ago at the simple first-sight observation that during certain periods of European history a higher quantity of literary works were produced whose plots, characters, imagery, and settings circle around urban environments than during others. On closer analysis, it has become obvious that these historical periods were times in which German speaking societies were undergoing substantial change caused by the appearance and spread of new ideas, like religions, political ideologies and inventions, or by events, like wars. For the German speaking European areas such times are in particular: the New Modern Times (late 15th and most of 16th century), when towns were establishing themselves as places of a socially emancipating citizenship, and a religious as well as a social revolution was on its way due to Martin Luther's opposition to Catholic teachings and hierarchy; times of war (30 Years War, the Ottoman attempts to conquer the Eastern and South Eastern parts of Europe, the German French War of 1870-1871, and World Wars I and II); the second half of the 18th century, when the identity concept of the nation started to fill the ideological vacuum caused by the loss of religion-based identity after European elites had devoted themselves to the secular ideas of the European Enlightenment; the turn of the 20th century when Sigmund Freud's theory on the human nature and psyche opened up a then revolutionary perspective on people's lives and characters; the 1920s and 1930s when economic disaster met with controversial political ideologies in polarizing society; and last but not least, the awareness of a possible global destruction by nuclear weapons during the times of the Cold War and after.

Finally, this first finding has led the author to the conclusion that starting with medieval time urbanity has been perceived as a vital and decisive social and cultural force by the members of German speaking European communities. As a consequence, the fictionalised city has been considered a suitable medium for ideologically inspired political, social, and religious discourse conveyed by literary texts; the cities created and represented in these texts providing readers with manifold intellectual comments on decisive cultural developments as the cities' representation portrays, reflects on, and shapes these developments. In this way, fictional cities in German literature have helped to discuss and promote ideological concepts and strategies ranging from the creation of religiously motivated (urban) worlds to fictitious realisations of political ideas represented in fictitious urban communities.

The variety of ideas conveyed by fictionalised urbanity corresponds with a huge range of techniques used in fictionalising the particular cities. The main ones isolated by the author's study are the following six: idealizing the city; representing the city as a delusion; gendering and sexualizing the city; spiritualising the city; othering the city; and orientalising the city. Each of these techniques has been found to be linked to one or more discursive approaches, like taking sides in political, religious, moral and social discussion. This article deals with four of them. It provides a literary survey both on the texts shaped by using the techniques and on the concepts discussed. In most cases it deals with one or two texts in more detail.

Idealizing the City: White Cities as Cultural Safe Havens

White cities are a phenomenon of 20th century German and Austrian literature. In 1911 the German poet Georg Heym wrote a first sketch of a poem titled "Heroische Landschaften" (Heroic Landscapes)[3], in which white cities take a prominent position. They are part of sceneries and of a social context strongly reminding of ancient Greek myths, contrasting their own purity and tranquillity to a vague situation of warlike apocalypse. Gottfried Benn has also created a white city in his novella *Geburtstag* (Birthday)[4]. His white city is a place where traditional patterns of heterosexual relationship are shattered, and the ideal woman is modelled intellectually. She is a blond; she is both sexually and intellectually demanding and liberal; and she is desired by a disillusioned male mind. Following a trip to the Provence in 1925, the Austrian writer Joseph Roth wrote a travel report newspaper serial for the *Frankfurter Allgemeine*, titled *Im mittäglichen Frankreich* (Travelling Mediterranean France). He later transformed these texts into a philosophical piece of literature (*Die weißen Städte*/ White Cities)[5]; yet, he did not publish it during his lifetime. In this text Roth reflects on the impact of World War I on a whole generation's belief in traditional values. Shortly after World War II, Ernst Jünger's novel *Heliopolis*[6] was published. It depicts life in a multicultural maritime city of predominantly white buildings after a sequence of destructive, and partly nuclear, wars. The city is dominated by two opposing powers; one vicious, and the other one devoted to humanistic values. Both are striving for the rule over the city; the vicious power finally gaining it. The Mediterranean and ancient ambience of the place, which suggests an overall humanistic quality, is mere fake serving as a shop-window-like disguise for the dark power's political agenda. It is established by a literary vocabulary and by literary fixtures referring to traditional contents but being applied on an alien situation and environment. Milo Dor's novel *Die weiße Stadt* (The White City)[7] was published in 1969. It tells the story of a politically active Serbian migrant in post-1945 Austria, who tries to cope with his present life in Austria and the experiences of his past life back in Serbia.

Let us have a more detailed look at Roth's text. Roth's text *Weiße Städte* introduces a narrator who feels that his existentialist experience of World War I has shattered both his intellectual identity and integrity. The cruelty of war has put all common values he and his generation had been brought up to into perspective. Traditional humanistic values have deteriorated to illusions. Dreaming has established itself as the only suitable means of perceiving and coping with what is considered reality. The narrator – in representing his generation – lacks continuity in almost all fields of life and installs himself in the position of an intellectual sceptic. Just the white cities of his youthful imagination and dreams are still able to provide the continuity he is longing for. As their utopian potential materialises in the Mediterranean cities of Southern France for him, those French cities are fit to mediate between past and present, and dream and reality. In this way they are able to re-establish the humanistic categories which are felt to have been destroyed by war. Encountering the white cities of Mediterranean France serves as an act of liberation for the narrator in Roth's text.

What all of these texts, hence, have in common, is the fact that a fictionalised white city is linked to the discourse on ancient culture and/ or the past in general, and that in all of these texts both the discourse and the fictitious city life is of a utopian quality. The utopias created idealize the white cities. They present them as cultural safe havens in which people either find their cultural values represented (as with Heym's, Roth's and Jünger's texts) or are free to experiment on their ideas and desires (as with Benn's and Dor's texts). Within this scope Benn's text applies a Dionysian quality of sexual liberty and sexual liberalism to ancient culture whereas Heym's, Jünger's and Roth's texts underline its humanistic quality. Dor's and Roth's texts add the general aspect of a desired past which is seen as a cultural value to the list of qualities attributed to white cities. With Dor it is the past of a youthful ideological idealism; with Roth it is the past of a cultural tradition rooting in the achievements of ancient and medieval Europe.

Representing the City as a Delusion: Adapting the Spiritual Idea of the *Arabian Nights*' City of Brass

Representing the city as a place of delusion is another technique to be met in 20th century fiction. It is closely linked to the discourse on the aspects of human vanity, the transitory quality of human existence, the relativity of common values and on human perception in general. One of the best examples to analyse and discuss both technique and discursive approach is the adaptation of the *Arabian Nights*' story of the city of brass[8]; the several adaptations appearing at different times throughout the 20th century. In the 1920s Friedrich Wilhelm Mader published his version of the *Messingstadt* (City of Brass)[9]. In the late 1970s Ernst Jünger integrated the story in the concept of a mythical theory of human history in his novel *Eumeswil*[10]. In 1991 Christoph Meckel published his novel *Messingstadt*[11], which tells the love story of a gambler of dubious reputation and a prostitute after a nuclear catastrophe has managed to invert all traditional categories and put all of human perception into perspective.

Before turning to the adaptations let us have a look at the original story, though. As the *Arabian Nights* have it, Sherezade spends thirteen subsequent nights telling her husband, the revengeful king of Samarkand, the story of the city of brass. It is a mythical place in the west of 'Adb el-Malik ibn Marwan's empire, on whose beaches bottles sealed with the wise king Salomon's sign have repeatedly been washed ashore. In order to find the city and the bay the Khalif of Damascus sends out Emir Musa, who, indeed, finds the place. However, it is no longer a flourishing city, but has turned into a city of the dead instead. It is a ghost town where "owls were howling" and "ravens croaking". The late inhabitants are sitting, lying or standing mummified at their work places being surrounded by inestimable wealth. They died of starvation during a drought which lasted for several years. To tell the world of their destiny they left numerous verses glorifying religious belief for its support in reducing and minimizing their needs and desires. The original story in this way uses the *vanitas*-motive to glorify Islam and to hint at the transitory nature of all human life and efforts.

Mader's text eliminates the spiritual and philosophical quality of the original and turns the story into a piece of adventure literature praising European, and, in particular, German cultural hegemony. It does so by defaming oriental culture as weak, negligent and effeminate (explicitly including its spiritual aspects) and by representing Europeans (both male and female) as strong and manly.

Jünger's text *Eumeswil* adapts the original text by neglecting its chronological structure and by focusing on its philosophical and spiritual message instead. As a consequence the action is moved to inside the city walls, and the plot as well as the phrasing of some passages is changed. The inscription on the table of Chinese Iron (respectively, yellow marble), for instance, at which originally "die tausend einäugigen und (die) tausend Könige mit gesunden Augen"[12] had been dining, reads the following way with Jünger's text: „An diesem Tisch haben tausend Könige gespeist, die blind waren auf dem rechten Auge, und tausend andere, die blind waren auf dem linken Auge – sie alle sind dahingegangen und bevölkern die Gräber und Katakomben."[13] In this way the passage is turned into a political allusion on post WW II German right- and left-wing political ideology and debate. Apart from making the story politically topical, the original story's quality of interpreting human life as a delusion is underlined. As the narrator points out, the story was not told for the sake of Emir Musa's adventures but for his encounter with the world of history; the world of history – in total inversion of common categories of perception – showing to be of virtual quality while the world of the fairy tale had to be seen as reality.

Meckel's adaptation of the story turns this particular aspect into the central issue of philosophical discourse. The city of brass is identified with B. C. (Babylon City). B. C. is a place situated on the way to Jerusalem. It is described in terms of stereotypical metropolitan life during the 1920s and 1930s. The collage of life styles it represents may strongly remind readers of the atmosphere in Otto Dix's triptych "Großstadt" (metropolis) of 1927-28. The main fields of life in B. C. are prostitution, gambling, alcoholism, violence, crime and anonymity. Life is without ties to traditional values and takes place in an environment constantly bordering on illegality. This is the surface level of the text, on which the plot is developed. It tells Jean's (alias Benjamin's) story, who earns his money rather dubiously. He frequently changes hotels and flats he stays at; he gains and loses numerous women, but still cannot forget the single one. Finally, he moves in with Saba (alias Gabriella), a prostitute, for an experiment and falls in love with her. He cannot resist returning to B. C. whenever he has left her. City life in B. C. is shown at extremes, be it excessive night-life, an ecstatic carnival or, finally, the existential situation of nuclear disaster. Nuclear disaster turns B. C. into a ghost town; however, for the first time also into an illuminated place. Only those inhabitants stay alive who till then had only gone out in the dark, if at all. The total inversion of the laws of nature is the discursive instant where the philosophical level of the text meets the surface level of the plot told. Like the original fairy city of brass B. C. is of symbolic quality. The individual city has been turned into a phenomenon. By integrating Christian tradition and symbolism (Babylon, Jerusalem, Saba) the text establishes B. C. as a threefold symbol. B. C. is the city of brass and Jerusalem at the same time combining the symbolic qualities of both. As in Christianity Jerusalem is a symbol for people's souls, B. C. consequently stands for Jean's concept of life: It is shown as a shining and glittering cover without substantial contents. As the fictitious reality of Babylon City overlaps with the illusion of the city of brass the text brings together discourse on knowledge with discourse on a human existence of commonly shared values and ideas.

If run down to central discursive issues the adaptations of the *Arabian Night's* story of the city of brass and the original story include and promote the following ones: firstly, the religiously inspired ideas of human vanity, of the transitory quality attributed to human existence, and of the moral concepts of good and evil, of the devout and the sinful; and secondly, the philosophical issues of a relativity of common values and human perception.

Othering the City: Cities as Reflections of the Self and the Other

A still other technique of representing urbanity integrates the city into the psychoanalytical concept of the Self and the other, i. e. it represents the city as the other, be it the city in general or a particular city. Although the historic adaptations of the Babylonian image and the Heavenly Jerusalem correspond with this concept as do the depictions of exotic cities in travel writings from the late 18th century onwards, othering the city is predominantly a phenomenon of 20th century fiction and poetry. Here cities of exotic quality are represented as projections of the narrator's alienation from his (or her) culture of origin. The alienation may refer to certain aspects of the culture (attitude towards taboos, sexuality, history, minorities) or to the culture in general. Gerhard Roth's *Eine Reise in das Innere von Wien* (A Journey into the Inside of Vienna)[14], Alfred Kubin's *Andere Seite* (The Other Side)[15], Paul Nizon's *Jahr der Liebe* (Year of Love)[16], Waltraud Anna Mitgutsch's *In fremden Städten* (In Alien Cities)[17], and Walter Meckauer's novel *Gassen in fremden Städten* (Side Streets in Alien Cities)[18] can be mentioned as classical examples.

Mitgutsch's text, which was published in 1992, tells the story of a young U. S. American woman who follows her Austrian husband to Austria and finally leaves him. The protagonist of Mitgutsch's text may well serve as an example of disillusionment resulting from migration, or rather, disillusionment resulting from disappointed expectations linked to migration, and of not being able to "get back to the roots": When Mitgutsch's protagonist leaves her husband, children and Europe after fifteen years of marriage, she returns to the U.S. just to find herself isolated and misunderstood there as well. She feels to live her father's life, the life of a want-to-be writer who never reached real popularity. Instead of committing suicide she finally burns her father in order to free herself. The several cities she moves to live in serve as projections of her logic of blaming others for her frustrations.

Walter Meckauer's novel deals with anti-nazi emigrants who live in Italian and French exile. The autobiographical protagonist of Meckauer's text lives a life of a step-by-step exile which was neither expected nor wanted but forced upon him by circumstance. Everything starts with a journey to Italy, which is supposed to last for a few months until Hitler would have disappeared again from the political stage, and finally ends in Vichy-France with the narrator-protagonist being arrested in order to be deported to Nazi-Germany and just being rescued by chance. The protagonist's story is a story of political and ideological miscalculation, in which the different cities serve as stimulators for the narrator's reflections on his Self. The protagonist feels the alien cities to represent his Self in a better way than the current culture of his native country.

Summing up, othering the city can be a positive concept of reflecting life and reality (like with Meckauer, and also with Roth and Nizon); but it can also be a negative one like with Mitgutsch (and Kubin).

Orientalising the City: Freud's Impact on the Early 20th Century City Concept of Fictionalised Venice

A very special technique of othering the city has been orientalising it. This technique was particularly prominent at the turn of the 20th century when Freudian thinking was just becoming up-to-date. By then the Orient had been stereotyped the European Other in travel writings and religious polemics for centuries. The additional quality which was attributed to it following Freud's theory on the levels of human consciousness was that of the unconscious. In a Freudian understanding the Orient was claimed to classically combine Eros and Thanatos, i. e. sexuality (including all types of then commonly not accepted sexual habits, like homosexuality, sadism and masochism) and death as well as morbidity. This also meant sexualizing the Orient within a concept of linking sexuality to committing violence. This was supported by the traditional stereotypical image of the Ottoman (and Muslim) Turk, who was said to be violent and cruel, sexually aggressive, and open to pervert sexual practices. Exploiting this imagery, at the turn of the 20th century two cities became the Orient's (fictional) European representatives, so to speak: Vienna and Venice. Both cities were seen to exactly represent the qualities mentioned; with Vienna the stress rather being on morbidity, though.

This article concentrates on Venice because the orientalising city representations of Venice are the more striking and obvious ones. At the turn of the 20th century Venice in a way had taken Rome's place in German literature in terms of integrating Southern cities into alternative concepts of sexuality. Wolfgang von Goethe's *Römische Elegien*[19] had established Rome as the place of extra-marital sexuality in German literature at the end of the 18th century; Venice has becomes the site of an eventually admitted homosexuality in Thomas Mann's text *Der Tod in Venedig* (Death in Venice)[20], which was published in early 20th century.

Interestingly enough, at the end of the 18th century Venice had still conveyed discursive issues like politics, religion and culture in Goethe's *Venezianische Epigramme, 1790* (Venetian Epigrams)[21]. Starting during the 1820s, however, Venice was increasingly seen as a (symbolic) link between the Occident and the Orient. This was partly inspired by Venice's prominent position in eastern trade and by her numerous battles with the Ottomans in the past. Apart from this journeys to the Orient had increasingly come into fashion by this time, and Venice became the main starting point for these journeys. This also added to the perception and representation of the city in an oriental context. One of the texts illustrating this approach very well is Alexander Freiherr von Warsberg's travel account *Homerische Landschaften* (Homerian lands)[22] of 1882, which tells the reader about an archaeological expedition to Kilikia.

Throughout the 19th century Venice was also increasingly attributed the quality of being two-faced, or rather, two-levelled: showing the elegant face of her imposing palaces, on the one hand, and the face of her dark and smelling side streets and canals filled with decaying rubbish, just like the Venetian carnival masks may hide a banal reality by displaying a shining façade. Texts which attribute this quality to Venice have been written by August Graf von Platen (*Sonette aus Venedig*/ Sonnets from Venice, 1824)[23], Hugo von Hofmannsthal (*Cristinas Heimreise*/ Christina's Journey Home, 1910)[24], and Rainer Maria Rilke (Venice-poems in *Neue Gedichte*/ New Poems)[25].

In Thomas Mann's novelette *Der Tod in Venedig* (Death in Venice) of 1912 Venice, finally, is a genuine place of the Eros. The narrator-protagonist of the story is Gustav Aschenbach, a highly decorated German artist of puritan attitude. He has been aware for long that he has homosexual desires but due to the moral and gender code of German society of the time he does not dare to admit this openly – not even to himself. Homosexuality was supposed to be morally rejected and considered un-manly. Men were expected to be manly providers of families and courageous soldiers. Venice becomes the symbolic place of his capitulation to his desires. He had been fleeing the city for years, officially because he did not feel fit for the humid climate. Actually, however, he is afraid of the impact which the special nature of Venetian culture has on him. He feels Venetian culture to be a combination of occidental soberness and oriental sensuality.

When he finally decides to go to Venice this journey becomes his very private and secret coming out: He sees (and watches) a young Polish aristocrat there, whom he both admires and desires. As he does not dare to address the youth he instead follows him all over the city secretly. In doing so he ignores all rules of dignity and even health; he makes up and dresses up like a young beau, and although the cholera is virulent at the time of his stay he eats fresh, i. e. un-cooked and un-washed fruit from a market while walking, just to be able to follow the young man. Indeed, he gets infected with the disease and finally dies of it.

The text by this links love, sexuality and desire to death, and both of them to the Orient which is identified with the unconscious. The cholera is said to have reached Venice by merchants who transported goods from the Orient to Venice on their ships. This has been kept secret from the public for a long time in order not to worry and disturb people. Venice by this is integrated into a fatal line of flight, disease, fear, lust, realization, beauty and abyss. Within this scope the death in Venice does not mean physical death but the death of a particular social behaviour. The city is the Freudian link between Eros and Thanatos. It is not before the protagonist is dying that he realizes how little sense his life of hiding and subliming his sexual orientation has made.

In this way Mann's text nicely shows how at the turn of the 20th century the technique of orientalising the city allows to convey and discuss issues like social codes, sexuality and its socially accepted and non-accepted practices, discrimination, cultural stereotyping concerning sexual preferences and habits, and existential situations in life.

Final Remarks

As is shown in this survey it is possible to isolate a number of techniques which have been used in fictionalising the city in German fiction and poetry throughout the centuries. It is also shown that these techniques are applied both on fictitious and authentic cities, and that they create and exploit (cultural) myths about these cities. It finally becomes obvious that the techniques do not appear isolated from each other; they both overlap within certain texts and are linked to each other within the scope of a larger discursive system which both reflects and inspires relevant issues of European thinking on society.

NOTES

[1] Veronika Bernard: Das emotionale Moment der Veränderung. Stadt als Dichtung (English equivalent: The Emotional Momentum of Change – The Fictionalised City), Bonn: Bouvier 2000.

[2] Veronika Bernard: Das emotionale Moment der Veränderung. Stadt als Dichtung (English equivalent: The Emotional Momentum of Change – The Fictionalised City), Bonn: Bouvier 2000.

[3] See Heorg Heym: *Das lyrische Werk*, München 1977, 467-469.

[4] See Gottfried Benn: *Gesammelte Werke*, Bd. 5, München 1975, 1230-1232.

[5] See Joseph Roth: *Werke*, Köln 1990, Bd. 2, 456-506.

[6] See Ernst Jünger: *Heliopolis. Rückblick auf eine Stadt,* Salzburg, Wien 1950.

[7] See Milo Dor: *Die weiße Stadt*. Salzburg, Wien 1994.

[8] See Anonym.: *Die Geschichte von der Messingstadt*, in: *Die Erzählungen aus den Tausendundein Nächten. Vollständige deutsche Ausgabe in sechs Bänden*. Zum ersten Mal nach dem arabischen Urtext der Calcuttaer Ausgabe aus dem Jahre 1839 übertragen von Enno Littmann, Bd. 4, Wiesbaden [2]1954, 208-259.

[9] See Friedrich Wilhelm Mader: *Die Messingstadt*. Stuttgart. Berlin, Leipzig 4. Auflage o. J.

[10] See Ernst Jünger: *Eumeswil,* Stuttgart 1977.

[11] See Christoph Meckel: *Die Messingstadt* (1991), Frankfurt am Main, 1993.

[12] See *Die Geschichte von der Messingstadt*, 224.

[13] Ernst Jünger: *Eumeswil*. Stuttgart 1977, 26.

[14] See Gerhard Roth: *Eine Reise in das Innere von Wien*, Frankfurt am Main, 1991.

[15] See Alfred Kubin: *Die andere Seite. Ein phantastischer Roman* (1909), Ungekürzter Neudruck, München 1962.

[16] See Paul Nizon: *Das Jahr der Liebe*, Frankfurt am Main 1981.

[17] See Waltraud Anna Mitgutsch: *In fremden Städten*, München 1994.

[18] See Walter Meckauer: *Gassen in fremden Städten* (1959), Frankfurt am Main, Berlin, Wien 1985.

[19] See Johann Wolfgang Goethe: *Werke*. Münchner Ausgabe. München. Wien 1985 ff, Bd. 3.2., 38-77.

[20] See Thomas Mann: *Der Tod in Venedig*, Frankfurt am Main, 1993.

[21] See Johann Wolfgang Goethe: *Werke,* Münchner Ausgabe, München, Wien 1985 ff, Bd. 3.2., 24.

[22] See Alexander Freiherr von Warsberg: *Homerische Landschaften*, Wien 1884.

[23] See Max Koch und Erich Petzet (Eds.): *August Graf von Platens sämtliche Werke in 12 Bänden*. Bd. 1. *August von Platens Leben und Schaffen*, Leipzig o. J.

[24] See Hugo von Hofmannsthal: Hugo von. *Cristinas Heimreise*, München 1908.

[25] See Rainer Maria Rilke: *Neue Gedichte*, Frankfurt am Main 1979.

Cityscapes as Statements

THE SLEEPING BEAUTY – IMAGING THE CITY IN THE CONTEXT OF NEO-COLONIALISM

Peter Volgger

University of Innbruck, Innsbruck/Austria
Peter.Volgger@architecturaltheory.eu

FWF Der Wissenschaftsfonds.

ABSTRACT

Asmara contains one of the largest collections of early modernist architecture and might therefore gain the status of a "World Heritage Site". Asmara has not only preserved this architecture, but also a 'modernist programme', which is generally seen as an emancipatory development. In contrast, the state of Eritrea today intervenes in the most intimate sphere of its citizens in the name of national sovereignty. Architecture is no longer seen as a representation, but as an ordering technique. The Eritrean government currently uses its heritage by applying the colonizers' rhetoric, and thus displays the 'World Heritage' in a new light.

Asmara vereint in seinem Stadtgebiet die größte Sammlung früher modernistischer Architektur und könnte deshalb den Status des Weltkulturerbes erhalten. Asmara hat nicht nur diese Architektur bewahrt sondern auch ein ‚modernistisches Programm', das allgemein als emanzipatorische Entwicklung gesehen wird. Im Gegensatz dazu interveniert der Staat Eritrea heute im Namen der staatlichen Souveränität in den intimsten Bereichen seiner Bürger. Architektur wird nicht länger als Repräsentation gesehen sondern als Mittel der Ordnungsschaffung. Die eritreische Regierung benützt ihr Erbe derzeit dahingehend, dass sie die Rhetorik der Kolonialmächte anwendet und so den Begriff des Weltkulturerbes in neuem Licht erscheinen lässt.

Introduction

Asmara owns an internationally renowned architectural ensemble that ranges among the highest concentrations of modernist architecture in the world. The city centre hosts an exceptional variety of architectural styles, including a number of iconic buildings from the 1930s that have remained largely untouched. The Italian-built city and its formal, colonial buildings already seem to belong to a different and distant age. The reason for this lies in a 30-years civil war against Ethiopia and – as a result – in the poverty of the country. In 1952 the United Nations decided that Eritrea be federated with Ethiopia as an autonomous unit. By 1961 the federal arrangements were so emasculated that the autonomous status of Eritrea was non-existent. The final act of dismemberment came with the dissolution of the Eritrean Assembly; Eritrea was declared the 14th province of Ethiopia. One of the longest wars of independence of the 20th century followed and ended in 1991 when Eritrean freedom fighters marched into Asmara, ending Ethiopian rule. The result of this war was the country's independence in 1993. In the early 1990s when Eritrea got independent researchers from all over the world 'rediscovered' Asmara. In 1997 the state of Eritrea invited the World Bank to collaborate in order to create a preservation programme and thus initiated the *Cultural Assets Rehabilitation Programme* (CARP). This programme has led to the production of a number of important publications, films and studies, particularly related to the image of *bella Asmara* (beautiful Asmara). CARP's ambition to forge Eritrea's national identity through the valorization of the colonial heritage coincided with an upcoming interest in colonial architecture in Africa among global heritage organizations (EU, World Bank, UNESCO).

In 1993 Eritrea declared its independence from Ethiopia after decades of violent conflict. Eritreans use the *Italian icon* of the city to establish a sense of superiority against the Ethiopians. A symbol of Eritrea's newly won sovereignty is *bella Asmara*. The *Asmarini* describe their city as the embodiment of Eritrea, not Italy ("Asmara is Eritrea").[1] They see their city as the embodiment of the country, not as something alien; it is seen as an expression of "national sacrifice", and thus as an integral part of the national development.[2]

In this article we will be concentrating on one of the key processes in the *cultural circuit*: the practices of representation. Besides being an 'image' which shows us/ represents the city, *bella Asmara* is also an image which tells us about how representation works. It produces its own kind of knowledge. Representation here is not a 'true' reflection or imitation of reality; the discourse of imaging in *bella Asmara* is going far beyond simply trying to mirror accurately what exists. [3]

The concept of representation through images has come to occupy a new and important place in the study of the colonial city. It is a 'system of representation' because it does not consist of individual concepts, but of different ways of organizing, clustering, arranging, and classifying concepts, and of establishing complex relations between culture, society, economy, politics and ideology. It explores the relationship between modernism and the project of modernisation in architecture; intertwining these in the context of colonialism and decolonisation and trying to look beyond the history of building and the format of a standard interpretation of architecture in the sense of architectural history.

The article is the result of an ongoing research project funded by the *Austrian Science Fund*[4]. The crisis in high modernism that came about in the era of decolonisation prompted us to begin an investigation into the housing developments under colonial rule, mainly in Asmara in the 1930s. Our study well explains this period and place as a laboratory, as an incubator, and a site for investigation that would later influence a rethinking of the international role of the modern movement in architecture. It also presents ideas about human and artistic development, but foremost gives an in-depth re-visit of the modern movement; the idea of the habitat, the transfer of ideas from one continent to another, from one generation to another, from the objectives of the military to those of the organizations of modern planning. It does so with an almost-candid and surely critical rereading of architectural history.

Asmara illuminates the urban transfiguration of the colonial dilemma, and thus the dilemma of every European city. On the one hand, we can hence investigate this architectural ensemble as time seems to have stopped. Hence, it is easy to create a set of cliches that reach into the micro texture of Asmara: *Espresso* machines, *Cappuccino*, *Cinquecento* taxis and the daily *passeggiata* melt into a specific atmosphere. Gebremedhin, one of the initiators of the preservation programme for Asmara, gets to the heart of it: "Eritreans [...] have [...] successfully adopted the modernist architecture of Asmara and reinvented its life space in their own manner!"[5] Many visitors are surprised by Asmara's illusion of a parallel universe; one that can only be described in terms of 'time having stopped'. The city centre seems to resemble an Italian one.

In his paper Gebremedhin presents arguments why the colonial city should be preserved although it was deliberately created as the abode of a racist and Fascist regime that wanted a place under the African sky for Italians and excluded Eritreans.[6]

In 1997 the city listed its buildings and thus revealed that the historic centre consists of about 400 buildings, which are architecturally significant. The survey showed that 40 per cent of the buildings were owned privately.

The *Cultural Assets Rehabilitation Programme* (CARP) came into being in 1997 when the State of Eritrea invited the World Bank to collaborate with it in forming a strategy for the preservation of Asmara's architectural heritage. A 'Historic Perimeter (HP)' was established immediately, covering an area of five square kilometres. A moratorium on new buildings within the 'Historic Perimeter' was proclaimed. The CARP survey examined the style of the buildings under three headings: Eclecticism; Modernism with its subset of styles including *novecento*; and Art Deco, *razionalismo*, *futurismo* and *monumentalismo*.

Of course, the colonial time represents a key stage in the emergence of Eritrean modernism, and the colonial architecture demonstrates a broad range of responses to complex ideological and cultural conditions. Eritrea conserves those modernist tendencies within a post-modern world as an experiment which uses political strategies in order to defend the *nation-building-project* against the influence of globalization. Asmara presents itself as *paradigmatic space*. Therefore, this city allows an analysis of our quotidian reality in a sarcastic way like no other does. Asmara provides space for reflection as well as for an empirical analysis of contemporary society. It is no archive of memories, but rather an incident that is constantly repeating itself.

The book *Asmara, Africa's Secret Modernist City*, describes this as follows: "Asmara is, by any standard, not simply a most convivial city, well planned and executed; its physical character – its architecture and urban spaces – also reflects strongly a range of international influences."[7] In reality, Asmara has totally changed over in the last 30 years. Asmara is now *Greater Asmara* – one of the fastest growing cities in Africa. How can we define the position of CARP within the context of *Greater Asmara*? What is the relationship between this centre and the rest of the city? Is CARP a World heritage or an African heritage?

Our project takes up the idea that Asmara is not only the *frozen city* that preserves the past. The tension between the formal and the informal city, between architecture by architects and architecture built without architects has existed since the very beginning of the modern project of urbanism as a profession of town-creation, but in the romantic representation of *bella Asmara* – the *frozen city* – it did not exist. We should turn our views from the grand master narratives and superpowers to the art of minor practices and everyday improvements.[8]

The notion of *new discovery* should not obscure the fact that it is not simply a return to Italian architecture originating from the interwar period. Created in a laboratory of European modernist fantasies, the 'historic perimeter' of

Asmara stands for a timeless example of modernity. Rabinow in his work *French modern* extends Foucault's rather Eurocentric scope and zooms in on urbanization in France's African colonies. He argues that the colonies "constituted a laboratory of experimentation for new arts of government capable of bringing a modern and healthy society into being."[9] Based on ideologies of progress and development through the organization of urban space the state developed the norms and forms of modernity. In her study Mia Fuller applies Rabinow's theories on Italian colonialism in Asmara and indicates how the Italian colonial government relied on practices of modern architecture. In the 1930s Asmara experienced a building boom as Italy invested in its infrastructure in Eritrea in order to invade Ethiopia:[10]

> The colonies served the colonisers as a 'laboratory' for testing modern techniques, which they regarded as being easier to realise in reference to the legal 'state of exception'. The laboratory paradigm had to be expanded, however. On the one hand it presumed a binary structure which equally underestimated the contradictions on the part of the colonial power and on the part of the colonised.[11]

The Secret Modernist City – The Romantic Image of Asmara

Today, the Eritreans have inherited the modern architecture of Asmara and many of them live in the former colonizer's houses. The description of Asmara generated a set of tropes such as the *Secret City*, the *Forgotten City*, the *Frozen City* or the *City of Dreams*. In most cases those images are a combination of a romantic spirit of discovery, and an exploration of the exotic, combined with colonial nostalgia.

How can we interpret the city of Asmara? Mia Fuller describes today's Asmara as a vehicle of complex local appropriations and rejections of the past against a larger backdrop of the future that is not linked only to Italian colonialism. The "photographic representation" – the icon of the Italian city is the "perfect snapshot of the past"[12] – is the result of many local and foreign actors who have developed their own strategies for the appropriation of Asmara.

Realizing Asmara's potential Gebremedhin's (who was the manager of CARP) first decision was to hire Edward Denison, a British photographer with a background of travelling in Eritrea: "A big part of our work […] was about getting (the modern heritage of Asmara) into the international domain: We gonna get the support of UNESCO, we gonna get the support of the World Monuments Fund. […] So we sent out masses of emails to these organizations."[13]

In 2003 Denison and Gebremedhin co-authored a book with the title *Asmara. The Secret Modernist City*. This book was meant to celebrate Asmara. The book literally reads like a call for support. The rhetoric, combined with the aesthetic appeal of the highly visual content created the romantic image of *bella Asmara*. Indeed, CARP capitalized on the popular reception of the book to create global support.[14] Denison attributes the development potential of the modern architecture of Asmara to his perception of the city as a 'nice' and 'safe' place to live. Therefore, he emphasizes the European character of the city.[15]

The Shared Heritage

The ambition to forge Eritrea's national identity through the valorisation of the colonial heritage of Asmara coincided with an upcoming interest in colonial architecture in Africa among global heritage organizations.

Culture should be regarded as a direct source of inspiration for development; and in return, development should assign a central role as social regulator to culture. In the late 1980s the World Bank announced a *holistic approach* to development and turned its attention to *cultural heritage* as a tool for what was called *post-conflict reconstruction*, *poverty reduction* or *nation building*.[16] The World Bank considered Eritrea a *natural experiment* for testing this new approach (the same rhetoric was used by the Italian colonizers!). And even the UNESCO World Heritage list entry of the historic perimeter of Asmara refers to an era when "Italian architects could [...] realize modern ideals."[17]

Somewhat paradoxically, for transnational organizations the appeal of the modern architecture of Asmara appears to be *nostalgia*[18]. The historic perimeter of Asmara stands for the colonial utopia of progress. According to Boym, "restorative nostalgia" manifests itself in the total reconstruction of monuments of the past.[19] The "untouched" historic heritage can reconstitute the "blank canvas" allegedly available to colonial architects in the past. This time Asmara would be a field of a new experiment for transnational organizations to test their approaches to *nation building*. [20] After the World Bank in Washington had terminated its loan to CARP in 2007, the European Union launched a follow-up *national heritage programme*. Five million Euro were invested exclusively in the restoration of modern architecture in Asmara.

The modern architectural heritage of Asmara is instrumental both to the transnational organizations and to the national Eritrean government. In particular, we want to know what happens when a young nation state in Africa is forced to operate in the same global space as the emergent transnational players. More specifically, the Eritrean government crucially depends on the appropriation of the modern architecture of Asmara as national heritage for the re-territorialisation of sovereignty. On the other hand, national and international organizations – with their approaches to *nation building* in Africa – are essentially dependent on Asmara's colonial heritage.

CARP's policy of creating a global sense of *shared heritage* lead to the governmental reaction of a radical policy of self-reliance in which the government crushed down on CARP's rallying of global assistance. Authorities became more and more apprehensive about foreign influence. Globalisation is the third phase in the relationship between the dominant countries and the dominated. The search for and the reconstruction of identity has become paramount. Now that national independence has been achieved, problems of national and community harmony have begun to surface.

The National Heritage

The *no-peace-no-war-situation* in contemporary Eritrea leads to a less hopeful situation. Of course, national identity as perceived by a government is inherently tied to the image of a splendid cultural past. According to Wallerstein, a state can create a national culture through its monopoly of policies:[21] "A national identity based on shorter-term political interest and the ideology of struggle emerged as the driving force behind most nationalist movements. Once independence was achieved, the glue that bound together the various groups no longer held."[22] One Eritrean commentator put it right when he said: "Asmara is our Jerusalem, the goal of our pilgrimage!" Eritrean people see their city as an expression of "national sacrifice", and thus as an integral moment of Eritrean nationalism. *Bella Asmara* has become a symbol of Eritrea's newly won national sovereignty.[23] Eritrea's government has turned the cultural capital of Asmara into the static symbol of Eritrean nationalism. In turn, Eritrea's policy of self-reliance at all cost (including serious human rights violations) disappoints the World Bank's interest in *post-conflict reconstruction* and the concept of the *shared heritage*. The Eritrean government sustains on-going conflict over its border with Ethiopia.

Identities and aesthetics in today's Asmara still demonstrate references to the colonial past.[24] In a *high modernist mission* the government never distinguishes between physical and moral pollution. Plastic bags are forbidden, beggars and prostitutes are transferred to the countryside or to the military camp of Sawa. Features of architecture become features of the nation. Cleanliness, order and security lead to a restrictive definition of urbanity and public space in Asmara.[25] Our project, therefore, centres on the relationship between the aesthetic regime of modernism and the project of modernisation – as well as on the highly charged intertwining of both in the context of colonialism and neo-colonialism.

The major and visible alterations of Asmara's street view concern the walls around properties, which many owners heightened for reasons of safety under the Ethiopian occupation. Actually, the global call to preserve the modern heritage of Asmara has effectively provided the Eritrean government with a concrete means to discretely exercise disciplinary power domestically. An orchestrated press campaign was launched to reduce the height of walls around private houses: "Asmara is an open city, so walls should only be one meter and twenty high. The 1938 master plan dictates this. [...] The government is now urging to abolish the walls."[26]

The *Asmarini* "imitate the colonial master" and his rhetoric, and, therefore, we can speak about neo-colonialism. Strong elements within the revolutionary forces inspire the nationalization of society in the name of progress. It is the rationalization – usually also conceived as the solution to problems of poverty and *backwardness* in the periphery – that provides the impetus for revolution. Eritrea, therefore, exemplifies features of modernity that have already disappeared from the Western world. This results from an interest in the symbolic value which was attributed to architecture as a means of urban planning in the colonial period; a concept which not only stood for the aesthetic project of modernism, but also represented the *planability* of social progress and the dawn of a new society. A naturalized belief in progress is used against the influence of globalization.

The Eritrean government but also the transnational organizations like the EU, the UNESCO, and the World Bank base their problematic politics of national sovereignty on colonial nostalgia. There is belief in the capacity of cultural heritage to transform Asmara into "a most modern city" again. Boym understands heritage as "institutionalized nostalgia". This time Asmara is a field of experimentation for national and transnational organizations to test new approaches to *nation building* through cultural heritage and its representation.

NOTES

[1] M. Fuller: Italy's Colonial Futures: Colonial Inertia and Postcolonial Capital in Asmara, in: http://escholarship.org/uc/item/4mb1z7f8?query=Asmara%20is%20what;hitRank=1#page-1 (12/ 10/ 2011), p. 8.

[2] Rausch C.: Modern Nostalgia: Asserting Politics of Sovereignty and Security in Asmara, Washington and Brussels 2011.

[3] S. Hall: *The Work of Representation*. In: Hall, S. (Ed.): *Representation. Cultural Representation and Signifying Practices*. London: Sage 1997, p. 16-61.

[4] see also: www.architekturtheorie.eu / txt.architekturtheorie.eu / www.architekturtheorie.tv

[5] Gebremedhin N.: Asmara, Africa's Secret Modernist City Prepared for the *African Perspectives: Dialogue on Urbanism and Architecture*, The Faculty of Architecture, TU, Delft 2007, in: http://www.bk.tudelft.nl/fileadmin/Faculteit/BK/Actueel/Symposia_en_congressen/African_Perpectives/Programme/Built_Heritage/doc/APD_wp_5_gebremedhin_paper.pdf

[6] Gebremedhin 2007.

[7] E. Denison., G. Y. Ren and N. Gebremedhin: Asmara, Africa's Secret Modernist City, London: Merrell Publishers 2003, p. 50.

[8] Also see: P. Volgger: The Sleeping Beauty, in: txt.architekturtheorie.eu

[9] P. Rabinow: French Modern. Norms and Forms of the Social Environment, Chicago: The University of Chicago Press 1989, p. 289.

[10] M. Fuller: Moderns Abroad: Architecture, Cities and Italian Imperialism, London 2007, p. 144.

[11] S. Karakayali: Colonialism and the Critique of Modernity, in: T. Avermaeta, S. Karakayali and M. von Osten: Colonial Modern. Aesthetics of the Past – Rebellions for the Future, London 2010, pp. 39.

[12] B. Groys: Die Stadt im Zeitalter ihrer touristischen Reproduzierbarkeit, in: Groys, B.: Topologie der Kunst, München/ Wien: Hanser 2003, p. 145.

[13] Interview Denison, in: C. Rausch: Modern Nostalgia, p. 8.

[14] Also see: Travelling exhibition 'Asmara – Africa's Secret Modernist City'. Various locations starting 2006; R. Ofori, and E. Scott: Asmara – City of Dreams. Washington 2005.

[15] Denison, p. 8.

[16] J. D. Wolfersohn: The Challenges of Globalization: The Role of the World Bank/ Address to the Bundestag, Berlin/ Germany: The World Bank Group 2001, in: C. Rausch: Modern Nostalgia 2011, p. 5.

[17] Tentative UNESCO World Heritage List Entry, The Historc Perimeter of Asmara and Its Modernist Architecture.

[18] S. Boym: The Future of Nostalgia, New York: Basic Books 2001.

[19] C. Rausch: Modern Nostalgia: Asserting Politics of Sovereignty and Securita in Asmara, Washington and Brussels 2011.

[20] C. Rausch: 2011, p. 20f.

[21] I. Wallerstein: The Nation and the Universal. Can There be Such a Thing as a World Culture?, in: A. D. King: Culture, Globalization, and the World System, London 1991, pp. 91-106.

[22] N. Alsayyad: Culture, Identity and Urbanism. A Historical Perspective from Colonialism and Globalisation, in: T. Avermaete, S. Karakayali, M. von Osten (Eds.): Colonial Modern. Aethetics of the Past Rebellions for the Future, London: Black Dog Publishing 2010, p. 80.

[23] Ibid, p.83

[24] C. Rausch 2011, p. 24.

[25] M. Treiber: "The choice between clean and dirty. Discourses of Aesthetics, Morality and Progress in Post-revolutionary Asmara, Eritrea", In: Dürr, Eveline; Jaffe, Rivke (Eds.): Urban Pollution. Cultural Meanings, Social Practices. Berghahn Oxford 2010, pp. 123-143.

[26] C. Rausch 2011, p. 14.

THE MILITARISED IMAGES OF THE CITY

Mladen Stilinovic

Independent researcher and architect, Brussels/ Belgium
mladen.stilinovic@gmail.com

ABSTRACT

This article is part of a research on the spatial interactions between the military and civil society. The development of both case studies – Skopje and Bitola – has been characterised by periods of war and strong army presence. The focus is on presenting the local productions of urban imagery by observing the specific agency of the military. Throughout the examined events and periods, army-related images became elements of the local palimpsests of urban and territorial narratives. The present urban context is analysed as well, as the current 'absence' of the military leads to new forms of (violent) spatial contest.

Dieser Artikel ist Teil einer breiter angelegten Forschung zur räumlichen Interaktion zwischen Militär und Zivilgesellschaft. Die Entwicklung beider Fallstudien – Skopje und Bitola – ist gekennzeichnet durch Perioden kriegerischer Auseinandersetzung und starker Armee-Präsenz. Das Augenmerk liegt auf der Präsentation der vor Ort entstehenden städtischen Bildlichkeit unter besonderer Berücksichtigung der spezifischen Wirkung des Militärs. Während aller untersuchten Ereignisse und Zeiträume wurden mit der Armee verknüpfte Bilder zu Elementen des örtlichen Palimpsests städtischer und territorialer Texte. Gleichzeitig wird der gegenwärtige städtische Kontext analysiert vor dem Hintergrund einer Zunahme (gewalttätiger) Formen des räumlichen Wettbewerbs angesichts der derzeitigen „Abwesenheit" des Militärs.

Introduction

The exploration of the militarised urban imagery, presented in this article is part of a research that focuses on the spatial interactions between the military and the civil society in the context of the Western Balkans. This context is rather peripheral to the existing scholarship on militarised spaces, however, the events in the last century placed it on the margins of both the 'occidental' and 'oriental', alternating between the two, thus providing this analysis with an abundance of content. The military related urban imagery was looked upon by focussing on two interrelated case-studies: the cities of Skopje and Bitola, both situated in the present-day Republic of Macedonia. Much alike the Western Balkans, these two cities are characterised by frequent and often abrupt changes of resident or occupying military power, the definition of which depends upon the historiographical discourse. Therefore, the militarised images of the city and their shifting agency are important components of Skopje's and Bitola's palimpsests of urban and territorial narratives. The following periods and transitory events were taken into consideration:

- The ultimate decline of the Ottoman Empire
- The two Balkan Wars and the First World War
- The Interwar period – Royal Yugoslavia
- The Second World War and the Skopje Earthquake
- The Cold War period – Socialist, non-aligned Yugoslavia
- The break-up of Yugoslavia and the armed conflict of 2001 in Macedonia
- The present-day context – abandonment of military domains

Urban Manifestations of the 'Military'

The arguments in this article are outlined with the objective to underpin the shifting agency of the military present in the production of urban imagery. Such agency will be traced using imagery from selected periods, which is analysed in relation to the changing entanglement of military and civil society. In certain cases I will also examine how the transitory events (military conflicts or other military activities) have been used as a leverage to embed these army-related images into the local palimpsests of urban and territorial narratives.

In doing so, the modernisation of warfare will be used as an important notion, as it has drastically altered the spatial impact of military strategies. Nowadays, as the military strategy is less often founded on actual army presence in the urban environment, the military apparatuses are moving out of sight, thus leaving behind vast remains of the 'glorious' past, such as walls and fortifications, as well as abandoned barracks and training grounds. Many military infrastructures are rendered obsolete, landscapes are left scarred. Bearing this in mind, the present-day urban context is taken into as one of the key considerations, since the current 'absence' of the military is often masking new forms of (violent) spatial contest.

The Town beneath the Ottoman Fortress

The declining Ottoman Empire is the first of the four aforementioned periods, in which I will look upon Skopje as an example of a military agency producing a dominant urban image, without following any 'modernising' tendencies. Skopje, known as Uskub at the time, kept the appearance of a rather isolated Oriental town up until the very beginning of the 20th century. The 'time-immemorial' fortress was a dominant element in the urban landscape, and as such it was overwhelmingly present in the urban imagery of the time (see fig.1).

However, given that the concept of the fortress as a part of the military apparatus was already an anachronism in terms of warfare techniques, such urban setting held only symbolic value. In this case, the military agency should be regarded in the light of the representation of military dominance over the different religious and ethnic groups, exercised by the late Ottoman Empire (Akhund 2009, p. 450).

Fig.1: Old postcard depicting the declaration of the constitution in 1908, beneath the fortress in Skopje (Uskub) – source unknown (old postcard – public domain of the Ottoman Empire)

The Modern Garrison City of the Ottoman Military

Unlike Skopje, in the case of Bitola the Ottoman Empire introduced the concept of modern military forces in order to pursue a different goal: displaying its modernisation (Akhund 2009, 450). Around the middle of the 19th century, as the declining Empire was trying to achieve a better governance over the inland areas, Bitola – also known as Monastir – was designated an administrative capital. Large public works were conducted, introducing Western-influenced urban and architectural elements, amongst them being the construction of a new military domain which was to represent an 'Ottoman city of the future' (Cohen 2000, 13). A thriving urban milieu was formed by the simultaneous presence of high-ranking military officers and bureaucrats, rising bourgeoisie of diverse origin and above all – foreigners: diplomats, missionaries and traders. In such context, the military agency became a competing segment within the production of urban imagery, sharing a common aspiration towards being 'occidental' (see fig.2).

Fig.2: Ottoman military parade in Bitola (Monastir) in 1906, taken from a motion picture by Manaki brothers (image source: Cinemateque of Macedonia in Skopje)

The Memorials of the City as a Theatre of War

The turn of the historic events brought the prosperous period of Bitola to an abrupt end. During the course of WWI Bitola suffered great urban destruction, followed by an exodus of the population. Times of war bring examples of military-related urban imagery being produced both during and following the actual act of warfare. As trenches were in the very outskirts of the city, the presence of different armies virtually transformed the urban landscape into a huge barrack. Such transformation produced images of soldiers taking part in everyday activities; the background being bombed buildings. In the aftermath of the war, different memorials and military graveyards, all depicting the heroism and patriotism of the troops, became prominent in the urban imagery (see fig.3). However, because the everyday urban life could not easily relate to such narratives, the military agency pursued a rather self-contained and implicit agenda regarding the production of urban imagery.

Fig.3: The WWI German military graveyards overlooking Bitola around 1930 (image source: Museum of Bitola)

The Royal Army

Once it became a regional capital of the Kingdom of Serbia (later of Yugoslavia) in 1910, Skopje was to emulate the national narrative through its urban imagery. This is the second period looked upon more closely, and it is an example of a military agency displaying both modernizing and a dominant role in the production of urban imagery, while re-contextualizing certain structures in order to fit them within the nation-state's overall narrative. The parallel processes of nation-building and de-Ottomanisation both had a significant military component. The existing fortress was named 'city of Dusan', a symbolic appropriation relating to pre-Ottoman medieval narratives. Furthermore, as a part of the urban expansion across the river, military-related buildings were erected in prominent locations. Especially important was the House of the Officers at the city's main square, which became one of the key features of the urban imagery from the time (see fig.4).

Fig.4: A view of Skopje from the fortress around 1930: House of the Officers on the right, retrieved from http://www.skyscrapercity.com/showthread.php?t=252159&page=3

The Provincial Garrison Town of the People's Army

Being a non-aligned country, Yugoslavia was an ever-prepared for war society that relied mostly upon guerrilla tactics, as an infliction of the WWII partisan narrative. Partly due to the country's constrained geography, the People's Army was using barracks in urban environments for both training of the troops, as well as symbolic presence. The case of Bitola during the third analysed, socialist period, presents the effects of such a hegemonic constellation that led to a dominant role of the military agency, which in turn allowed for a significant control over the production of urban imagery. Just like many other provincial garrison cities, Bitola was to replicate the state model based on the trinity of youth, workers and soldiers, displayed by the omnipresence of the People's Army in everyday urban life (see fig.5). At the same time, the military domain itself was a restricted area, accessible to military personnel only. Finally, the military maintained its representative features, by preserving the House of the Officers as an elite cultural and entertainment centre.

Fig.5: Workers, youth and soldiers parading in Bitola (1984) (image source: Museum of Bitola)

The International City of Solidarity

Meanwhile, the profound changes in Skopje's urban setting were marked by the modernisation process that took place in the aftermath of the Skopje earthquake of 1963. The military agency in this case makes a turn towards depicting itself as a 'builder' of the modern urban identity, even at the expense of its previous urban features. When in the aftermath of the Cuban missile crisis military units of the opposed Cold War blocks joined in relief efforts, the image of reconciliation captured the world's attention (see fig.6). The subsequent renewal plans brought the idea of rebuilding Skopje as a 'city of the future', a symbol of the international solidarity, which would also feature as a 'grand national capital' (UNDP 1970, 31). The military buildings situated in the fortress and the House of the Officers were both torn down by the earthquake, and there were no reconstruction efforts. Instead, the military retained its symbolic presence in the urban imagery through a multitude of domains, administrative buildings and housing districts for the officers and their families, all featuring pioneer modern architecture.

Fig.6: "Soldiers left their arms to help re-build Skopje" a scene from the movie 'Skopje 1963', directed by Veljko Bulajic (image source: Cinematheque of Macedonia in Skopje)

Contested Landscapes

Lastly, in the present context of Skopje, outlining the fourth analysed period, the passive role of the military agency leads to various conflicts. Since the independence of Macedonia and the withdrawal of the People's Army, the military agency lost its dominant role in the structure of the society. The territory around Skopje became subject to various appropriations: NATO and the UN have deployed their units, and, furthermore, areas surrounding the city were the scenery of the armed conflict of 2001. The former military-related urban imagery is subject to contestation as well, an example being the new US embassy situated near the fortress. Moreover, the very remnants of the fortress are claimed by both dominant ethnic communities as a part of their respective national narratives – culminating in public unrest and effectively restricting the access to the fortress. On the other hand, there is an on-going construction of a House of Officers replica which is to serve as a City Hall, within the scope of the Skopje 2014 project, which is in turn contested on multiple levels (Kotevska 2011).

The Afterlife of the Militarised Landscapes

During the last two decades, the military presence in Bitola has been gradually fading as well until it disappeared completely a few years ago. In the absence of the military agency, its remnants are re-contextualised as a part of the production of urban imagery. The vast interiors of the once enclosed domain are now in continuous state of decline (see fig. 7). The intent to transform the area into a 'new town', declared by the local government, could be considered as a tendency to create a post-transitional elite society, by spatially replacing the former one. On the other hand, the 'reductionist exclusion' tendency found in the current local production of urban imagery rejects both the military memorials as well as the more recent militarised urban imagery, in favour of urban features and structures that relate to the perceived 'cosmopolitan' period of the city (Stilinovic 2013, 49). Such a structure is the House of the Officers, which is seen as a hallmark of the current, 'occidental' urban image of Bitola – despite being part of the Ottoman legacy.

Fig.7: A Sight from the abandoned military domain in Bitola in 2011 (source: Mladen Stilinovic)

Conclusion

In conclusion, this article provides a different reading of the urban imageries by trying to better understand the changing relations between the military and the civil society. Also, it identifies the agency of the military and the shifting roles it had in the overall production of urban imagery.

Primarily, as the modernisation of warfare drastically alters the spatial impact of military strategies, it also has a subsequent effect on the military agency. However, throughout different periods, the military maintains a representation of itself as a dominant force within the urban society. Therefore, the military introduces and preserves 'representational' structures in the urban imagery (such as the House of the Officers), while the actual military domains are often transformed into restricted areas.

Furthermore, some fragments of military-related imagery are erased from the urban narrative (the WWI memorials in Bitola), while others become recontextualised, depending on the entanglement of military and civil society and their respective historiographies (the fortress in Skopje during Serbian rule).

Finally, the physical absence of the military leads to various claims upon the ex-militarised territories and structures – the transformation of which proves to be a substantial urban issue. In this present context, the tendency of the current local productions of urban imagery is to integrate the former military-related fragments, albeit with a new meaning.

BIBLIOGRAPHY

Akhund, Nadine. 2009. "Muslim Representation in the Three Ottoman Vilayets of Macedonia: Administration and Military Power (1878-1908)". *Journal of Muslim Minority Affairs*. 29: 4, 443-454.

Cohen, M. 2000. "Monastir: Oasis of Civilization, 1839-63". *The Turkish Studies Association Bulletin*. 24: 2, 3-22.

Kotevska, Jasna. 2011. "Troubles with History: Skopje 2014". *Art Margins*. http://artmargins.com/index.php/2-articles/655-troubles-with-history-skopje-2014.

Stilinovic, Mladen. 2013. "Bitola: Shifting Images of a Western Balkan City". *Oase Journal for Architecture* (89). 40-53.

United Nations Development Programme. 1970. *Skopje Resurgent: The Story of a United Nations Special Fund Town Planning Project*. 383.

HORROR VACUI

Farzaneh Bahrami

Federal Institute of Technology (EPFL), Lausanne/ Switzerland
farzaneh.bahrami@gmail.com

Shaida Ghomashchi

Artist and independent researcher, Tehran/ Iran
shaida.ghomashchi@gmail.com

ABSTRACT

In the context of over-densification in Tehran, it is unlikely to have an urban landscape free of cranes. Cranes pop up and disappear in the skyline of Tehran, but their image goes beyond the construction sites and urban development. The authors understand the crane as a visual element and explore its multiple-faceted presence in the social-urban fabric of today's Tehran. The article will take the 'Horror Vacui' beyond its conventional implication (in visual arts) and exploit various meanings of horror in this context.

Angesicht der herrschenden Überbevölkerung in Teheran ist es unwahrscheinlich im Stadtbild keine Kräne zu entdecken. Kräne erscheinen und verschwinden in Teheran, aber ihr Bild weist über Baustellen und Stadt-Entwicklung hinaus. Die Autoren verstehen den Kran als visuelles Element und erforschen seine facettenreiche Präsenz im sozio-urbanen Gewebe des heutigen Teheran. Der Artikel fasst den Begriff des „Horror Vacui" weiter als es in den bildenden Künsten üblich ist und widmet sich in diesem Zusammenhang unterschiedlichen Spielarten des Schreckens

Between Past and Future

The city, like a mental organism, has access to its previous states of existence. Its spatiotemporal depth may depend on the number of military occupations, fire cuts and revolutions it has witnessed[1]. The patterns of the urban growth are determined by a variety of factors, including geography, history, and the economics of the city. Often there is a certain continuity in a city's development. Tehran, however, has systematically overwritten its past, creating a hardly legible palimpsest by favouring destruction over conservation. The anti-mnemonic character of Tehran might be the expected consequence of a constant rupture in the political power during the relatively short history of the city, but also the outcome of the actions and choices of individuals within society. The choice stretches from active and ideological destruction to careless development.

In the time span of some two hundred years Tehran has evolved from a typically traditional Islamic city of 15,000 inhabitants to a growing metropolis with snaking highways cutting through the city, hosting almost one sixth of the country's population and extending on a surface of 700 km^2.

In the late eighteenth century Tehran was demarcated as the capital by the Qajar kings who sought to maintain the traditional alliance between religion and politics. The city inherited its architectural language from its predecessors with a hierarchical streets layout, inward looking individual houses to ensure privacy, i. e. to create a smooth transition from private (Andarouni – feminine domain) to public (Biruni – masculine domain) – and all buildings composed around the main Bazar and the Friday mosque.

The city developed at a slow pace during the first decades of the Qajar Dynasty. The universal Exhibition of Paris carried out by Baron Haussmann impressed Nasreddin Shah, who began to tear down old city walls after his return from Europe and set out new urban policies[2]. This increased the city's total area to 18.4 km^2, making it four times bigger than before. In the new northern quarters, foreign embassies were established, the first modern or multi-storey buildings were built and new streets were laid out.

Despite the growing population and new urban development Tehran remained a rural city, especially in comparison with other cities which had become much more prosperous by then, like Tabriz with its more international character. However, after the constitutional Revolution in 1906 and the discovery of oil in 1908, Iran found a new international role, and Tehran rapidly out-grew other cities. Since then it has experienced different political structures; it has hosted several revolutions, upheavals and urban movements, each leaving a trace on the city form.

With the wave of modernization in the first decades of the twentieth century the traditional city of Tehran was transformed radically. The transformation, however, was not an evolutionary process but rather a conscious, radical move initiated by Reza Shah. The walls' gateways were destroyed, private houses and their relation to the street were redefined and the orthogonal grid of streets was superimposed upon the existing dense and irregular pattern of the traditional Islamic city.

Perceived as regressive and contradictory to the image of modern Tehran, manifestations of Islam were suppressed. Anything on the way was simply and unceremoniously demolished.[3] For example, *Tekyeh Dowlat*, a theatre constructed in the years 1867-1873 for the performance of different forms of the Ta'ziyeh (the passion-play performed annually during the month of Muharram to commemorate the martyrdom of Imam Hossein), was demolished during the first Pahlavi period, and on its ruins new buildings were built to house the modern bureaucracy.

The second Pahlavi period coincided with the nationalization of the oil industry. Oil income financed extensive programs of industrialization as well as urban development. In this context the first comprehensive plan was drawn up by the American architect Victor Gruen, who sought to reshape Tehran into a Los Angeles-type suburban entity. He envisioned a city divided into ten different districts linked to one another through a network of freeways and a rapid transportation system.[4] Even though the master plan was never fully achieved and implemented, the Tehran of today is very much the result of this vision.

The socio-economic reforms and, particularly, the land reforms under the second Pahlavi in the 1960s caused massive migration to the cities, especially to Tehran. The immigration rate increased in the aftermath of the Islamic revolution; the new arrivals were mostly settled in the peripheries and created the new sprawling capital whose dramatic physical expansion and densification continues to this day.

The densification has taken a new turn in the recent years; it mostly consists of a self-managed and self-initiated process by individual property owners who tear down their old houses within the legal terms and reconstruct new ones to increase the total floor area.

These buildings, which are called 'pick-axe buildings', are no more than thirty (even twenty) years old, and they are normally sound in foundation and structure or in a few cases may simply need a renovation. However, they are condemned to be demolished as their land value and the potential square-meters surpass the value of the current material structure and the immaterial values such as identity or memories, both individual and collective ones.

The city's spatial framework is where the collective memory unfolds, thus the destruction of its physical body is the destruction of the supporting basis of the collective memory. The old urban fabric metamorphoses into a range of new fabrics at a breakneck speed; neighbourhood characteristics disappear in the homogeneity of new trends in architectural style and material. Katouzian, an Iranian historian and political scientist, takes this phenomenon to be a manifestation of his perception of Iran as a short-term society, where "political, social, educational, literary [elements] are constantly in danger of receiving the pick-axe treatment by short term whims of fashion"[5]. In his article on this issue, written almost a decade ago, Katouzian explains the pick-axe attitude by urges of fashion. Today, one might attribute this phenomenon to economic instability, land speculations and urban policies. This, however, does not mean that individuals are mere victims of vicious political or economic circles since "the society, including at its heart, ordinary citizens should not be seen as inactive in their own choices. If there are city centers, suburbs, suburban spaces, if there are open or closed blocks, if people get around on foot, by car or by tram, it is the choice of urban society (or, at least, that of a part of it)"[6].

Horror Vacui

Fashion: don't you remember that we are both caducity's daughters?
Death: what can I remember, I who am memory's greatest enemy?
(Giacomo Leopardi, nineteenth century)

In the context of Islamic art, 'Horror Vacui' is not the individual motif such as a flower, an arabesque, a geometrical design or a hunting scene which asks for our attention and possible interpretation, but rather the whole ensemble (Gestalt). It expresses itself on our sensibilities and represents our aesthetic experience. It is only by a secondary act, a close viewing that we are led to examine the separate details. In case of Tehran it is the pick-axe buildings, reconstructions and the geometrical presence of cranes. Confronted with the question of their possible significance, Richard Ettinghausen argues that one of the factors which lead to 'Horror Vacui' in Islamic art is that life in the cities was crowded, and this was seen as natural and appropriate to civilization. So art itself as the prime result of civilization should be similarly crowded.[7]

'Horror Vacui' is an attempt to re-narrate the pick-axe Tehran, through the omnipresence of its cranes as symbolic elements representing life-death cycles, both in the body of the built environment, and the imagination of its inhabitants.

It is unlikely to capture a landscape frame in Tehran without a crane as a visual element. Even amidst the cacophony of the city one cannot ignore their vertical presence. Cranes are being placed in various different layers, contributing to the ceaseless construction. There is no absolute pattern to follow them but rather a complex interplay which occurs on the surface of the town.

Cranes pop up and disappear in the skyline of Tehran, but their image goes beyond the construction sites and urban development. We render existence to a "skeletal scheme" – a structural figure of a geometric nature which has straight linear outlines, being more dead than alive depending on whether it is regarded from a physical or mental point of view. In Islamic art it is only by secondary act, a close viewing of the object and its decoration, that we are led to examine the separate details and are then confronted with the question of their possible significance; but when it comes to the cranes in the context of an urban landscape we will be concerned with the manner of arrangement of the various, yet, similar units in a larger setting. The skyline of Tehran is covered by these straight geometrical lines of an abstract nature which have been merged with the background of the horizon.

Besides, the image of the crane is entangled with the dramatic public scene of executions. The Iranian regime's preferred method of execution is public hanging from a construction crane. To address this egregious phenomenon UANI launched its "Cranes Campaign" in 2011 in order to put pressure on leading crane manufacturers to end their business with the Iranian regime.[8]

Here again the question arises of how individuals contribute to this "public" spectacle by their participation as the audience. When it comes to participation in social acts, does it really matter whether you are a part of the spectacle as an executor or a mere witness to the crime who maintains neutral in times of moral crisis?

In his well-known text *Introduction to the reading of Hegel* Alexander Kojeve shed light on this matter: "Si la réalité humaine est une réalité sociale, la société n'est humaine qu'en tant qu'ensemble de Désirs se désirant mutuellement en tant que Désirs".[9] Moreover, cranes metamorphose into Shi'ite ritual artefacts during the holy month of Muharram. During this period they serve as sacrifice stones. Each neighborhood sets up its own 'Tekkiyeh' for the ceremonial processions of the month of the same name. They are venues for gathering of mourners known as 'Heyat' (literally meaning 'group' or 'delegation') who honor the life of Imam Hossein (Hussein is an important figure in Islam as he is a member of the *Ahl al-Bayt*, the household of Muhammad, and the third Shia Imam). Religious ceremonies more than often include food offerings held at both public venues like mosques and at private residences. These communal gatherings are also a kind of forum where friends, acquaintances and neighbors meet over food that is served after the ceremonies. During Muharram cities are abuzz with the preparation for food offerings known as Nazri, the processions which are usually sponsored by wealthy benefactors. Sheep, cows and other Halal animals are specifically and ritually sacrificed for this purpose.

Most of these 'Heyats' usually own cranes which are being used in the process of making Nazri (charity food); as if every neighbourhood has its own foundation stone (قُبَّة الصّخره) . A rock which connects the earth to heaven and from which, according to the Quran, the prophet Muhammad ascended to heaven is the very same stone on which Abraham fulfilled God's test to see if he would be willing to sacrifice his son Isaac but sacrificed the ram instead.

In Giacomo Leopardi's prose magnum opus "Operette morali" (1824) the dialogue between Fashion and Death goes on:

> Fashion:but I remember well, and I know that you and I together keep undoing and changing things down here on earth although you go about it one way and I another… I'm saying it is our custom to keep renovating the world. … I persuade and force all genteel men to endure daily a thousand hardships and a thousand discomforts and often pain and torment.
>
> Death: so, if you feel like running next to me, be sure you don't croak for I go fast.

The cranes of Tehran are messengers of two sisters: death and fashion. They symbolize the thrill and the dread of a world in which *all that is solid melts into air*. Their presence is somewhat of a reminder, aide-mémoire of a *paradoxical unity, a unity of disunity.*[10]

NOTES

[1] Marot, Sébastien. *Sub-urbanism and the Art of Memory*. Vol. 8. AA Publishing, (2003), p. 41.

[2] Sluglett, Peter (Ed.). "The Demography of Cities and the Expansion of the Urban Space", in: *The Urban Social History of the Middle East 1750 – 1950*. Syracuse: Syracuse University Press (2008), pp. 164-181.

[3] Marefat, Mina. *Building to Power: Architecture of Tehran* 1921-1941, Massachusetts Institute of Technology, Department of Architecture (1988), p. 72.

[4] Bayat, Asef. "Tehran: Paradox City". NEW LEFT REV 66 (2010), pp.99-122.

[5] Katouzian, Homa. "The short-term society: a study in the problems of long-term political and economic development in Iran". Middle Eastern Studies 40.1 (2004), pp.1-22.

[6] Lévy, Jacques. *Urbanité/s, Urbanity/ies*, [DVD], Lausanne, Chôros-École Polytechnique Fédérale de Lausanne (2013), 1:07:03.

[7] Ettinghausen, Richard. "The Taming of the Horror Vacui in Islamic Art", Proceeding of the American Philosophical society, Vol. 123, no. 1 (Feb. 20, 1979), pp.15-28.

[8] http://www.unitedagainstnucleariran.com/cranes

[9] Kojeve, Alexandre. "Introduction a la lecture de Hegel", Paris (1978), p.13.

[10] Berman, Marshall. "All that is solid melts into air", Penguine books (1988), p.15.

The Psychology of the City/ Urbanity as an Issue of a Developed Society

THE NATURE AND THE CITY – THE PICTURE OF NATURE IN ISTANBUL

Z. Nilüfer Nahya

Erciyes University, Kayseri/ Turkey
nlufern@yahoo.com

Fulya Anılır

Yeni Yuzyil University, Istanbul/ Turkey
fulyaanilir@gmail.com

ABSTRACT

This article aims to examine the picture of nature and city dwellers, and the image of nature in city life. The questions of how human beings use and modify nature and, accordingly, what kind of a picture of nature can be observed in a city are answered by analyzing the observations of some Istanbul districts. Although Istanbul is mostly known for its historical heritage, this article also focuses on the impact of industrialization and modernity in natural places.

Dieser Artikel zielt darauf ab, das Bild der Natur und der Stadtbewohner im Kontext des Stadtlebens zu lesen. Die Frage, wie der Mensch die Natur gebraucht und modifiziert, und welches Bild der Natur in diesem Sinne in der Stadt zu finden ist, wird durch die Analyse von Beobachtungen in einigen Istanbuler Stadtteilen beantwortet. Obwohl Istanbul in erster Linie für sein historisches Erbe bekannt ist, konzentriert sich der Artikel auch auf den Einfluss der Industrialisierung und der Modernisierung auf inner-städtische Naturräume.

Levi-Strauss identifies the distinction between humans and nature by opposing nature and culture; also distinguishing humans from animals. He defines a human as “both a biological being and a social individual”.[1] The role of the human as a natural being has changed when humans started to modify nature. The domestication of natural elements is the other relationship of humans and nature. Many plants and animals have been domesticated and even new kinds of animals have been developed by humans.

Today city-dwellers create their own relation with nature in modern cities. City-dwellers live within nature by modifying, controlling, recreating, and re-establishing it. They also assign meanings to this relationship which can be observed in their city life. Observations, photos, gravures, pictures, symbols and possible meanings behind people's attitudes can be combined to understand the general picture and any image of nature.

This article aims to analyse the picture of nature and city dwellers, and the image of nature in city life. Nature-human relations defining the look of nature can be seen in different parts of the cities in several ways. 60 photos have been taken in Istanbul and have been analysed in the context of nature and the city for this article.

Istanbul and Nature

Istanbul, the focus of this article, is one of the oldest cities of the world. The establishment of Istanbul dates back to the 7th century BC. The city was named *Byzantion* then. *Byzantion* became a Roman city in the 2nd century BC and was transformed into the new capital by Emperor Constantin and named *Constantinopolis* in 324.[2] The city has had a cosmopolitan structure since that time. After the conquest of the city in 1453 Sultan Mehmed II renamed it Istanbul.

The look of Istanbul was changed further during the Ottoman era by construction activities, and the cosmopolitan structure of the city was expanded in time too. But the look of Istanbul was changed mostly due to big or small fires, and the city was reconstructed many times in the Ottoman era.[3] But the greatest change came with modern industrialization during the 19th century. The industrialization process especially affected mansions, gardens and old palaces: they were demolished in favour of military buildings, new factories and terminals. Barracks and factories became the symbols of Ottoman industrialization.[4] The change in Istanbul further intensified in the new Turkish Republican period. Istanbul remained the Republic's industrial centre. Yet, the biggest change in terms of urban planning was experienced in the 1940s and 1950s. Constructing big avenues and streets changed and damaged both the historical and the natural configuration of the Istanbul city.[5] By the 1980s the rise in population created a housing shortage, and resulted in the construction of apartment buildings and *gecekondu*s – self-constructed squatter housing. *Gecekondu*s and apartments were often built in the empty spaces of the city, which were sometimes natural areas, such as forests, stream banks and the seaside.[6]

The sea, and especially the Bosporus, has been crucial in history. The Asian and European continents meet in Istanbul and make it a strategic place from a military and commercial perspective. The Istanbul ports were used for national and international transportation of goods and people.[7] In addition to its beauty, the seaside was a marketplace where goods were sold in boats on the sea.[8] Moreover, the sea defines the climate in the city.[9]

Although Istanbul is often imagined and presented as a historical centre, this city has another face: it is modern, industrial and commercial. But nature remains an important dimension of both historical and modern images of Istanbul.

The Image of Nature in Istanbul

Nature is considered in between wild and domesticated classifications. As mentioned above, early domestications show humans' desire to control nature. These control or domination processes continue inside the cities. Cultured plants, landscape designs and the meanings behind them are the results of this process of control of nature. Natural arrangements constituted and conducted by human intervention can be classified as 'controlled nature'.

The controlled nature of Istanbul can be seen mostly in the parks, gardens, apartments and streetscapes of the city where district and city municipalities have control of the green areas; but city-dwellers can also interfere in the usage of the natural places of Istanbul. Most common parks are not only the natural places to stay and to spend time but also the places where animals and humans come together. City-dwellers bring their dogs to the parks and socialize with each other. Parks are also the places for street animals. City residents bring animal food or their own leftovers to feed the animals in these spaces. Thus it is possible to see humans including children and adults and animals together in the parks.

Although millions of people live in the cities, loneliness is one of the main problems of city life, and owning animals as pets is one of the ways in which urban residents deal with loneliness. Conditions of the city force pet owners – especially dog owners – to go out for a walk in their neighbourhoods for their dogs' socializations and needs. In fact, this socialization is not only for the dogs but also for their owners. They meet with the other pet owners in the parks, on the roads and at veterinary surgeries, and make new friends as well. There is also a phenomenon of collective pet ownership – when several people voluntarily look after dogs or cats living in the parks, streets, or cafes; they not only feed them, but also provide veterinary care, walk them, and name them.

Homelessness is another result of city life. Homeless people offer yet another picture of the human relationship with street animals and green spaces in the city. Like in all other global cities homeless people live around Istanbul. They live in the parks and in the green spaces near the roads. Often, homeless people share these spaces and their food with street animals, mostly cats and dogs. In Istanbul this picture represents both the human-nature relation and the life of urban society. They also live outside of the regular city life, not conforming to the social norms and lifestyle. Herewith they are considered dangerous, weird, and addicted to alcohol and/ or drugs, and are alienated from mainstream society. But at the same time they take part in the city life because they live in the cities, and their settlement in the parks and near the roads makes them visible to society.

Another common picture in Istanbul is house cats sitting inside flats near the windows watching the roads, the people, the other cats, and the birds. Some of these cats can go out of the apartments and come back to their houses at night. But some people prefer to look after their cats in front of their apartments. They take them to the vets, feed them two or three times a day together with the other cats, and provide shelter for them, often inside their apartment buildings in rainy or snowy weather. It is also possible to see some cats living in the shops, sleeping in the show glasses, sitting on the books of bookstores, and cleaning themselves on chairs, cars and motorcycles.

Many people feed domestic birds such as canaries, budgerigar and zebra finches as pets, but also wild birds such as pigeons, seagulls, sparrows, crows and Eurasian collared doves in Istanbul. The urban environment is "a new habitat that has the potential to support diverse bird communities" and "birds respond to urban ecosystems by either avoiding cities or by adapting or exploiting the urban landscape".[10] Urban spaces – parks, gardens and apartments – become environments for wild urban birds where they survive and have contact with city dwellers.

Gardens, usually located in front or behind the apartment buildings or private houses, are another type of natural places controlled by city-dwellers. In the Ottoman era the concept of home (*ev*) included the garden and the house.[11] House gardens were the outdoors in which women could spend time.[12] Today, the main aim in laying out a garden is mostly to create or to live in a 'beautiful' environment. Backyard gardens of some apartments are even used for agriculture with the purpose of growing organic food. Urban residents often prefer to grow vegetables such as tomatoes, cucumber, parsley, mint, spring onions, spinach and purslane themselves rather than buy them in supermarkets. Yet, most gardens are spaces for briers and ornamental flowers like rose, chrysanthemum and viola. Winders and vines can also be seen in some gardens. Ornamental flowers are also seen in front of the apartment windows and balconies.

Though Istanbul's long history of ancient trees is a notable natural element in the image of nature, Istanbul loses them day by day. The most characteristic trees of Istanbul are cypresses and sycamores.[13] The sycamore has been associated with the State and history since Ottoman times. Its look reflected the power, dominance and challenge of the Empire.[14] But historical sycamore trees were also destroyed because of the growing city population and settlement problems.[15] Now they can be seen in the historical gardens, parks and near the roads in old neighbourhoods of Istanbul. Unfortunately, these trees, the witnesses of the developing city, are forgotten and harmed during the change of settlements, by building roads and rail lines, and by increasing pollution.

Green areas near the roads and streets are the streetscapes where the nature of the city becomes visible. These well-kept places are used not only for beautification of the city but also for giving messages to the city-dwellers or tourists. For example, while Istanbul was a candidate city for the 2020 Olympics, and the International Olympic Committee members examined the candidate city's suitability, the Olympic rings, the tulip figure as a symbol of Istanbul 2020, and finally "Istanbul 2020" were depicted with flowers on the green streetscapes of heavy-traffic roads.

These spaces are also used for promotion of Turkish tourism. For example, Istanbul Municipality pictured a sailboat by using flowers near the street on the way to the Fatih Sultan Mehmet Bridge leading from the European to Asian side. This kind of flowering is also used to write "Turkiye" close to Gümüşsuyu Street and Inonu stadium in Dolmabahçe.

The "Wild" Nature of Istanbul

Cities grow faster in the era of globalization because industrialization and migration open new regions for settlements. This means more human intervention in nature. However, this intervention cannot be successful or dominant where wilderness still remains. Benton Short and Short figure that cities "are seen as much natural as wilderness and the environment as much social as the city" hence, "the city is an integral part of nature and nature is intimately interwoven into the social life of cities".[16] This wildlife has successfully colonized the urban environment, and urban areas serve as suitable habitat for many species.[17]

Wilderness, or uncontrolled nature, is present in the cities as well. As Istanbul grows it incorporates parts of the countryside which can contain forests or meadows. It is common to see many "wild" animals in Istanbul. For example seagulls are identified with Istanbul and seen in the films, paintings, gravures and photos of Istanbul. They have developed new types of behaviour with the new industrial city. Today they are fed like pigeons, collared doves and sparrows by people in the streets and in front of windows. There is a popular Istanbul tradition of feeding seagulls with bagels during the ferry travels and to take photos of these moments.

Street animals such as cats and dogs are other "wild" animals trying to find food and shelter in the city. The difficulties of these animals uncover and show the picture of nature in the city. For instance, cats and dogs have problems disposing of and covering their excrement in the city. In the central parts of the city sometimes cats cannot find a place to bury their excrement because of the concrete floors of the city. They use the small soil spaces at the bottoms of trees, city parks and gardens. Since no street animals are inoculated they can be classified as 'wild' animals of the city.

Animal shelters play an important part in animals' lives in the city. The concept of "animal shelter" arose as a result of modernization and urbanization. As the people had occupied the animals' natural habitats, the freedom of the animals became limited and the animals were obliged to steer away from their instinctive behaviour.

In Istanbul, the animal shelters are affiliated to the district municipalities and as such are generally located far from the city centre. Most of the animals housed in the animal shelters are dogs, though in some shelters cats are also housed. Animals such as rabbits, turtles, seagulls, crows, hamsters, horses or donkeys can be temporarily housed during their treatment periods or until a person is found to claim such animals. Animal shelters must release healthy animals back to the streets after sterilizing and treating them and also deal with abandoned pets which are not accustomed to stray life.

Some of the cats and dogs are brought to animal shelters wounded due to being hit by cars. Highways present one of the greatest threats to life for animals living on the streets. Some of these wounded animals lose their lives and others have to continue disabled or paralyzed.

The Meaning of Nature in Istanbul

In today's Istanbul most of the green spaces are parks and cemeteries. In Turkish tradition trees are associated with cemeteries, and they are grown in many cemeteries in Turkey. A tree that is commonly found in cemeteries, as well as mosque yards, is the cypress.[18] According to Dursun, in Islamic mysticism the cypress is the symbol of *Allah* because of its similarity to the letter *elif*[19], and therefore cypresses are grown in cemeteries because they symbolize the return of man to God.[20] Kuban points out that cemeteries looked like small forests in Ottoman Istanbul.[21] The gravures of 18th and 19th century cemeteries of Istanbul show many trees that cover the whole area of the graveyard.[22] Cemeteries are still green places in Istanbul, like a green veil; a reminder of death in very busy city life. This symbolism can also be seen in the cemetery walls. Trees and ivies covering the cemetery walls both from inside and outside hide the graveyard like veils shading death.

However, in the tombs of Ottoman sultans and their family members, trees and ivies turn into decoration elements. For example, the tomb of Mahmud II in the Cemberlitas district, which also hosts members of his family, draws attention with its magnificent construction. The graves of some other Ottoman dynasty family members and famous bureaucrats of the Ottoman Empire are found in the graveyard of the tomb. Greenery was put in the graveyard not as a veil of death but as a beautification element. This comparison shows differences of class and power in the city.

The relation of policy and nature in the city continues in today's Istanbul. Due to its position as a historical capital both in the East Roman and the Ottoman Empires, people come across the manifestations of power in many parts of Istanbul. For example, tulips are favourite and historical flowers of Istanbul. Tulips were popularized in Europe by Dutch merchants. However, they were transported to the Netherlands by Ottomans. In the Ottoman Empire itself tulips became popular only during the Tulip Era at the beginning of the 18th century.[23] The Tulip Era was also the period when people spent more time in the private and public gardens. New gardens and pavilions were built; some of them renewed; and seaside villages and river sides became popular places for city-dwellers.[24]

In order to support this historical connection, Istanbul Municipality started a Tulip Festival in 2006, and tulips became more popular in Istanbul. In April the Istanbul Municipality plants tulips of many colours in the parks and streetscapes. Besides concerts, panels and exhibitions are organized during the festival. According to the municipality's official page, the festival is part of "both the vision and mission of preserving our (Turkish) cultural heritage" and it aims to remind people of these traditional flowers, which were decorating the city of Istanbul for thousands of years" and to "convey these beauties for the future generations".[25] Therefore, the aim of this Tulip Festival is reviving Ottoman culture is in line with government policy.[26]

Conclusion

According to our observations, the relationship between humans and nature is largely determined by the conditions of modern city life. Istanbul is both a historical and an industrial city. The people of Istanbul and the government are the actors modifying nature in the city according to their policies, lifestyles and needs. City-dwellers establish special relations with nature in the city independently from the government, the municipality, and even from construction companies. They feed animals, grow plants, domesticate wild animals, and own pets. While the patterns of control of nature are similar in most modern cities, the human-nature relationship in each city is also unique because it is shaped by the unique combination of historical, geographical and cultural conditions.

The picture of nature presented here shows that the meaning of nature in the city of Istanbul is different from the meaning of nature outside of the city. Istanbul's natural objects can be considered representations of wild nature. Representation is one of the features which define an image.[27] But an image not only represents, but also imitates 'the real'; it even creates the illusions of the objects.[28] Thus, in many parts of Istanbul nature represents, and sometimes imitates, 'the real' nature. Designed landscapes that imitate wild nature are a widespread feature of contemporary urban planning in Istanbul.

NOTES

[1] Levi-Strauss, Claude. 1969. *Elementary Structures of Kinship*. Boston: Beacon, p. 3.

[2] Genim, M. Sinan. 2012. "Istanbul ve Mimari". *Şehir ve Kültür: Istanbul*. Ahmet Emre Bilgili (Ed.). Istanbul: Profil, pp. 266-270.

[3] Kuban, Doğan. 2000. *Istanbul Bir Kent Tarihi: Bizantion, Konstantinopolis, Istanbul*. Istanbul: Tarih Vakfı Yurt. 271.

[4] Kuban, 2000, p. 349.

[5] Kuban, 2000, p. 389-399.

[6] Tuna, Korkut. 2012. "Istanbul'un Sosyolojik Dönüşümü". *Şehir ve Kültür: Istanbul*. Ahmet Emre Bilgili (Ed.). Istanbul: Profil, pp. 376-383.

[7] Kuban, 2000, p. 110-112.

[8] Çelik, Zeynep. 1998. *19. Yüzyılda Değişen Osmanlı Başkenti-Değişen Istanbul*. Istanbul: Tarih Vakfı Yurt, p. 61.

[9] Eyice, Semavi. 1993. "Istanbul". *Istanbul*. Ankara: Kültür Bakanlığı, p. 23.

[10] Shochat, Eyal, Susannah Lerman and Esteban Fernández-Juricic. 2010. "Birds in Urban Ecosystems: Population Dynamics, Community Structure, Biodiversity, and Conservation". *Urban Ecosystem Ecology*. J. Aitkenhead-Peterson and A. Volder (Eds.). Madison: American Society of Agronomy, p. 76-77.

[11] Işın, Ekrem. 2006. *İstanbul'da Gündelik Hayat*. Istanbul: İletişim. 4. Baskı, p. 205.

[12] Kuban, 2000, p. 342-343.

[13] Eyice, 1993, p. 23.

[14] Dursun, 2012, p. 170.

[15] Eyice, 1993, p. 26.

[16] Benton Short, Lisa and John Rennie Short. 2008. *Cities and Nature*. NY: Routledge, p. 5.

[17] Also see Ditchkoff, Stephen S., Sarah T. Saalfeld and Charles J. Gibson. 2006. "Animal behavior in urban ecosystems". *Urban Ecosystems* No: 9, pp. 5–12.

[18] Eyice, 1993, p. 23.

[19] For *Elif* or *Alif* in Islamic mysticism see Schimmel, Annemarie. 2001. *İslam'ın Mistik Boyutları*. Istanbul: Kabalcı, p. 403-412.

[20] Dursun, A. Haluk. 2012. "Tarih, Mekan ve Kültür: Istanbul". *Şehir ve Kültür: Istanbul*. Ahmet Emre Bilgili (Ed.). Istanbul: Profil, p. 172.

[21] Kuban, 2000, p. 342.

[22] See Sevim, Mustafa (Ed.). 1996. *Gravürlerle Türkiye in Gravures: Istanbul*. Ankara: Ministry of Culture. Vol. 1 and Vol. 2. Dursun (2012, p. 171) also underlines that it is hard see sycamore trees in Istanbul today when compared with gravures of Ottoman Istanbul.

[23] For more about the Tulip Era see Kuban, 2000, p. 309-317.

[24] Genim, 2012, p. 293.

[25] "Tulip Time in Istanbul". http://www.ibb.gov.tr/sites/istanbuldalalezamani/en-US/Pages/BaskaninMesaji.aspx, accessed on 23-08-2013.

[26] Some scholars name this ideology *Neo-Ottomanism*. See Yavuz, Hakan. 1998. "Turkish Identity and Foreign Policy in Flux: The Rise of Neo-Ottomanism". *Critique: Critical Middle Eastern Studies*. Vol. 7, Issue 12, pp. 19-41.

[27] Marin, Louis. 2013. *İmgenin İktidarları*. Ankara: Dost, p. 14.

[28] Wulf, Christoph. 2009. *Tarihsel Kültürel Antropoloji*. Ankara: Dipnot, p. 282.

The Image of Contemporary Warsaw in the Context of Architecture and Local Discourse

Magdalena Łukasiuk

University of Warsaw, Warsaw/Poland

mlukasiuk@wp.pl

Abstract

In this article the author proposes a theoretical approach to analysing the image of the city. The empirical base for statements made is research conducted by the author into the environment of migrants in contemporary Warsaw, the capital of Poland. The research combines the perspective of the sociology of architecture and the category of discourse to create a theoretical approach adequate to grasp a mechanism responsible for the construction of the image of the city. This eclectic approach connects the individual perspective with the social representations, as well as the spatial phenomena with meanings inscribed in them.

In diesem Artikel verfolgt die Autorin einen theoretischen Ansatz zur Analyse des Stadt-Bildes. Die empirische Grundlage für die getroffenen Aussagen ist eine Studie, die die Autorin aktuell unter Migranten in Warschau durchgeführt hat. Die Studie verbindet die Perspektive der Architektur-Soziologie mit der Kategorie des Diskurses, um einen theoretischen Ansatz zu formulieren, der geeignet ist jene Mechanismen zu erfassen, die für die Konstruktion von Stadt-Bildern verantwortlich sind. Der eklektische Ansatz verbindet individuelle Perspektiven mit gesellschaftlichen Darstellungen und räumliche Phänomene mit den ihnen eingeschriebenen Bedeutungen.

In her book *Soziologie der Städte* (*Sociology of Cities*) Martina Löw claims that various scientific disciplines considering the subject of the city offer three ways of understanding the notion of the city as:

- a graphic picture diffused by the media: painted, drawn, photographed

- a built city space; in Europe circulating around the old town
- a cognitive map or a depiction[1]

In this article the last two notions will be interesting for me, and especially the relation between them. My objective is to reconstruct the mechanism responsible for unifying the image of the city within the social environment of migrants. This image results not only from the material circumstances of the city and the meanings inscribed in them, but also from some social phenomena grounded in this material base and exceeding it.

Methodological Remarks

My findings are founded on empirical studies carried out in Warsaw among domestic migrants: adult and educated people (with MA degrees) who came to the capital from other parts of Poland after their education approximately in the year 2000 and later. The presented material is based on 50 IDIs, 60 autobiographies sent as a response to the contest I published in one of the newspapers (*Gazeta Wyborcza*) and also on an analysis of the internet forums dedicated to the Warsaw migration phenomenon. Although the research did not relate to one environment in the traditionally phenomenological sense[2], it did include a group of people with a similar biographical experience of migration, living in the same city, being in similar life situations and – what is important for me – to a large extent remaining in their social environment, i. e. mostly or almost exclusively staying in social relations with other migrants.

The Image of Warsaw in the Environment of Migrants

Which image of Warsaw emerges from the responses of the interviewees? Below I present some representative examples:

> The truth is, today's Warsaw is repulsive in the spiritual realm, the practices and architecture. Let me start with the latter one. [...] The arguments that the capital was rebuilt from cinders as some kind of explanation of the hasty chaos, along which the socio-realistic bunkers that were developed, and the past years, prove that the head architect was a great pretender with some kind of dispiriting variation of bravado. A couple of minutes spent waiting for a bus is more than enough to let the mixed landscape of concrete blocks of flats, glass skyscrapers, omnipresent shoe-lace stalls, Vietnamese booths, shouting billboards and boiling garbage baskets provoke even the most peaceful sensitive person, just after her confession[3].

> What irritates me in Warsaw is rather a lack of an urban idea for this untamed capital energy. Warsaw is a kind of a wild garden full of weeds which, on the

> one hand, is attractive with its wildness, but on the other wearing after some time: these booths located on the corners of the roads – the constraint of the view, limitation of space, or those so called merchant houses, as if hiding the ugly things, and maybe they're ugly because they're unskilfully hidden. Warsaw is like a warehouse, littered by more or less useful things in the course of the past 50 years. But why is it still being littered? Inertial force? Warsaw is a difficult city ... All the known cognitive tools that would normally be used in a situation of exploring a new territory, fail here. You wouldn't go for a walk to the city centre; you don't take a walk through the centre. Anyway, the centre does not exist here. The centre is the metro station, [...] the marketplace? There's no marketplace. The Old Town? For tourists[4].

> Because Warsaw is most probably the ugliest city in the world, I would like to live in a city founded on the Magdeburg law, with a marketplace, streets, a town hall, something medieval[5].

Following Kevin Lynch's notion, Kirsten Wagner indicates that the legibility of the city in its physical and material sense connects to its possibly largest order, coherence, explicitness and lucidity[6]. At the level of city reception by the interviewed new inhabitants, the dominant impression of Warsaw is one of chaotic architecture, resulting in a lack of cognitive tools enabling the construction of the whole mental scheme of the city. This chaos emerges in a multitude of eras, styles and mixed functions in one place, composite colours, unclear location of buildings in space, differences in qualities of finishing materials and the preservation conditions. In this way the city is received as illegible, appalling or even hostile. The spatial distribution and the size of Warsaw are not meaningless here.

Chaos as a General Rule of the Perception of the City

The image of the city, developed on these foundations, is a chaotic one, and the chaos is elevated to the rank of a rule pervading all perception aspects. The perfect examples of the general perception of the city as a chaotic one are the migrants' statements on the city symbol. It is neither the Old Town, nor the Royal Castle, nor the City Hall, but the labyrinth of underground passages under the Central Train Station, *nota bene* located in the sacred area of the city centre, which today is suffering from atrophy[7]. It may be described as an eradiation of chaos and lack of legibility. This theme emerges in many statements:

> The very exit from the Central Station was unpleasant for me. I was always getting lost in those tunnels[8].

> I got out at the Central Station, and of course I got lost in the underground, I was walking round and round in circles, not knowing how to get out, I felt like [I was] in a trap. Everyone's running somewhere, rushing with their suitcases,

> shopping nets, shopping bags, dogs, children … It is a weird place, so colourful and so grey at the same time, so world-wide and [yet] provincial, you'll meet a prince and a beggar here; it is a train station for some and a home for others. I was walking round for several minutes asking how to get out from time to time. Warsaw for me seemed not as the promise of paradise, but as the place of exile[9].

According to Ewa Rewers, "the traditional city does not exist anymore and its reconstruction is not possible"[10]. This fact leads to some sort of nostalgia which affects the perception of today's city by the migrants interviewed. The expected order inscribed into the "traditional city" and its lack in contemporary Warsaw induce migrants to perceive the city automatically in contradiction to the ideal image which does not exist, but is still used for comparisons.

The Theoretical Approach

To build an interpretative model, I would like to propose two perspectives, which enable the theoretical 'grasp' of a mechanism responsible for developing the image of contemporary Warsaw by the migrants.

The first is the sociology of architecture. In general it assumes that the architecture itself is a "heavy communication medium", which is not only the "developed environment for interactions", but also belongs to the "co-world of communication"[11]. Joachim Fischer enumerates what is communicated by architecture and also what is forced on people for approval in the form of so called *offers of sense*. He creates a catalogue of problems or gravity points in the framework of the sociology of architecture. Fischer mentions functional differentiations, according to the logics of Luhmann's social systems, the division into spheres: sacred and profane; private and public; work, production, entertainment and consumption. The social equality or inequality; the authority relations evident, for instance, in the land ownership; the location of the place of residence with reference to the city centre and outlying areas, as well as the *Beletage* phenomenon, are also communicated by the architecture. In addition, generations speak through the architecture since there are buildings from different times, standing side by side[12]. These are manifested uses of different building technologies, preferences and, unlike lifestyles, connected with the buildings. Architecture perceived this way pre-codes people's actions. Not only does it reflect the society of its time but it also solidifies and even enhances the existing social relations (as well as the relations of power, dependency, and axiologies)[13].

The second perspective I would like to call upon here is the perspective of discourse. The research of discourse is an examination of the world's vision as shared and reproduced inter-subjectively by a society, a community or a group. Cezary Trutkowski combines the notion of social representations developed by Emilé Durkheim[14] with the category of discourse in its Foucaultian version[15]. As it was noted by him:

> the world of discourse outlines the world of our social representations – these are imposed in the framework of constant communication which is conducted with the outside world and by this communication these representations are modified and complemented. [...] By analysing the discourse outlining the everyday communicative actions of the individuals, we may get to the content and the scope of social representations – we can recreate the way of social reconstruction of the world based on the available transmissions, with the components of this world being contained in[16].

The vision of the world, and so the image of the city too, mutually exists in the discourse: on the one hand it is revealed in the discursive events, on the other hand the discourse itself creates, shapes and changes it. That is why analysing the discourse of the city means researching the dynamic image of the city currently shared by the participants. The discourse analysed here is the environmental discourse which I was referring to in the methodology. The migrants' discourse on the image of Warsaw is not any dominant or officially confirmed image of the city. Although, as it is noted by Cezary Trutkowski;

> in every society, we obviously encounter the everyday situation, where there's a competition of different, often opposing methods of defining the reality and establishing the laws governing it. Nevertheless, from the viewpoint of the social representations theory, each opinion, shared by a very small number of persons or being even a singular opinion, as much as it will be included in the realm of the public discourse (declaimed in front of other persons), yet by the very fact becomes a component of constant process of shaping of the social representations[17].

Kirsten Wagner, when commenting on Kevin Lynch's approach, claims that he excludes the problem of meanings from his analysis and concentrates only on the material aspects – the spatial forms and structures[18]. Following her statement I suggest that the combination of over-mentioned perspectives connects both the physical realm and the meanings in the image of the city.

Returning to the question on the mechanism of development and re-creation of the city image among the interviewed migrants, I would like to propose a theoretical, eclectic approach.

In my opinion, the integration of the individual and the social perspective seems to be crucial. The sociology of architecture and also the methodology of Kevin Lynch's research[19], focus on the interaction of the object with the individual. The object might be a building, a road, a bridge, a district or a larger development complex. Here, from joined phenomenological and semiotic approaches, a mechanism emerges in which the inter-subjective meanings are inscribed into the object and decoded by the individual recipient, according to his/ her *habitus*.

This process is not free from a number of nuances. For example, the class diversification in the methods of decoding those meanings, or the routine of using objects inscribed in the body, pre-reflexive and extra-verbal, differentiate the way of the decoding process. The emphasis is on the analysis of the object-human relation, which means that objects are not understood as mere containers of coherent meaning.

This way of thinking enables us to make the first step to diagnose the messages decoded by the particular migrants from these parts of the city they were able to get to know.

The second step requires a social level of interpretation. It is this level – in the form of migrants' discourse of the environment – where the social representations are solidified in their collective emanation. Decoded meanings, impressions and feelings caught in the articulated form, adopt the shape of generalized city representations. Its image, which is built in various personal experiences with the architecture and also reversibly marking those experiences, influences and pre-codes the perception of the city. This is why I was amazed by the repetitiveness and uniformity not only of the opinions quoted above but also the examples and even the linguistic formulations used by the interviewees while I was analysing the enumerated sources.

Final Remarks

Such construction and confirmation of the city image is inter-subjectively shared, self-reproducing and self-returning. Migrants come across it many times, even before they are able to experience the city itself; hence, their own feelings obtain the discursive framework where they are being inscribed, and also the method of evaluating. In such a way a coherent image of the city emerges – an image accurately representative of the researched migrants' environment. However, the perspective of discourse and the category of meaning could suggest that the image of the city would be a cognitive one. I understand it similar to *the local structure of feeling* under the assumption, that thoughts have been felt and feelings have been thought (*Gedanken gefühlt und Gefühle gedacht werden*)[20], which is closely connected with the materiality of the built space.

In the end, for a bit of a contradiction, I would like to quote some characteristic opinions on the same subject from another research project of mine; focusing on another environment, which is fascinated with modernistic architecture in Warsaw and immersed in different discourse:

> I have an image of Warsaw ... It's an emotional image. Because I come from Warsaw, I was born here and have lived all my life in Warsaw. For me, sometimes it is a beautiful city. It's just untidy, undeveloped, not thought out, and broken here and there but in general it is an interesting city, there's positive energy in the city. For me it is positive.[21]

> [Warsaw] is pretty in its chaos, because in my opinion it is not ugly – for sure it is chaotic – but chaos can also be of some value. [...] Above all, Warsaw is perceived as a city of great opportunities, and maybe when you arrive here, the chaos may be interpreted as the very opportunity. Simply everything is possible here, you can have the worst, stalemate situation but also you can encounter something very pleasant, simply everything can happen here and this is what is evident on the streets.[22]

NOTES

[1] Löw Martina, *Soziologie der Städte*, Suhrkamp Verlag, Frankfurt am Main, 2010, p. 141.

[2] See Grathoff Richard, *Środowisko i społeczeństwo* [in:] Świat przeżywany. Fenomenologia i nauki społeczne, Krasnodębski Zdzisław, Nellen Krzysztof (Ed.), Państwowy Instytut Wydawniczy, Warsaw 1994, pp. 244-275.

[3] Autobiography 1 sent for the contest announced by *Gazeta Wyborcza*, polish newspaper.

[4] Autobiography 2 sent for the contest announced by *Gazeta Wyborcza*.

[5] An interview with a man from Nowy Sącz.

[6] Wagner Kirsten, *Die visuelle Ordnung der Stadt. Das Bild der Stadt bei Kevin Lynch*, http://hsozkult.geschichte.hu-berlin.de/forum/id=774&type=diskussionen, 11/ 12/ 2013.

[7] See Jałowiecki Bohdan, Szczepański Marek S., *Miasto i przestrzeń w perspektywie socjologicznej*, Wydawnictwo Naukowe Scholar, Warsaw 2006, p. 391 passim.

[8] An interview with a woman from Kielce.

[9] Autobiography 3 sent for the contest announced by *Gazeta Wyborcza*.

[10] Rewers Ewa, *Post-polis. Wstęp do filozofii ponowoczesnego miasta*, Universitas, Krakow 2005, p. 281.

[11] Fischer Joachim, "Architektur: 'schweres' Kommunikationsmedium der Gesellschaft", *Architektur der Gesellschaft*, APUZ (Aus Politik und Zeitgeschichte), 2009, Nr. 25, p. 8.

[12] Ibid, p. 9.

[13] See Fischer Joachim, Delitz Heike (Ed.), *Die Architektur der Gesellschaft. Theorien für die Architektursoziologie*, transcript Verlag, Bielefeld 2009; Frank Susanne, "Architektur: mehr als ein Spiegel der Gesellschaft", *Architektur der Gesellschaft*, APUZ (Aus Politik und Zeitgeschichte), 2009, Nr. 25.

[14] See Durkheim Emile, *Elementarne formy życia religijnego. System totemiczny w Australii*, transl. into Polish Anna Zadrożyńska, Wydawnictwo Naukowe PWN, Warsaw 2010.

[15] See Foucault Michel, *Porządek dyskursu. Wykład inauguracyjny wygłoszony w College de France 2 grudnia 1970*, transl. into Polish M. Kozłowski, słowo/ obraz terytoria, Gdańsk 2002.

[16] Trutkowski Cezary, *Społeczne reprezentacje polityki*, Wydawnictwo Naukowe Scholar, Warsaw 2002, pp. 109-110.

[17] Ibid, p. 120.

[18] Wagner Kirsten, *Die visuelle Ordnung der Stadt.*

[19] Lynch Kevin, *The Image of the City*, MIT Press, Cambridge 1960.

[20] Löw Martina, p. 62.

[21] NGO 1.

[22] NGO 2.

Bibliography

Durkheim Emile, *Elementarne formy życia religijnego. System totemiczny w Australii*, transl. into Polish Anna Zadrożyńska, Wydawnictwo Naukowe PWN, Warsaw 2010.

Fischer Joachim, "Architektur: 'schweres' Kommunikationsmedium der Gesellschaft", *Architektur der Gesellschaft*, APUZ (Aus Politik und Zeitgeschichte), 2009, Nr. 25, 6-10.

Fischer Joachim, Delitz Heike (Ed.), *Die Architektur der Gesellschaft. Theorien für die Architektursoziologie*, transcript Verlag, Bielefeld 2009.

Foucault Michel, *Porządek dyskursu. Wykład inauguracyjny wygłoszony w College de France 2 grudnia 1970*, transl. into Polish M. Kozłowski, słowo/ obraz terytoria, Gdańsk 2002.

Frank Susanne, "Architektur: mehr als ein Spiegel der Gesellschaft", *Architektur der Gesellschaft*, APUZ (Aus Politik und Zeitgeschichte), 2009, Nr. 25, 16-21.

Grathoff Richard, *Środowisko i społeczeństwo* [in:] Świat przeżywany. Fenomenologia i nauki społeczne, Krasnodębski Zdzisław, Nellen Krzysztof (Ed.), Państwowy Instytut Wydawniczy, Warszawa 1994, pp. 244-275.

Jałowiecki Bohdan, Szczepański Marek S, *Miasto i przestrzeń w perspektywie socjologicznej*, Wydawnictwo Naukowe Scholar, Warszawa 2006.

Löw Martina, *Soziologie der Städte*, Suhrkamp Verlag, Frankfurt am Main, 2010.

Lynch Kevin, *The Image of the City*, MIT Press, Cambridge 1960.

Rewers Ewa. *Post-polis. Wstęp do filozofii ponowoczesnego miasta*, Universitas, Krakow 2005.

Trutkowski Cezary, *Społeczne reprezentacje polityki*, Wydawnictwo Naukowe Scholar, Warsaw 2002.

Wagner Kirsten, *Die visuelle Ordnung der Stadt. Das Bild der Stadt bei Kevin Lynch*, http://hsozkult.geschichte.hu-Berlin.de/forum/id=774&type=diskussionen, 11/ 12/ 2013.

METAMORPHOSIS AND MULTIPLICATION OF AN *IMAGINAIRE*

Giovanni Comoglio

Politechnic University of Turin, Turin/ Italy

giovanni.comoglio@polito.it

ABSTRACT

This article deals with the shaping of an image for mutations in the urban habitat and the town-countryside distinction in contemporary Shanghai. Contemporary Shanghai, as re-started in 1990 by a political planning decision, is undergoing a process of reconstruction of the idea of the city itself, of its *imaginaire* of the city. This process has led to several redefinitions: inhabitants are redefined in their role, status, and relationship with the perceived urban environment. A new urban habitat is shaped, and the idea of countryside is translated into a planning/ building issue, designed by the most powerful actors. All these images converge in Urban Planning Exhibition Centers, i. e. public spaces where *imaginaires* become promotional experiences.

Dieser Artikel beschäftigt sich mit der Schaffung eines Bildes für Veränderungen im urbanen Habitat und in der Abgrenzung von Stadt und Land im zeitgenössischen Shanghai. Das zeitgenössische Shanghai, wie es 1990 durch eine politische Planungsentscheidung wieder-begründet wurde, durchläuft einen Prozess der Re-Konstruktion der städtischen Idee, des *imaginaire* der Stadt. Dieser Prozess hat zu mehreren Neu-Definitionen geführt: Einwohner werden in ihrer Rolle neu definiert ebenso wie der Status und die Beziehung zur städtischen Umwelt. Ein neues urbanes Habitat wird geformt, und die Vorstellung von einem ländlichen Gebiet wird übersetzt in eine Frage von Planung und Bebauung, an der sehr einflussreiche Akteure beteiligt sind. Alle diese Bilder vereinigen sich in Stadtplanungsausstellungszentren, dies sich als öffentliche Räume präsentieren, in denen die *imaginaires* zu werbewirksamen Erfahrungen werden.

The redefinition of an urban habitat entails the redefinition of imageries, which will be made of some persisting elements and some other elements following the mutation from the start. When images are considered as a foundation for a new identity of spaces and populations, the creation of an *imaginaire* can become one of the most relevant concerns for governments.

The city of Shanghai is one of the most suitable and interesting cases[1], as dealing with Shanghai means dealing with the "re-started" city par excellence. This concept is strongly linked to the issue of a pervading presence of a top-down unidirectional planning attitude which is clearly mirrored by the history of Shanghai during the Twentieth Century: Contemporary Shanghai is the result of political planning decisions about both local and national economic development.

Between 1949 and the early Nineties, the development of this urban reality has been stopped for reasons of national and international trade exchange, and Shanghai has been levelled to the general Chinese urban context in terms of housing and industrial production policies. At the end of the Eighties, even though, Hong Kong was about to return under the control of Chinese government, it remained the most powerful business centre on Chinese territory, with a persistent presence of western capital. A "made in China" business city, an alternative guiding light for development was required: That is where the history of "re-started" Shanghai begins[2]. During the last twenty years, the city has undergone a massive phenomenon of service sector and real estate development. Capitals related to land development and building development have operated on the urban reality matching the interest of government in carrying out great development projects. The Chinese State has had the unique chance to reshape the habitat it had already shaped in a former historical phase. The most effective instrument employed to perform such a fundamental transformation has been, as in many other cases in China, the possibility of displacing large amounts of people within the urban space, thus clearing entire areas to be drawn back to a dimension of *tabula rasa*, where new buildings or infrastructures can be realized. A potentially unlimited possibility of redefining landscape, interior balances, fluxes and network within a context whose dynamics were almost completely defined opened up.

Inhabiting contemporary Shanghai is synonymous with inhabiting transformation: this statement involves all the aspects of the spatial and social system, starting at the composition of an almost completely new population. Shanghai metropolitan area has reached 23 million inhabitants in 2010. This number has a historical and sociological relevance, mostly because it is a constantly increasing value[3], and in its recent development it mirrors a modification of practices and policies towards a formerly constant phenomenon, i.

e. rural-to-urban labour migration. This phenomenon, which was already considered a normal trend during the late Fifties, has undergone several political and cultural reinterpretations from the after-Mao period on. The re-definition of the newly emerging population by authorities aims to create a third subject: a floating population, neither urban nor rural[4].

Picture 1: A commercial street in the borough of Hongkou, Shanghai: 'floating population' generating a mixed use of urban space (Giovanni Comoglio, 2012)

It is a matter of establishing and keeping divisions, thus achieving a more effective action of control on the whole urban system, which keeps on being composed by separate groups sharing a common space. As this article will show, the strategies carried out by State and Municipalities to consolidate this new hybrid urban identity involve different paths, dealing with rights, space, communication and media.

Nonetheless, before considering governmental planning strategies one has to face the most important and actual fact about Shanghai, that is the hybrid nature of its urban reality. It is a hybrid habitat created by both old and new inhabitants; a habitat made of a set of practices (use of spaces, individual building and re-building techniques, co-existing lifestyles), and the use of rights and possibilities that urban population is allowed to access. Contemporary Shanghainese urban space is shaped by the cross effect of two different relationships, i. e. the interaction of inhabitants with the everyday habitat and the interaction of the government and the power elites with precise visions of the city which are supposed to quickly achieve a realization. In this cross-effect framework, the government is in fact giving inputs to development. However, it would not be correct to think of this urban building process as something linear and unambiguous, proceeding straight from the input to a concrete structure without any modification or intervention by different actors.

Several ways of governmental intervention or partial retreat from the construction of urban landscape have followed one another. During the Fifties and the Cultural Revolution, a standardized industrialization was introduced in housing construction[5], with prefab blocks and “modernist villages”. Nevertheless, the reception of this technical imposition – rather than innovation – was not an automatic effective answer to an order of change: construction knowledge and methods were developed, codified and spread all over the country by central authorities. The task of the realization of new housing compounds, however, was often given to local firms and builders, thus setting the base for a perceivable intervention of local practices on national planned programs. From the late Seventies to the early Nineties the situation grew more and more hybrid, with the first efforts of an experimental market economy showing, fostered by the government to match the potential of a global context. This process lead to the Nineties, when the institutional framework of urban dwelling went through a crucial change: even though not in a complete form, private property was allowed on real estate units. The State remains the owner of the land, with no room for any emphyteutic lease, but citizens can become the owners of their own houses, and construction firms can keep the ownership of their own developments.

Everything changed from that moment, even though a single element remained unmodified: the trending form of settlement, the compound. What changed was the form of assembling dwellings, shifting from the small block to the standard 20-30-storeys “tower”, and the way of living in these redefined spaces. Common circulation and service spaces were affected in particular; these spaces being considered something public or private, open or closed.

Planned policies introduced large changes in the built urban fabric[6] and requestioned the issue of an identity for Shanghai as a place that has to assume a clear and common meaning for people. Whose city is this city? Whose space is this space?

The government has given the input for the generation of this hybrid reality but it is not the only player within this process, as mentioned before. In this reality the need of a strong form of control was therefore felt by public authorities. An instrument as well as the identification of a common ground was necessary in order to gather a multitude of tendencies around a definition of future urban development in which the government and its partners could have a definitely leading role.

In the end, all this required the invention, the planning itself, of an *imaginaire* as well as a vehicle of change, and a strategy to communicate this in order to consolidate consensus.

Collected data, but mostly experience, i. e. the chance to share the lives of the Chinese urban population, are essential in demonstrating and exploring the fact that the media and entertainment are chosen as the common grounds on which the two main actors of these dynamics encounter and agree.

All the data exposed and the phenomena explored so far identify this creation of an imagery, which is the result and the point of intersection of two different paths: the first one made of practices of living and perceiving, inhabiting changes and new scenarios; and the second one linked to a dimension of planning, basically including politicians and allied economic powers. These paths are expected to converge in an instrument made both of public space and media space. This is the fundamental vocation of an Urban Planning Exhibition Center, an institution born for an image, the image of the city(-ies).

In order to better understand the contents and programmatic layout of such places a brief excursus must be dedicated to the components of the mentioned paths, which constitute the raw material for the generation of the U.P.E.C. It is a set of built and intangible data and classifications capable of leading to the definition of an imagery.

The first path, created by inhabitants, by both the "old" and "floating" population, is made of a perceived and lived-in landscape originating from the interaction of people with the modification and expansion of the so-called "urban" Shanghai. Here we recognize some different typologies of attitude towards urban living. A first one can be identified in the persistence of formerly consolidated habits in common use of space even after the introduction of private property. The pre-existent urban space, built from West-open nineteenth century to the early-republican 1970s is the favourite scenery for this approach to urban life. Another attitude is an evolution of the latter one, as it is mostly settled in those parts of town characterized by the coexistence of new and old urban fabric, often mixed in a thick and complex new reality.

Different conceptions of private and common find a way to exist side by side, interpreting quite often the built context as an infrastructure for evolving practices.

Picture 2: Coexistence of old and new urban fabric in Shanghai: Mutation gets in touch with everyday practices (Giovanni Comoglio, 2012)

A third attitude is living in the *ex novo* city, the new outer developments driving the expansion of contemporary Shanghai. It can be quite properly interpreted as the less defined form of real urban life. As the stabilization of a shared conviction about concepts like *neighbourhood* or *quarter* works at a different speed from the typical speed of contemporary construction and settlement dynamics in Chinese cities, this is a long and still uncertain road to the definition of a solid urban identity.

On the other hand, the second path is the track on which groups of power operate, where one can find both local and central government acting together with economic allied players. It is the basic matrix for two relevant aspects in the shaping of modern Shanghai. A first aspect is the frequent recourse to the technique of creating *tabulae rasae* inside the city for public interest, in order to enable the establishment of public venues (Expo 2010) and infrastructure or the realizations of private interventions implying particular financial advantages for city development policies (business centres, housing compounds). This kind of scenario preserves nevertheless a hybrid nature because in these cases new rights and possibilities given to urban population modify the linearity of a top-down reshaping process: Property gives the right not to be displaced for public utility without compensation, thus transforming a formerly immediate translation of visions into actions in a more delicate matter of negotiation and feasibility valuation. Furthermore, the issue of town-countryside relationship itself stays in this path: In the areas under urban influence countryside becomes something planned in comparison with towns or, at least, in a close relationship to them. It becomes some kind of another urban issue as it is planned and determined by reflections which are developed within an urban cultural framework. This is the case with Chongming Island, which is situated at the estuary of the Huangpu river. It has been identified by Shanghai authority as the future Shanghai countryside including agricultural productive areas, preserved/ spectacularized "nature" parks, trade logistics infrastructures (harbours), and newly developed residential areas; the latter aiming to be appealing for Shanghainese urban population searching for a more relaxed and "natural" environment for life. Countryside, therefore, becomes a town-based statement.

In order to unify the different imageries in a uniform and controllable proposal the choice of political players has been the interpretation of the issue in terms of communication. A single image has to be shown to the public acting as an audience which has to be built and gathered. Urban Planning Exhibition Centers demonstrate that a media-dominated or even an entertainment-dominated dimension is intended to be the main place where the two players currently building the urban imagery of Shanghai must get in touch. Their conception as well as their very existence demonstrates that these are the places where the building of the *imaginaire* happens. This is expressed by some of their basic components, which are strongly linked to a communication-planning attitude[7].

A first element is the place itself in its relationship with the urban context as well as in its physical features: the building, in the end. Shanghai Urban Planning Exhibition Center and Chongming Island Urban Planning Exhibition Center are located in buildings which are characterized by a visually relevant and distinctive image. The future of a place is kept and shown inside a landmark, showing contemporary features and recalling tradition at the same time. It is placed in a significant position within the city, from both a symbolic and small-scale-geographic point of view.

Other elements are directly related to the concept of exhibition: Exhibition in U.P.E.Cs is largely relying on digital and visual media. Visitors can access a series of sensorial inputs that quickly turn the experience into a uniquely rendered movie of a future city.

Picture 3: Chongming Island Urban Planning Exhibition Center: future development physical and digital rendering (Giovanni Comoglio, 2012)

Nevertheless, the sensational core of the exhibition remains the physical model. By the use of a scale model showing the urban area stretched along its most relevant development sites, the city is resumed, synthesized and made possible to explore in its current shape, and in its suggested future dynamics. Relevant points and places as well as possible outstanding lines of circulation and trending expansion, are selected and shown by thematic lightings or animations inside the model. Future is predicted.

Picture 4: Shanghai Urban Planning Exhibition Center: the main scale model (Giovanni Comoglio, 2012)

Exhibition is also the clear term of the one-way approach to the dynamics of imagery building shown by Shanghai authorities. Public power communicates, and the citizens must see. Visits to S.U.P.E.C.[8] are a relevant part of almost all guided tours to Shanghai for both Chinese and foreign tourists. The city confirms an *imaginaire* to be shown to strangers, thus consolidating its own self-image. The aspect of exhibition is therefore capable of covering almost all aspects of planned Shanghai, including the most specific ones. The Chongming Island Urban Planning Exhibition Center, for instance, explains the future development of the area, thus explaining, as a consequence, the methods, tendencies and instruments of a planned solving approach to the town-countryside issue in the whole region. *Past* is also considered and re-proposed. It is widely diffused, though, through U.P.E.Cs in many different forms of expression, without neglecting the most cheerful and commercial ones: Pictures, timelines and interactive digital reconstructions of urban scenarios are considered with the same respect as integrated small-scale shopping malls built as sceneries showing an Early Thirties Shanghai commercial street.

Structures like the S.U.P.E.C. are specifically related to single cases like the Shanghai one, but their particular nature has the advantage of letting this spectacular and imperative attitude come to the surface in such an evident way. It is a rare case in which an often claimed hidden message of planning communication is made evident and shown with no retention in broad daylight.

This may not be the only field where an image of Shanghai is built, and it is probably not going to be the only stand-alone one. This exploration of the topic may be suspected of operating on a methodological simplification; doing an analysis based on a division between *planners* and *people*. But still, it mirrors a radical simplification that has been actually carried out in developing nowadays Shanghai. It mirrors the current state of urban conception in Shanghai in factual, political and cultural terms.

As a "young" reality, Shanghai is surely going to change its self-perception, its cultural framework and its ways of expression as its new identity has only been built since the Nineties. Nevertheless, Urban Planning Exhibition Centers are the actual places where planning meets the population. Their current role will have to be considered also when urban culture and cultural playgrounds have changed. Part of that future culture will in some way be the result of this phase based on communication and spectacularization as the ingredients of an urban imagery – of an *imaginaire*.

NOTES

[1] This research has been developed as both an academic and field research in 2012, as a result of an international exchange established between the Polytechnic University of Turin and Tongji Unversity in Shanghai.

[2] Comparisons and interpretations of data about the "Shanghai restarted" phase can be found in Edward Denison, Guang Yu Ren, *Building Shanghai, The story of China's gateway,* Chichester, Wiley academy, 2006. 214-225.

[3] According to Shanghai 2010 Census Data population in Shanghai Municipality was at 9, 5 million in 2005.

[4] Also see Li Zhang, *Strangers in the City*, Stanford CA, Stanford University Press, 2001.

[5] Florian Urban: *Tower and Slab*, London, New York, Routledge, 2012.

[6] This is referring to the real estate boom in Shanghai in the 1990s, with its introduction of new building typologies within a consolidated 20th century context.

[7] Programs and components of the exhibitions are often resumed by promotional publications which are available inside the U.P.E.Cs

[8] Shanghai Urban Planning Exhibition Center.

KOLKATASCAPES – IMAGES OF AN INDIAN CITY

Sandra C. S. Marques
Centre for Research in Anthropology at the University Institute of Lisbon, Lisbon/Portugal
sandrasimoesmarques@hotmail.com

ABSTRACT

"Too much poverty", "too crowded", "too dirty", "too polluted" are the expressions most used by international tourists when describing the city of Kolkata (formerly Calcutta), the capital of West Bengal, India. In order to reflect on such representations, the article will focus on analysing visually exposed spaces in which a certain ambiguity, a dissociation between the vocation for which they were configured and their appropriation by social agents is present. The author of the article argues that this ambiguity in Kolkata's public spaces is the causal factor behind the great anxiety shown by foreigners in the appropriation and representation of this city.

"Zu viel Armut", "zu viele Menschen", "zu schmutzig", "zu viel Umweltverschmutzung" – das sind die von internationalen Touristen in der Beschreibung der westbengalischen Hauptstadt Kolkata (früher Kalkutta) am häufigsten genannten Attribute. Um solche Repräsentationen zu reflektieren, wird sich der Artikel auf die Analyse visuell exponierter Orte konzentrieren, denen eine gewisse Ambiguität und Diskrepanz zwischen ihrer ursprünglichen Bestimmung, die ihnen ihre Gestalt verlieh, und ihrer aktuellen sozialen Nutzung eignet. Die Autorin des Beitrages vertritt dabei die These, dass diese Ambiguität in Kolkatas öffentlichen Räumen der ursächliche Grund für die große Angst ist, die sich bei ausländischen Besuchern im Herangehen an die Stadt und in ihrer Darstellung zeigt.

Introduction

Kolkata, the capital of the State of West Bengal, India, is hardly a sought after destination for international tourists, serving as an in- and outbound gateway to the northeast of the country and used by many of them only as in-transit stopover (two to six days) for the Buddhist religious tours and the adventure and eco-tourism circuits in the region east of the Himalayas or in the Andaman and Nicobar islands lying in the Bay of Bengal. The small numbers of tourists that choose to stay in the city for longer periods of several weeks or months are usually involved in academic or professional projects or they may be on vacations complemented with social volunteering work.[1]

"Too much poverty," "too crowded," "too dirty," "too polluted"; these are the expressions most used (often cumulatively) by international tourists when describing Kolkata. The regularity and persistence of these discursive formations in representations of the city is so dominant that they occurred – every time, at some moment – not only among tourists I came into contact with in the city but also among others I met in different places in India, as they explained why they refrained from visiting this city. Now, these are not hallmarks exclusive to this city. Many other places in the world may be described in similar terms. Just as certainly, too, Kolkata can be represented by many other traits. What then is so particular about Kolkata that may explain such persistence in the choice of images used by Western tourists to represent it?

In order to reflect on such representations and the way cultural practices are articulated through the creation/ appropriation of public space in this large metropolis, I shall attempt to introduce the reader to the sensory landscape of the city and its meanings. I shall focus on the analysis of visually exposed spaces (those spaces more immediately accessible to tourists) in which a certain ambiguity, a dissociation between the vocation for which they were configured and their appropriation by social agents, is present. I think that this ambiguity or subversion of visibilities, in the city's public spaces is the causal factor behind the great anxiety shown by foreigners in their appropriation and representation of this city.

Notwithstanding the importance of the visual aspect in touristic experience (amply argued by John Urry in *The Tourist Gaze* 1990), I emphasise that I do not consider it in one-dimensional terms. Tourists are not "disembodied eyes". They are bodies in which visual images are converted into the primordial mediator of communication in order to gather information and knowledge; and in which the visual and textual image is used as a metaphor and means of expression for a phenomenological whole of bodily experiences.

As defined by Elizabeth Grosz: "The body becomes a human body, a body which coincides with the 'shape' and space of a psyche, a body whose epidermal surface bounds a psychical unity, a body which thereby defines the limits of experience and subjectivity" (Grosz 1992: 242).

In the context of tourism, the subject-bodies experience and somatise the sensation of the other, of the difference, of the diverse sensory landscapes (*sensescapes*, as Rodaway calls them). As I see it, they move in between and through, they experience and embody the different sensations of external reality, which are mediated subsequently through narrative constructions using visual (usually photographs) and discursive images (oral and written storytelling). By making use of the relative autonomy of the possibilities of "saying"/ "telling" shared by the community to which they belong, the tourists try to construct narratives that will unify the ambivalences and contradictions of meanings, offered by ideological formations and fragmented knowledge of their repertoire, and translate their mental representations of wonder, pleasure, discomfort, fatigue, desire, repulsion, identity or difference experienced *in situ*.

Kolkata *Sensescapes*

> Kolkata the giant sucks you into its universe, chaotic, swarming, polluted and above all full of life! An ants' nest of menial labourers bustles in every direction. How can India generate such total disorder?! [transl. by the author from French] (T5 - French, M, 1 day in Kolkata, 2004);
>
> Crowded streets, every one of them, bustling with people […] the rickshaw rocks to the rhythm of the wallah's pace. The wallah has a little bell in his hand that he rings to let people know he is coming. It's a pleasant, gentle ring, against the background of honking traffic and loud music coming from the shops (T9 - North-American, M, 8 days in Kolkata, 2006);
>
> Imagine your local high street on a Saturday afternoon, now imagine it half as wide put a few more taxis in it, some cows, some rickshaws, and throw in some street stalls just for the fun of it. Now imagine being in a taxi going 80 km/ h (no exaggeration) through that lot dodging and weaving like a computer game ... we were scared and he didn't understand when we asked him to slow down! (T13 - English, F, 3 days in Kolkata, 2005);
>
> We had a quick kip as neither of us managed to sleep much on the plane, and then (against all sane judgement) went off to explore. [...] We have decided that Kolkata is maybe just one step too far on the side of extreme travelling and are jumping on the next available train to Nepal (T7 – English, F, 3 days in Kolkata, 2004).

Images of Population Dynamics

Throughout its 300 years of existence, Kolkata has gone through several changes in dimensions and configuration. Nowadays, it occupies a central area (KMC) of approximately 187 km^2, with a fixed population density of over 4.5 million[2]. If we refer to the metropolitan area covered by the city (KMA), then we are looking at an area of 1,785 km^2, numbering close on 14.7 million inhabitants. These figures attest the situation of over-population in the city's central area, i. e. the area which tourists usually visit. On any given day, counting for the fluctuating population, it harbours roughly six million people, with some areas reaching a population density of 100,000 individuals per km^2 (see Chakraborti 1997, 15).

Public transport is abundant, low-priced and varied. Besides the subway network (the first in India, and in constant expansion), there is a tram system (70 km in length with about 28 km on segregated track), a circular system of train lines, whose two major train stations serve two million passengers daily, an extensive bus system (Whitelegg 1997: 13) and over 20,000 taxis (Bhattacharyya 1997: 39). In 2005 between buses, taxis, auto-rickshaws, private cars, goods trucks and others, only about a million motor vehicles circulated on the surface daily (Jana *et al* 2008, 1). However, the ubiquitous pedestrians overflow from the sidewalks onto the wide roads which also accommodate ecological bicycles, an assortment of hand-pulled goods transportation vehicles, rickshaws and cycle-rickshaws, all rigged with horns or bells.

In India, noise pollution became an offence only a couple of decades ago, through the enactment of the *Environment (Protection) Act* of 1986, and vehicles continue to hoot ceaselessly at every manoeuvre, at any time of day or night. Hooting is understood, apparently, as one of the skills in the art of driving, and the legitimacy of the procedure is reinforced by the slogan "Please Blow Horn" written on the back of most heavy trucks throughout the country. In Kolkata, despite the control measures in force, the noise in the city in many places and at many times of the year continues to exceed in practice the levels deemed tolerable to human hearing. In my experience, however, with the exception of agents of the West Bengal Pollution Control Board, this is an issue of little relevance among residents, and it has never been included as a problematic or offensive issue in their discourses on the quality of life in Kolkata. Indeed, to my surprise and that of many international visitors it is common to see residents sleeping soundly through their mid-day siesta in public spaces where the noise is far above 75 decibels (the highest permissible limit of noise pollution in India).

As expressed by these tourists, to circulate on the broad avenues and busy intersections of Kolkata may become a daunting task for the inexperienced traveller. It demands boldness, a sharp sense of opportunity and sharp perception. The sensory stimulation is overwhelming and the difficulty of processing information due to the non-recognition of meanings in this realm that is strange causes feelings of disorientation, insecurity, irritability and dismay – of "too much..." – in a body that is tired and maladjusted.

In addition to this, international tourists are confronted with a considerably different understanding of inter-personal distance, spatial experience and spatial zones of privacy – intimate, social and public (as defined by T. Hall). As demonstrated in T. Hall's theory of proxemics (1990), differing cultural frameworks for defining and organizing space, which are internalized in all people at an unconscious level, can lead to serious failures of understanding in cross-cultural settings. As he describes it, to the Westerner, "crowding" is a word with distasteful connotations. And yet, a young Indian researcher residing in Switzerland confessed to me: "I never knew what loneliness was until I left India. In here, there is always someone around you. In Switzerland I have experienced the sense of solitude for the first time in my life!" (Si, Kolkata, 2004).

Indeed, the comfort inherent to a desirable physical distance that subjects deem to be desirable for the different levels of privacy, involvement and interaction is translated into concrete implications in the planning of space – private and public – and in the normative rules of accessibility. Different spatial symbolisms are materialised in discordant configurations, uses and metrics. Even if for the foreigner coming from a "Western society", Kolkata presents itself as chaotic, excessive, crowded and hard to access, it has an order based, precisely, on the accessibility of physical proximity and on the comfortable advantages of the flexible, multimodal, inclusive, free or low-cost use of public space.

> Especially the females come from far away from Kolkata by train; they carry all their vegetables they have picked up from the village – fresh ones – […]. They sit on the road, either in the footpath or in the road, only in the morning time or in the evening. Maybe these hawkers – we call them hawkers, because they come and sell and go away –, they have spoiled the habits of Kolkata's people. I have heard from a lot of Bengalis and non-Bengalis staying in Kolkata 'I like my house very much!' I said 'why?' [they answer] 'if I go out, I get bread, I get eggs, vegetables, fish and chicken, […] I get pan, I get cigarettes and sweets, I don't have to go to the market and walk long distances'. That's why they have taken the maximum area of the road and the footpath everywhere, whether they are selling vegetables or garments or some kind of any other items (R6 – Bengali resident, M, 2006).

In this organisation ruled by the logic of physical proximity and accessibility, markets and street vendors that also offer all kinds of services are met at each step. Kolkata is a city of immigrants and the Bengali population makes up less than 45 per cent of the inhabitants. The remainder comes from other states of India and other countries such as Bangladesh, China or Nepal, in a continuous influx, requiring a place to live and a place to work in a space that is increasingly scarce. In exemplary mutualism, the working immigrants start colonising the areas adjacent to those where their services are demanded and, around them, a giant network is formed to purvey their basic needs at even lower prices, including food, clothing, bodily functions, hygiene or religious worship. As its inhabitants keep boasting, Kolkata is a singular city, in which any individual manages to survive with hardly any possessions by resorting to the use of public space to exercise all his bodily and spiritual functions. Bengalis define it in one sentence: *Shantipurna shohabosthan* – "the land of peaceful coexistence".

> A large percentage of the people live in poverty previously beyond our comprehension (T7, 2004).

> I didn't visit the goonda-controlled slums, the bustees [...]. I'm reluctant to go with no greater purpose than picturesque poverty (T2 – Canadian, M, 2 days in Kolkata, 2004).

Indeed, the income distribution in KMA was estimated by KMDA in the *Report on Socio-Economic Profile of Households in Kolkata Metropolitan Area: 1996-97*. On the basis of the then defined poverty line of Rs. 308.20 (or less) per-capita the report estimated that 19 per cent of households in KMA belonged to the category of the poor. However, on the basis of "calorie intake criteria" the estimated poverty level was found to be 34 per cent for KMA.[3]

According to another Kolkata Metropolitan Development Area (KMDA) report for the same period (1996-97) roughly one-third of the inhabitants lived in *bustees* or *slums,* which made up 42 – 45 per cent of the residential area of the great metropolis.[4] Yet, contrary to these tourists' hasty judgment and those of many other tourists I met, only 30 per cent of this population lives below the poverty line, and it is not always possible to establish a direct correspondence between a low occupational prestige, residence in a *bustee*, and standard of living.[5]

> She [her neighbour] is paid 7000 Rs, per month, to work from 6.00 a.m. to 9.00 a.m. – 3 hours per day, sweeping the street. She has a good house with colour TV and fridge, CD player, bangles made with gold and silver anklets ... She is a 'low caste government employee'; her husband also has the same job (...) My mother is a 'gentle lady' but no money! (R19, Muslim Bengali resident in a bustee, F, 2007)

Images of the Environment

By the end of the 1990s, statistics indicated that in a large modern metropolis the daily production of solid residues was roughly 1,800 tons per million inhabitants. In Kolkata at that time the city centre's six million dwellers produced only about 2,600 tons per day (Chakraborti 1997: 20), i. e. much less than in the large Western cities. In 2004, according to an agent of the West Bengal Pollution Control Board, Kolkata produced not more than 5,000 tons of garbage per day, but due to deficient management of human resources and available equipment, the state government only managed to collect about 20 – 30 per cent of the total (CPCB agent, personal interview, Kolkata, Dec 8, 2004). But beyond the difficulties in removing garbage, there is another reason for its display in several parts of the city: the recycling habit. This system of re-use, kept on the fringes of the formal economy, is very much part of the culture of the city and its inhabitants. It extends to all kinds of materials, goods and equipment of daily use, producing value in terms of the global economy at the same time that it preserves distribution of the wealth obtained among the underprivileged. This is contrary to what happens in the recently-created industry of recycling in "modern western societies", in which the value obtained – from the process and resulting products – is once more appropriated by the large economic corporations.

However, for most international tourists who have stayed only a few days, the meaning attributed to this universe of exposure, handling and reutilisation of garbage-materials – which subverts their logic of representation of the city as an object, i. e. the logic of the visibility and conventional uses of public spaces as they know them –, is reported through images of poverty, ignorance, negligence, and even malice, as presumed in the following appreciation by this tourist:

> Another tip is to smash any bottles you may buy and drink whilst in Calcutta; this applies to spirits, beers, coffee, aftershave and perfume. The reason for this being that unscrupulous people will collect the bottles and sell them for refilling with cheap, inferior goods to be sold on for high profit!! (T1 - English, F, one week in Kolkata, 2005)

Like for many international tourists my first contact with this tropical city took place just after the monsoon season (October 2004), when the ambient temperature is not too high (maximum 27 – 30º Celsius), but relative humidity reaches saturations of 90 – 100 per cent. Add to these weather conditions the high levels of noise and air pollution with high concentrations of noxious gases including benzene from the intensive combustion of coal.[6] In these cooler months it is usual to see residents in warm clothing and wrapped in scarves that cover head and neck, trying to prevent the seasonal respiratory and ear infections. It is an efficacious measure, which foreigners in the city, such as I, do not usually adopt and become sick. I needed a few weeks until my body started adapting to weather conditions, overcoming the feeling of permanent fatigue, adjusting its sense of orientation and acquiring references and skills that enabled me to move around, know where I was and use services and utilities. Even though, my four-month stay in this first period was not sufficient to fully eliminate sporadic feelings of disorientation and irritability as I moved around in public spaces. It was only during my second fieldwork at the end of the first month's stay that I finally could enjoy the constancy of feelings of security, pleasure and wonderment that became embedded in my experience of this extraordinarily rich public space.

Similarly to what is shown in numerous empirical studies regarding perceptions of other places, the factors of familiarity, the number of visits, and the duration of stays tend to be reflected in the creation of more holistic, complex and differentiated images (Chon 1991, Fakeye & Crompton 1991, Milman & Pizan 1995, Baloglu & Mangaloglu 2001). Although the "too much ..." kind of representation persists among tourists staying in the city for long, I found that it tends to be enriched with other dimensions of meanings and emotions. For most international tourists visiting Kolkata, though, this period of acclimatisation does not happen. Since their experience of the city is limited to only a few days, most "Western" tourists have to deal with the inexistence of an intrinsic relationship between this reality and their referents for city and public space, with the lack of reassuring referentials to let them understand and use this object which does not have the meaning they know. And the tourists' experience and somatisation of the sensation of alterity, of the strangeness of this dense sensescape on their tired, ailing bodies, as a tourist cited above put it, "is maybe just one step too far on the side of extreme travelling".

Conclusion

The reality of the city object results from a cultural act of classification: cities are subjects of representation and objects in such representations. To colonise a space for residence, leisure, labour, worship, or depositing waste, means setting an identity for the entire surrounding environment. Kolkata has countless grand edifices and beautiful mansions; it was laid out in broad streets flanked by spacious sidewalks that sometimes span over three metres. However, this is not its scenic portrait. From the start of the city's creation, the dispossessed have controlled and configured the appearance of the most manifestly public spaces – the streets, sidewalks and outer façades. Muffled by an uninterrupted skirting of tents, huts, shelters, stands, crowded pavements and extensions of shops and workshops, many buildings are reduced to amorphous vertical blocks. In this way, Kolkata has been reconfigured in a sort of open-mechanism landscape tableau, in which actors, processes, products and residues of their functioning are equally included and exposed and consequently impose sensory confrontation with them.

The search for exotic experiences is usually associated to the initial motivation to discover *the other*, when confronted with alterity, and is often converted into a primary reinforcement of the references to the reality one knows, i. e. to that which is familiar and provides security. As the tourist consumes travel experiences in terms of the matrices of knowledge and expectations formatted *a priori* in his/ her culture of origin (MacCannell 1992, Craik 1997), it is not surprising then that he/ she who is a native of "western societies" feels assaulted by this entity that ostensibly confronts him/ her with "too much …" of everything that was not supposed to be there.

NOTES

[1] On a global scale, India, despite its immense territory and tourism potential, is a destination in low demand (less than 0.5 per cent of international tourists choose this country as their destination); and in the national context Kolkata and West Bengal are even lower (about 0.5 per cent of all the international tourists visiting the country). Apart from neighbouring Bangladesh, which contributes nearly 30 – 40 per cent of annual entries with a tourist visa into West Bengal, most international visitors are from the USA, the UK, Australia, Canada, Germany, France, Italy and Japan (West Bengal Tourism Office, Kolkata, 2003-2007). Although also tourists from other places were contacted during this study (2004-2007), the majority of the sample is 'Western' tourists.

[2] "Population, Decadal Growth Rate, Density and Sex Ratio by Residence and Sex, West Bengal/ District, 1991-2001". Directorate of Census Operations, West Bengal, 2003.

[3] Jawaharlal Nehru National Urban Renewal Mission (JNNURM), Government of West Bengal. Ch I: "City Assessment: Analysis of the Existing Situation", 2007. 13.

[4] Kolkata Metropolitan Development Area Report in: JNNURM, Government of West Bengal. Ch I: "City Assessment: Analysis of the Existing Situation", 2007. 14.

[5] KUSP – Kolkata Urban Services for the Poor. Data provided by KUSP agents in the KUSP headquarters in Salt Lake and during the open discussions of the KUSP project to the local communities (Kolkata, December 2005 – January 2006).

[6] In 1995 an estimated 80% of families used coal as energy source in the city (Chakraborti 1997, 18).

REFERENCES

Baloglu, S. & M. Mangaloglu. 2001. "Tourism Destination Images of Turkey, Egypt, Greece, and Italy as Perceived by US-based Tour Operators and Travel Agents", *Tourism Management* 22: 1-9.

Bhattacharyya, D. 1997. "Unco-ordinated Public Transport: Calcutta Style", *World Transport Policy and Practice* 3(3): 38-41.

Bochner, S. 1994. "Cross-cultural Differences in the Self Concept: A Test of Hofstede's Individualism/Collectivism Distinction", *Journal of Cross-Cultural Psychology* 25(2): 273–283.

Chakraborti, Dipankar. 1997. "Calcutta in Pollution Perspective", *World Transport Policy and Practice* 3(3): 15-23.

Chon, K. 1991. "Tourism Destination Image Modification Process", *Tourism Management* 12: 68–72.

Craik, Jennifer. 1997. "The Culture of Tourism" in Chris Rojek & John Urry (Eds) *Touring Cultures: Transformations of Travel and Theory*. London, Routledge: 113-136.

Fakeye, P. & J. Crompton. 1991. "Image Differences between Prospective, First-Time, and Repeat Visitors to the Lower Rio Grande Valley", *Journal of Travel Research* 30(2): 10-16.

Goffman, E. 1963. *Behavior in Public Places: Notes on the Social Organization of Gatherings*. London, Free Press.

Grosz, E. 1992. "Bodies-Cities" in B. Colomina (Ed.), *Sexuality and Space*. New York, Princeton Architectural Press: 241-253.

Jana, B. et al. 2008. "A Review on GHG Emission as CO2 Equivalent from Transport System in View of Advanced Vehicular Technology and Improved Fuel Quality", PHILICA.COM Article nº 131. Available from: <http://philica.com/display_article.php?article_id=131>.

MacCannell, D. 1992. Empty Meeting Grounds: The Tourist Papers. London, New York, Routledge.

Milman, A. & A. Pizan. 1995. "The Role of Awareness and Familiarity with a Destination: The Central Florida Case", *Journal of Travel Research* 33 (3): 21–27.

Rodaway, P. 1994. *Sensuous Geographies*. London, Routledge.

Hall, T. E. 1990. *The Hidden Dimension*. New York, Anchor Books.

Urry, J. 1990. *The Tourist Gaze: Leisure and Travel in Contemporary Societies.* London, Sage.

Whitelegg, John. 1997. "Sustainable Transport Solutions for Calcutta", *World Transport Policy and Practice* 3(3): 12-14.

This study has been funded by FCT, Portugal.

Images of the City/ Urbanity in Literature

CELEBRATING MULTICULTURALISM – LONDON IN ZADIE SMITH'S *WHITE TEETH*

Hatice Övgü Tüzün

Bahçeşehir University, Istanbul/ Turkey
ovgu.tuzun@bahcesehir.edu.tr

ABSTRACT

Published in 2000, Zadie Smith's first novel *White Teeth* offers a picture of London at the turn of the 21st century, told from a range of viewpoints that represent various ethnic and cultural groups. Highly acclaimed by critics and readers alike, *White Teeth* tactfully deals with issues of race, ethnicity and culture, while celebrating the multicultural and cosmopolitan spirit of modern London. In such a setting, identities are presented as hybrid and fluid and space(s) as continuously negotiated by those who inhabit them. As the author of this article shall be arguing throughout, Smith embraces and promotes the vibrancy and heterogenity polyphonic and multiethnic London seems to embody.

Zadie Smiths im Jahr 2000 erschienener Erstlingsroman *White Teeth* bietet ein Bild der Stadt London an der Wende zum 21. Jahrhundert. Der Roman erzählt aus einer Vielzahl von Perspektiven, repräsentiert durch verschiedene ethnische und kulturelle Gruppen. Von Kritikern wie Lesern gleichermaßen hochgelobt, behandelt *White Teeth* in taktvoller Weise Anliegen wie Rasse, Ethnizität und Kultur. Gleichzeitig feiert der Text den multikulturellen Geist des modernen Londons. Vor diesem Hintergrund werden Identitäten als hybrid und fließend präsentiert, und der Raum als permanent von jenen verhandelt, die ihn bewohnen. Die Autorin dieses Artikels formuliert die These, dass Smith die pulsierende Lebensfreude und Heterogenität, die das polyphone und multi-ethnische London zu verkörpern scheint, erfasst und befördert.

Published in 2000, Zadie Smith's first novel *White Teeth* offers a picture of London at the turn of the 21st century, told from a range of viewpoints that represent various ethnic and cultural groups. The story revolves around Archie Jones, his Bengali Muslim friend Samad Iqbal and their extended families. Through their stories, Smith meditates on varieties of historical experience and the impact of socio-cultural dynamics on individual lives. Highly acclaimed by critics and readers alike, *White Teeth* tactfully deals with issues of race, ethnicity and culture, while celebrating the multicultural and cosmopolitan spirit of modern London. In such a setting, identities are presented as hybrid and fluid and space(s) as continuously negotiated by those who inhabit them.

In the words of Anthony Quinn: "Zadie Smith's debut novel is, like the London it portrays, a restless hybrid of voices, tones and textures. Hopscotching through several continents and 150 years of history, 'White Teeth' encompasses a teeming family saga, a sly inquiry into race and identity and a tender-hearted satire on religious antagonism and cultural bemusement" (Quinn, 2000, 1). As Quinn further notes: "That is why ''White Teeth', for all its tensions, is a peculiarly sunny novel. Its crowdedness, its tangle of competing voices and viewpoints, betoken a society struggling toward accommodation, tolerance, perhaps even fellowship, and a time in which miscegenation is no longer the exception but the norm" (Quinn, 2000, 1). As I shall be arguing throughout, Smith embraces and promotes the vibrancy and heterogenity polyphonic and multiethnic London seems to embody. Although she is acutely aware of the fact that all individuals are situated beings with identities that carry the burden of cultural history, her prose is informed by a deep belief in the idea that identities, especially in places like London, are always in the making and never fixed. Hence, the novel as a whole amounts to a celebration of contemporary London as a city that is formed by the mixing of cultures and races.

Writing about these contemporary themes and issues against the backdrop of modern London, Smith is in familiar territory. As the daughter of a black Jamaican mother and a white English father, she spent most of her life in London to which she feels deeply connected: "I find a lot to celebrate in the community I live in and the people I see around me ..." she said in an interview. "There's a red head [walking with] a Chinese kid, a black kid, an Asian kid, and it doesn't even seem to concern them. And it really lifts your spirits" (quoted in O'Grady 2000: 19-20). Arguably, the celebratory mood of *White Teeth* owes a lot to Zadie Smith's personal experiences growing up in London as well as her enthusiastic embrace of the multicultural ethos and hybridity as a person and as an intellectual. *Her* London is a city in which divergent paths intersect, voices merge and transform, human beings burdened by all kinds of historical baggage clash, love, hate, and evolve.

In his review of the book, Kakutai suggests that Smith sets her story in London, not the London of imperial monuments and long-running West End shows, but a cacophonous, Martin Amis-ish London of curry shops and pool halls and cheap hair salons. Here, frustrated waiters dream of making their mark on history, street people like Mad Mary and Mr. Toupee flaunt their eccentricities, and "Becks, B-boys, Indie kids, wide-boys, ravers, rudeboys, Acidheads, Sharons, Tracies, Kevs, Nation Brothers, Raggas and Pakis" swagger and limp their way, like Yeats's "rough millennial beast", toward their own purgatories and heavens (Kakutai, 2000,1).

Taking such a huge diversity of people as its subject, the novel is ambitious in scope as well as in execution. The main characters of the novel are Archibald Jones and Samad Iqbal who become friends during the Second World War but continue their friendship long after it comes to an end. When Iqbal eventually immigrates to England, he moves into Willesden, the Northwest London neighbourhood where Archie lives. They spend most of their free time at O'Connell's, the local Pool House. Half cafe, half gambling den, O'Connell's is owned and operated by an Iraqi family, Ali and his five sons (all named Abdul). We are told that "O'Connell's is no place for strangers. O'Connell's is the kind of place family men come to for a different kind of family. Unlike blood relations, it is necessary here to earn one's position in the community" (183). Admittedly, O'Connell's has a very peculiar vibe. It's full of men who seem to be in roughly the same social class but who are very different in many other ways. Still, no matter how different they are in terms of race, culture and worldview, they manage to find a common ground on which to stand. All in all, O'Connell's is a safe haven where its visitors feel momentarily (and rather comfortably) suspended in the present.

This cosy atmosphere does not necessarily mean that there are significant issues that lead to occasional moments of conflict between characters. Despite the obvious strength of their friendship, Archie and Samad have their differences of opinion especially around questions of identity:

> "You don't stand for anything, Jones," continued Samad. "Not for a faith, not for a politics. Not even for your country. How your lot ever conquered my lot is a bloody mystery. You're a cipher, no?" "A what?" "And an idiot. What are you going to tell your children when they ask who you are, what you are? Will you know? Will you ever know?" "What are you that's so bloody fantastic?" "I'm a Muslim and a Man and a Son and a Believer. I will survive the last days." (120-121)

Samad's passionate outburst aptly illustrates how strongly he feels about his given identity which for him is an existential issue. Being English, born and bred, Archie Jones is clearly not as concerned about his identity as Samad is about his. That is to say, no matter how close the two men might be, they cannot purge themselves of the historical and cultural baggage they have inherited. As the narrator suggests in Chapter eleven: "A legacy is not something you can give or take by choice, and there are no certainties in this sticky business of inheritance" (307).

Elsewhere, Samad bears his chest to Irie, Archie's daughter with Clara who is of Jamaican descent:

> "I sometimes wonder why I bother," said Samad bitterly, betraying the English inflections of twenty years in the country, "I really do. These days, it feels to me like you make a devil's pact when you walk into this country. You hand over your passport at the check-in, you get stamped, you want to make a little money, get yourself started ... but you mean to go back! Who would want to stay? Cold, wet, miserable; terrible food, dreadful newspapers – who would want to stay? In a place where you are never welcomed, only tolerated. Just tolerated. Like you are an animal finally housebroken. Who would want to stay? But you have made a devil's pact ... it drags you in and suddenly you are unsuitable to return, your children are unrecognizable, you belong nowhere. (193)

Samad talks to Irie about feeling that, in moving to England, he has had to give up the sense of belonging that is irrevocably attached to the place he is from. Samad strongly believes that one can only hold on to one identity at a time. Like many immigrants, especially those from the developing world, he feels displaced and that his identity is violated living in a foreign land, constantly having to interact with strangers. The more he feels his identity is threatened the more culturally conservative he becomes to the point that he turns into an oppressive force in the lives of his twin sons Millat and Magid who he wants to re-fashion according to an ideal he has cultivated in his mind. As second-generation immigrants who were born and grew up in London, his sons' sentiments about their identity is much more ambivalent although they, too, share their father's frustration regarding issues of identity and belonging.

Millat, for instance, feels that

> he had to please all of the people all of the time. To the Cockney wide-boys in the white jeans and the colored shirts he was the joker, the risk-taker, respected lady-killer. To the black kids he was fellow weed-smoker and valued customer. To the Asian kids, hero and spokesman. Social chameleon. And underneath it all, there remained an ever-present anger and hurt, the feeling of belonging nowhere that comes to people who belong everywhere. (269)

Despite the seeming ease with which Millat moves freely between various ethnic groups, he truly suffers from what we might call "his little sense of belonging". He is, in other words, wary of being a free floating signifier in whom everyone can see something else. Magid eventually becomes the opposite of what Samad had hoped whereas Millat grows into a rebellious man.

Their mother Alsana, on the other hand, chooses to undermine her husband's assumed authority by refusing to provide definitive answers to anything.

It is certainly ironic that in a novel that is so deeply marked by identity and one in which father figures cast such long shadows, Irie's child is in a way without a father.

> What she didn't know, and what she realized she may never know (the very moment she saw the ghostly pastel blue lines materialize on the home test, like the face of the madonna in the zucchini of an Italian housewife), was the identity of the father. No test on earth would tell her. Same thick black hair. Same twinkling eyes. Same habit of chewing the tops of pens. Same shoe size. Same deoxyribonucleic acid. She could not know her body's decision, what choice it had made, in the race to the gamete, between the saved and the unsaved [...] At first this fact seemed ineffably sad to Irie; instinctively she sentimentalized the biological facts, adding her own invalid syllogism: if it was not somebody's child, could it be that it was nobody's child? (515)

Irie does not, and will not, ever know the identity of her baby's father. Magid and Millat are the two possibilities, but being identical twins, they have the same DNA.

Notwithstanding the obvious appeal of a rich cast of fascinating individuals whose stories inform the plot, the main character of *White Teeth* appears to be contemporary London, the city which is made by them and which in turn has become an indispensible part of who they are:

> This has been the century of strangers, brown, yellow, and white. This has been the century of the great immigrant experiment. It is only this late in the day that you can walk into a playground and find Isaac Leung by the fishpond, Danny Rahman in the football cage, Quang O'Rourke bouncing a basketball, and Irie Jones humming a tune. Children with first and last names on a direct collision course. Names that secrete within them mass exodus, cramped boats and planes, cold arrivals, medical checkups. It is only this late in the day, and possibly only in Willesden, that you can find best friends Sita and Sharon, constantly mistaken for each other because Sita is white (her mother liked the name) and Sharon is Pakistani (her mother thought it best – less trouble). (326-327)

Smith seems to suggest that ways in which people think about and consequently read and express identity has changed drastically at the turn of the century in a place like London. What stands out as the most striking implication here is that this ethnic anonymity she foregrounds provides us with an opportunity to rethink identity by adopting new frameworks in tune with the spirit of changing times. Presenting a view of identity as an ongoing series of negotiations at particular points in time and space, Smith not only emphasises the contingency of identity but also promotes the idea of embracing diversity and change within ourselves as well as in others.

Upon its publication, *White Teeth* was widely hailed as an ode to contemporary London living, a highly optimistic rendering of the multicultural experience. Smith herself has endorsed these assessments saying:

> But I did want to try and say that there is a lot to celebrate. I find a lot to celebrate in the community I live in and the people I see around me. And it is very specific. I didn't want the community in *White Teeth* to be representative of immigrants in England, that's not my job really, I'm not a politician, and I wouldn't claim such an optimistic vision of other people's experience, but I have a good time. I love living here [London]. (quoted in O'Grady: 2002, 107)

Rather than asserting a space of her own in a society she is entitled to, Smith attempts to (re)define that space as a hybrid location that is an inherent part of British contemporary society. "This space is problematic; it is characterised by ambivalence and an ongoing process of juggling notions of belonging and exclusion; it is the outcome of processes of negotiation and change" (Fernandez: 2009, 144). In this context, Smith problematises contemporary British social space and reveals varied ways of dealing with being a first- or second-generation immigrant in Great Britain. At the same time she presents a diversity of ways of inscribing such experiences in space. Characters in *White Teeth* are, therefore, "heterogeneous and diverse and they approach their ethnically diverse origins (in the case of second-generation characters) or the diverse society they inhabit (in the case of first-generation ones) as part of their ordinary daily life" (Fernandez: 2009, 144). In this respect, the spaces where these characters are located are depicted as being in a continuous process of (trans)formation and change and their identities are represented as being fluid (Fernandez: 2009, 144).

In his book titled *The City of the World: A Book about London and the Londoner* published in 1912, Edwin Pugh observes that "London is a city of transitions. It is a city of a million houses – and no homes; of millions upon millions of inhabitants – and no natives ... London is at once the oldest, the newest, the most stable, and the most fictile of all cities. It is consistent only in its inconsistency" (quoted in Freeman: 2007, 1). I would suggest that, published almost a century after *The City of the World*, *White Teeth* is grounded in this perception of London as a city that is ever lastingly in the making, never complete and always changing. I would further argue that in favourably presenting London as an exemplary model and celebrating the multicultural spirit it embodies, Smith is in fact celebrating the existence of a certain kind of individual who, as a product of this multicultural city, is able to speak in various tongues. This individual is self-inventing, open-minded, and has gained the capacity to empathise quite a bit further than herself. In the words of Fernandez social spaces of interaction are depicted in *White Teeth* as offering people the opportunity of constant self-redefinition as the direct result of a society that, due to its multicultural nature, is in itself continuously open to adjustments (Fernandez: 2009, 153). Racial combativeness and confrontation that Smith occasionally hints at does not produce violence but reveals character and creates situation.

By the end of the novel the heroine, Irie, begins to notice certain kinds of very claustrophobic spaces that are made still more claustrophobic by the emotions and histories of people who occupy them. In this sense, *White Teeth* as a whole is informed by Smith's search for an alternative space that will make us feel at home without feeling choked or drowned. As she reveals in an interview: "The characters in *White Teeth* find the old world, the world we have lived in up to now – particularly the 20th century – tiresome and overwhelming, and they are kind of sick of dealing with it, but the new world is frightening to them. That kind of reflects my feeling about it" (quoted in Silverblatt 2000).

Given the unfolding of events in the post 9/11 era marked by talks of the clash of civilisations and the failure of multiculturalism, many would call into question Zadie Smith's optimism and regard it as naive and/ or premature. After all, the first decade of the 21st century has so far been host to several developments that call into question the claim that multiculturalist policies will pave the way for a harmonious world society. Within this context, cities have now became ambivalent places of both connection and confrontation, where the impermeability to novelty and otherness still hinders the European Union's efforts to promote a more integrative model, in an attempt to harmonize uniqueness with diversity. Consequently, multiculturalism today is at the heart of political debate and it is possibly the most challenging and vexing issue in contemporary democratic politics. The question of how individuals and governments might balance the competing claims, values and practices of different cultural groups will continue to engage contemporary writers in the years to come.

BIBLIOGRAPHY

Fernandez, Irene Perez. "Representing Third Spaces, Fluid Identities and Contested Spaces in Contemporary British Literature". *Atlantis Journal of the Spanish Association of Anglo-American Studies.* 31.2 (December 2009): 143-160.

Freeman, Nicholas. *Conceiving the City: London, Literature, ana Art 1870-1914*. New York: Oxford University Press, 2007.

Kakutani, Michiko. "*White Teeth*: Quirky, Sassy and Wise in a London of Exiles" *New York Times on the Web*. April 25, 2000. http://www.nytimes.com/library/books/042500smith-book-review.html

O'Grady, Kathleen. "White Teeth: A conversation with Author Zadie Smith". *The Atlantis.* Volume 27.1, Fall/ Winter 2002: 105-111.

O'Grady, Kathleen. "The Empire Strikes Back: *White Teeth* by Zadie Smith". *The Women's Review of Books*, Vol. 18, No. 1 (Oct. 2000): 19-20.

Quinn, Anthony. "The New England". *New York Times on the Web*. April 30, 2000 http://www.nytimes.com/books/00/04/30/reviews/000430.30quinnt.html

Silverblatt, Michael. "Zadie Smith on Bookworm (2000)". *YouTube* posted on 28/ 06/ 2012.

Smith, Zadie. *White Teeth*. London: Penguin Books, 2001.

THE INDUSTRIAL CITY IN CHARLES DICKENS' *HARD TIMES* AND ELIZABETH GASKELL'S *MARY BARTON*

Gönül Bakay

Bahçeşehir University, Istanbul/ Turkey
gonulbakay@gmail.com

ABSTRACT

Drawing on works by the famous critic Raymond Williams, this article examines the function and scope of industrial novels by focusing on two well-known examples: *Hard Times* and *Mary Barton*. As the author will be arguing throughout, the novels discussed in this article foreground the hard conditions working classes are subjected to and profess reform but they do not actually indicate concrete ways of undertaking such reforms. In this sense, these novels perform the important function of drawing attention to and raising awareness regarding the inhumane conditions working class English people were forced to live under in 19th century England.

Der vorliegende Artikel wendet die Theorien von Raymond Williams auf die Diskussion der Funktion und der Bandbreite des Industrie-Romans anhand zweier bekannter Beispiele an: der Romane *Hard Times* und *Mary Barton*. Die Autorin formuliert dabei die These, dass die in diesem Beitrag behandelten Romane die harten Bedingungen hervorheben, unter denen die Arbeiterklasse lebte, sowie deren Reformierung fordern, ohne aber konkrete Wege aufzuzeigen, wie diese Reformen zu bewerkstelligen seien. Die Romane erfüllen in diesem Sinne die wichtige Funktion, Aufmerksamkeit auf die inhumanen Bedingungen zu lenken, unter denen die englische Arbeiterklasse des 19. Jahrhunderts zu leben gezwungen war, und so ein gesteigertes Bewusstsein für diese Bedingungen zu schaffen.

Drawing on Raymond Williams' theories, this article aims to discuss the function and scope of industrial novels by means of examining two well-known examples: *Hard Times* and *Mary Barton*. Raymond Williams argues that industrial novels did not offer a viable solution to the problems of the age since in them "recognition of evil was balanced by the fear of becoming involved. Sympathy was transformed not into action but into withdrawal" (Williams, 1983: 6). As the author will be arguing throughout, the novels discussed in this article foreground the hard conditions working classes are subjected to and profess reform but they do not actually indicate concrete ways of undertaking such reforms. As Catherine Gallagher observes: "The industrial novels attempt to make a statement about the conditions of industrial England, to represent and give voice to the disenfranchised workers and present a vision of reform" (Gallagher, 83). In this sense, these novels perform the important function of drawing attention to and raising awareness regarding the inhumane conditions working class English people were forced to live under in 19th century England.

Raymond Williams explains in some detail the huge differences between cities and industrial towns. He suggests that

> for that, in this period, is the visible difference between London and the new industrial cities. London had a long history of radicalism significantly based mainly in the skilled craftsmen and the artisans: the older kind of working. class ... The rates of population increase in Manchester, Leeds, Bradford, Birmingham, Liverpool and Sheffield, especially between 1820-1850, were in the strickest sense phenomenal (some increased in a decade by more than forty percent). (Williams 1983, 220)

The relationship between classes during this period was highly strained and changing social and environmental conditions brought about rearticulations of social relations. Williams further points out to the inevitable consequences of rapid population growth as well as the environmental damage caused by industrialization:

> But it was not just matter of numbers: these were cities built as the places of work: physically in their domination by the mills and engines, with the smoke blackening the buildings and effluents blackening the rivers; socially in their organization of homes – 'housing'-- around the places of work that the dominant relation was so always there. It is no surprise that so many investigators and visitors reported 'no mutual confidence', no bond of attachment between the upper and lower classes of society. (Williams 1983, 220)

In this context, Charles Dickens' *Hard Times* can be read as a successful representaion of England in the throes of rapid social and economic change. The action of the novel revolves around two capitalists; Gradgrind and Bounderby. Gradgrind is a man devoted to facts and he has no place in his life for sentiments or other things that cannot be grasped rationally. The book begins with his words: "Now what I want is facts. Teach these boys and girls nothing but Facts. Facts alone are wanted in life. Plant nothing else, and root out everything else" (Dickens 1994, 1). However he cannot root out sentiment from his own daughter Louisa's life. In order to give her brother Tom the financial help he needs, she marries her father's friend Bounderby although she detests him.

Stephan and Rachel, on the other hand, are representatives of the working class. Louisa, Stephan, Rachel and Sissy Jupe represent fancy and emotion in this novel. Dickens' ending of the novel with Louisa remaining unmarried and the death of Stephan might attest to the fact that the author could not find a satisfactory answer the problems of the industrial age. In particular, he could not foresee a happy ending for working class individuals.

In his memorable description of Coketown, Dickens draws attention to the monotony, uniformity and the dreariness of the city. The town resembles Manchester or Peston:

> It contains several large streets all very like one another, and many small streets still more like one another, inhabited by people equally like one another who all went in and out at the same hours, with the same sound upon the same pavements, to do the same work, and to whom every day was the same as yesterday and to-morrow, and every year, the counterfact of the last and the next. (Dickens 1994, 19)

Arguably, *Hard Times* is informed by two different views regarding the nature of the interaction between the city and the individual. The city (environment) influences and shapes the character or the character can change environment. As Raymond Williams suggests: "It was no moral case of 'God made the country and manmade the town'. The English country, year by year had been made and remade by men, and the English town was at once its image and its agent (honest or dishonest, as advantage served)" (Williams 1975, 54).

In *Hard Times*, Dickens creates characters that do not seem to be human types but rather seem to be products of the industrial age. Dickens was searching for a theme for his magazine "Household Words" and settled to write a critique of life in industrial towns. He had lived through a 23 week textile strike in Manchester and had firsthand knowledge of its implications. He had also thought deeply about the Preston strike of 1853 – 1854. He was against strikes and believed in the necessity of negotiations. He also believed that strikes pulled the workers in two opposite directions. As a result, they were squeezed between their friends and their employers.

During the time of the industrial revolution, workers suffered because of hard living conditions and because by a wrong move or word, they could easily lose their jobs. In *Hard Times* Bounderby's relationship with Stephan is a good example to illustrate this point. Workers' unions were getting quite powerful in this era. Being a member of these unions gave workers the power to struggle against the injustice and exploitation by rich factory owners. However, if you did not belong to one of these groups, you would be left quite alone in the world. This is what happens to Stephan Blackpool when he refuses to participate in the collected riot of the workers because he had given his word to Rachel:

> Thus easily did Stephan Blackpool fall into the loneliest of lives, the life of solitude among a familiar crowd. The stranger in the land who looks into ten thousand faces for some answering look and never finds it, is in cheering society as compared with him who passes ten averted faces daily, who were once the countenances of friends (Dickens, 129).

Although Stephan tries to explain to Bounderby the dire conditions under which they live, his efforts do not yield any positive results. He cannot comprehend how the rich are always right and the poor workers are considered to be always wrong. He observes:

> Deed we are in a muddle, sir. Look round town – so rich as 'tis – and see the numbers o' people as has been broughten into bein heer, fur to weave ',an' to card, and to piece out a livin', aw the same way, somehows ' twixt their cradles and their graves. Look how we live and wheer we live an in what numbers, an by what chances, an wi' what sameness; and look how the mills is awlus a goin, and how they never Works us no niher to onny dis'ant object-ceptin awlus, Death. Look how you considers us, and writes of us, and talks of us, and goes up wi' your deputations to Swcretaris o' State'bout us and how yo are awlus right and how we are alwlus wrong (Dickens, 134).

Another important character in *Hard Times* is Mr Gradgrind who reflects the characteristics of the industrial town he inhabits in that he is orderly, emotionless and bases everything on facts. Industrial cities reflected the major characteristics of the era; hard work, utility, discipline and harshness. Gradgrind has built his life on strict principles which left no time and space for fun and fancy. Bitzer's description of a horse and Sissy's views on flowers and carpets reflect the irreconcilable opposition between fact and fancy. Gradgrind cannot comprehend that horses may mean a lot for some people, more than what Bitzer describes as "Quadruped. Gramivorous. Forty teeth, namely twenty-four grinders, four eye teeth and twelve incisive" (Dickens, 4). Similarly, according to utilitarian principles one could not cover one's room with wall paper with horse patterns on it since one could not have horses walking on the wall.

In *Hard Times,* Dickens also refers to Carlyle's 1829 essay "The Signs of the Times". Dickens admired Carlyle all his life. Carlyle criticized in his works the mercantile system that deprived people of sentiments, imagination and love. Dickens believed that imagination was necessary for the continuation of society. He also strongly believed that values such as compassion and understanding cannot be easily destroyed in a community. In this context, Coketown and Mr. Gradgrind reflect the destructive forces in a community. However, the novel has been criticized for not offering workable solutions that could improve the social condition of the workers in Coketown. Although Dickens like Carlyle attacked the mercantile system, he still opposed several of Carlyle's views. Contrary to Carlyle, for instance, Dickens professed that the positive aspects of human nature could not be easily destroyed. As Mildred C. Christian observes, "The negative forces depicted in Dickens' novel derive directly from Carlyle's work, the same cannot be said of the positive values which are opposed to them" (Christian: 1947, 241). Moreover, Dickens' "religious views were highly secularized and he showed little of Carlyle's stern Old Testament morality or his transcendental certainty of the existence of the living God" (Law: 1996, 6).

Published in 1848 under Elizabeth Gaskell's pseudonym Cotton Mather Mills, *Mary Barton* is another successful example of the industrial novel. The book takes place in Manchester and is inspired by the real life murder of a progressive mill owner in 1831. Peter Preston describes the industrial city of Manchester in the following words: "It is the philosopher alone who conceives of either the grandeur of Manchester or the immensity of its future. There are yet great truths to tell, if we had either the courage, to announce or the temper to receive them" (Preston: 1994, 37). Preston further observes that Gaskell was more able in describing the complexities of life in a cosmopolitan town. As he suggests: "Her knowledge of its life and people is too rich and complex to allow for easy contrasts, simple outrage, unqualified despair, fen or hope. She tries to go beyond the image in order to understand why things are as they are, why people behave as they do" (Preston: 1994, 40).

Elizabeth Gaskell, who moved to Manchester after she got married, knew the industrial city from the inside out. In *Mary Barton*, Gaskell examines the city as well as the country particularly in the light of their contrasting characteristics. Gaskell's novel begins with the introduction of the Martons and Wilsons. John Barton is an industrialist whose wife dies possibly due to "a shock to her system" caused by the sudden disappearance of her sister. After losing his Mrs. Barton and their baby in childbirth, John Barton is forced to raise his daughter alone. Mary Barton works as a dress-maker because her father does not allow her to work in the factories. She grows up to be a very attractive young lady and two men fall in love with her. One is Harry Carston, son of a rich mill owner, and the other Jem Wilson. Although Mary hardly speaks to Jem, she falls in love with him but rejects him when he confesses his love for her.

In writing this novel, Gaskell is fully aware of the harsh conditions of the city of Manchester where disease, filth and poverty are rampant: "But in Manchester, where alas, there are no flowers, the rain had only a disheartening and gloomy effect, the streets were wet and dirty, the drippings from the houses were wet and dirty and the people were wet and dirty" (Gaskell 1994: 140). At the end of the novel, Elizabeth Gaskell, similar to Lady Bruton in *Mrs Dalloway,* suggests sending a group of workers to Canada. This, however, was considered to be an evasive solution by readers and critics alike.

Elizabeth Gaskell saw troubles of the industrial city and tried to offer some solutions although, admittedly, these were not enough to remedy the situation at hand. Josephine Johnston remarks that Elizabeth Gaskell saw the potential in the individual. "She discarded all the social criteria such as wealth, position and religion; she judged man from the standpoint of what he might become not from viewpoint of what he was. In every person, there was some potential goodness which, if properly evoked and carefully handled, could solve many social problems" (Johnston: 1982, 124). She believed that work, institutions, friendly visiting of the poor, and reformation of the prisons could ameliorate the harsh conditions of the industrial era.

In her novel *Mary Barton* Gaskell examines one of the most serious problems of industrial towns; filth and dirt. According to Natalie Freeland Gaskell believed that outside dirt did not constitute the most serious problem of the industrial cities as people had got more or less immune to the dirt and pollution: "She believed that long exposure to unsanitary surroundings could result in immunity to disease" (Freeland: 2002, 801). Gaskell's more imminent concern seems to be the miseries that could be found in the interior of the houses. In fact, Gaskell appears to be suggesting that there are more serious problems inside the houses than outside. It is interesting to note that Barton and Wilson are not particularly bothered by the filth when they arrive at Davenport's door: "A door led into a back cellar with a grating of a window, down which dropped the moisture from pigsties and abominations. It was not avid. The floor was mass of bad smelling dung mud" (Gaskell, 801).

Gaskell examines in some depth the subject of social injustice in English society at the time of the industrial revolution. Life was difficult and the conditions harsh for the struggling poor in the new developing industrial towns. The towns housed the new factories which were a source of more serious work and at the same time places of danger. Like Dickens, Gaskell stressed in her novels the new dangers people were exposed to in the factories.

As in *Hard Times,* the contrast between the country and the city also shows in the characterization of individuals who come from one or the other.

John Barton, we are told, is a "thorough specimen of a Manchester man: born of factory workers, and himself bred up in youth and living in manhood, among the mills" (Gaskell, 41). John Barton symbolizes the ideal man. He is, at the same time, the symbol of defeat. "No haughty ghost could ave had less of the energy of life in its involuntary motions than he" (Gaskell, 407).

The demolition of home industry forced women to seek work outside their homes in the factories. Many claimed that factory work and industrial revolution caused havoc inside homes. Due to their unkept houses more men sought happiness outside their homes. Moreover, factories were considered to be dangerous places for women. Mary Barton's father was also against the idea of his daughter working in the factories, believing that this would lead to a loss of virtue.

Before Gaskell published *Mary Barton*, Britain had been mainly an agricultural country. Home industry was important; however, certain technological inventions changed the whole system. Spinning Jeny allowed for mass production of clothes and later, the steam engine and the locomotive allowed for rapid transfer of goods. Coal mines were also another factor that contributed to the development of industrial cities. Cities like Manchester, Birmingham, and Bradford became the main industrial cities where people sought work in the factories. Because many of the changes took place in a very short time, people found it hard to adapt to the new conditions. In the cities, they often led abominable lives, crammed in small dwellings living in filth and poverty.

Most of the workers depicted in *Mary Barton* were forced to work for twelve to thirteen hours with only an hour left for lunch. As Gaskell shows, there were also rich factory owners and skilled labourers that led comfortable lives. The striking contrast between the rich and the poor is thus the main theme of the novel. As Mary Lenard notes: "By the eighteen-forties, the idea that the rich and poor were two opposing camps, isolated from each other, dominated cultural discourse" (Lenard: 1999, 7).

Ultimately, Mary Barton is forced to face two choices; to continue living in poverty or find a rich lover and live like a duchess. Her aunt Esther tries to prevent Mary from making the same mistakes as herself. She observes: "what shall I do? How can I keep her from being such a one as I am, such a wretched loathsome creature. She was listening just as I listened and loving just as I loved, and the end will be just like my end. How should I save her? She won't harken to warning and heed it more than I did" (Gaskell: 170).

The bitterness and sharp differences between the two classes is illustrated in Barton's conversation with his friend about the wealthy. When his friend

Wilson comments that he could never abide the gentlefolk, Mr Barton observes:

> And what good have they ever done me that I should like them? If I am sick, do they come and nurse me? If my child lies dying as poor Tom lay, with his white wan lips quivering, for want of better food than I could give him, does the rich man bring the wine or broth that might save his life. If I am out of work for weeks in bad times and winter comes, with black frost and keen east wind and there is no coal for the grate, and no clothes for the bed, and thin bones are seen throug the rugged clothes, does the rich man share his plenty with me, as he ought to do? No, I tell you, it's the poor and the poor only, as does such things for the poor. (Gaskell: 9)

Besides being a worker, Mr Barton participates actively in many workers unions. He was a Chartist and ready to do everything for his order. Both his parents and his family suffered from poverty. His mother died from lack of nourishment. When the mill he was working for is closed, Jim Barton thinks he can still find some other work, but since the depression of the trade spreads, he cannot easily find another job and starts to live on credit. When his son catches the scarlet fever and Barton cannot find the means to feed him properly and sees the rich, in turn, spending their money lavishly on parties and luxuries, his hatred for the rich grows:

> You can fancy now the hoards of vengeance in his heart against the employers. For there are never wanting those who, either in speech or in print, find in their interest to cherish such feelings in the working classes; who know how and when to rouse the dangerous power at their command: and who use their knowledge with unrelenting purpose to either party (Gaskell: 22).

Through the portrayals of Jem and Harry Carson, Gaskell shows that dirt and hard work are morally preferable to cleanliness and riches. This view is manifest in the depiction of Jem and Harry Carson: "Jem put his black, working, right hand upon Harry's arm to detain him. The haughty young man shook it off, and with his glove pretended to brush away the sooty contamination that might be left upon his great coat's sleeve" (Gaskell: 208).

All in all, it is significant that the relationship between people is fundamentally shaped by economics. As John R. Harrison observes Dickens criticizes the utilitarian philosophy of these times mainly through his portrayal of capitalist characters:

> The Gradgrind – Bounderby philosphy is that the Coketown "Hands" are commodities, "something" to be worked so much and and paid so much, to be "infallibly settled" by laws of supply and demand and something that increased in number by a certain "rate of percentage" with accompanying percentage of crime and pauperism, in fact something wholesale, of which vast fortunes were made. (Harrison: 2000, 116)

In *Hard Times,* Dickens also addresses the alternative system advocated by socialism and the changes it will bring about. Dickens' views diverged sharply from his contemporaries on this issue. As Liam Brophy observes: "Dickens was aware of the approach of socialism with its interference in the lives of the poor and its microtomisation of the masses so that character and individuality which Dickens so dearly prized would be paved away to fit a sturn-lived society" (Brophy: 1946, 505).

As Lenard suggests, "Elizabeth Gaskell and Dickens share at least two significant qualities as novelists: namely, an interest in social issues and a corresponding conviction that fiction could change society by influencing the audience" (Lenard: 1999, 109). To conclude we can say that both authors supported the industrial revolution but saw clearly its devastating effects on the lives of the poor. However, they evaded suggesting viable solutions to the problems they examined in their work. Given their precarious situatedness as writers endowed with a sense of moral responsibility but who also depended on a largely middle class target audience, they raised important issues but could not go all the way to offer radical solutions.

BIBLIOGRAPHY

Brophy, Liam. "The Lesson of *Hard Times*: The social Novel from Dickens to Wells," *Irish Monthly*, vol 882, Dec.1946: 503-511.

Carlyle, Thomas. *Collected Works of Thomas Carlyle*. London: Chapman and Hall, 1858.

Christian, C. Mildred. "Carlyle's Influence Upon the Social Theory of Dickens," *Troloppian*. Vol 7, No.2 (March 1947): 1183-1185.

Dickens, Charles. *Hard Times*. London: Penguin Books Ltd., 1994.

Freeland, Natal. "The politics of Dirt in Mary Barton and Ruth", *Studies in English Literature 1500-1900*. Vol. 42.4 (Autumn 2002): 799-818.

Gallagher, Catherine. "Industrial Reformation of English Fiction: Social discourse and Narrative Form 1832-1867". Chicago: University of Chicago Press, No: 5, Comparative Literature (December 1985): 1183-1187.

Gaskell, Elizabeth. *Mary Barton*. London: Penguin Books, 1994.

Harrison, John R. "Dickens's Literary Architecture: Patterns of Ideas and Imagery in Hard Times". *Papers on Language and Literature: A Journal for Scholars and Critics of Language and Literature*. Vol. 36.2 (2000): 115-38.

Johnston, Josephine. "The Sociological Significance of the Novels of Mrs. Gaskell", *Social Forces,* Vol. 72 (December 1982): 224-227.

Law, Graham. "Industrial Relations: Carlyle's Influence on *Hard Times*", *Humanitas,* Vol. 34 (1996): 1-19.

Lenard, Mary. *Preaching Pity: Dickens, Gaskell and Sentimentalism in Victorian Culture*. New York: Peter Lang, 1999.

Preston, Peter. *Writing the City: Eden, Babylon and New Jerusalem.* London: Routledge, *1994.*

Raymond, Williams. *Culture and Society*. US: Columbia University Press, 1983.

Williams, Raymond. *The Country and the City*. New York: Oxford University Press, 1975.

WRITING ISTANBUL – A DIACHRONIC NARRATIVE

Burcu Alkan

Bahçeşehir University, Istanbul/ Turkey
burcu.alkan@bahcesehir.edu.tr

ABSTRACT

Istanbul has been a hub for cultural, artistic and literary production throughout its history and remains to be so today. It has also been the setting of many literary works. However, only in a way that a few cities achieve, it transcends being a mere setting and pervades both the imaginations of the writers and their narratives. In whatever genre they might have been written, in many narratives of the city, Istanbul becomes manifest as a construct of Romantic imagination. This article is a diachronic analysis of the narratives of the city, examining its Romanticised construction.

Istanbul blickt auf eine lange Tradition als kultureller, künstlerischer und literarischer Knotenpunkt zurück. Darüber hinaus wurde die Stadt als Schauplatz zahlreicher literarischer Werke gewählt. Allerdings überschreitet die Stadt die Qualität eines reinen Schauplatzes in einer Weise, die nur von wenigen anderen Städten geteilt wird, und durchdringt sowohl die Vorstellung als auch die Erzählweise der Schriftsteller. Welchem Genre auch immer die Texte entstammen mögen, in vielen von ihnen wird Istanbul zum Konstrukt romantischer Vorstellung. Dieser Beitrag bietet eine diachrone Analyse der romantisierenden literarischen Darstellungen Istanbuls.

"Writing Istanbul: A Diachronic Narrative" does not just refer to a historical analysis of the writing that is related to the city of Istanbul. It is also about Istanbul being a ceaseless, seamless narrative in and of itself. Literary or not, the narratives of the city often begin with how its geography and history blend to create a unique composition. Istanbul's cultural diversity with its many peoples, religions and traditions promises a rich narrative of history, set on seven hills and along the shores of the Bosphorus, Black Sea and Mar-

mara, whilst also expanding beyond the early borders due to a constant flux of immigration.

The earliest known settlers of the geography known as Istanbul today were the Ancient Greeks who migrated from Western Anatolia.[1] Dispersed around the region, several sites were populated, such as Khalkedon on the Asian and Byzantium on the European side. With the amalgamation of Byzantium and the Roman Empire, the fate of the area was decided. Having served as the capital of Eastern Roman and Ottoman Empires, the city grew to become an important political centre, trading port and cultural hub. It also witnessed the end of the imperial era with the foundation of modern Turkey and finally acquired its current postmodern dynamism. Being a narrative palimpsest as such, the 2500-year history of the city "defies categorization". As Doğan Kuban notes in his "Ode to Istanbul",[2] written for Habitat II, since

> each layer of civilisation sits on the decomposed previous one, the urban history of the city cannot be reconstituted. No archaeological research on a site inhabited continuously for 2500 years would yield the discovery of its hidden secrets. Hence, its urban history will be written as a literary model, embellished by interpreted fragments taken from historical sources. An unpretentious model, but one which may help to define a literary paradigm of a lost image.

Kuban's "literary model" points to a methodology that also encourages a conversation between the history and the literature of the city, which are intermingled. As such, an attempt at constructing a "literary paradigm", whereby the narrative of its history and history of its narratives come together, would promote more than a search for "a lost image". It would enable the unearthing of one that has been agglomerating and transforming through time.

Legends, Personifications and the Romantic Istanbul

The earlier narratives of Istanbul emerge from the tales of Ancient Greeks. For instance, whether it is the love story between Leandros and Hero, or the story of the King who wanted to protect her daughter from her fated death with the bite of a snake, the stories that surround the Leandros/ Maiden's Tower of Istanbul are among the many popular myths of the city. Both names of this tower, which is located on a set of rocks on the Bosphorus, come from these tales. Similar to the many such stories, these narratives blur the boundaries between reality and fiction. Still, that the boundaries between reality and fiction are blurred as such somewhat loses its significance once factuality is considered secondary to another kind of reality: a narrative reality that emphasises the condition of being human.

The story of Leandros and Hero, if it ever happened, has also been associated with the Dardanelles. The stories travel, as do the storytellers. Walter Benjamin points to the importance of storytellers who "come from afar", along with those who stayed to collect the "local tales and traditions".[3] In the light of Benjamin's travelling storyteller, it could be suggested that a bard, who had been telling the story of the love between Hero and Leandros, might have changed the setting to make it more attractive to the local audiences. Similarly, are not there many other stories of fathers and their attempts at protecting their beloved daughters from undesirable ends? Rapunzel, for instance? Yet, there is no avoiding one's fate, the tales tell us, even though a castle on a bunch of rocks in the middle of the water might appear inaccessible, when fate wills, the snake will travel in a basket of fruits. Not surprisingly in this regard, in Mersin, on the Mediterranean coast, there is a castle on a small rock formation in the middle of the sea, which is renowned with a story similar to that of the Maiden's Tower. It is even called by the same name: the Maiden's Castle. The stories and their tellers seem to have travelled from coast to coast around Asia Minor.

Benjamin argues that wisdom is the knowledge of folk culture.[4] It is created, perpetuated and disseminated through the telling of stories. Narratives are one of the most humane realities of our existence. It is how we define and understand ourselves, how we express our humanness and how we make sense of our existence. To put it in a Wildean manner, narratives, studied as a form of literature are more real than the so-called reality. It is not about factuality *per se*, but a kind of truth that because narratives (literature) do not claim anything beyond what they are (compared to official historiographies) are in some ways closer to a sense of reality based on a particular kind of truthfulness.

This humanness of the narratives makes the stories travel not only geographically, but also temporally. The story of the girl being bitten by a snake is often resurrected. A recent comic book publication, *Çiztanbul* brought together several artists in Istanbul to draw their versions of Istanbul narratives. In his "Kuledeki Miras", one of the eight artists, Alberto Jimenez Alburquerque reminds his protagonist, Ragıp and the readers of the myth of the girl who was put into a special coffin after having been bitten by the snakes.[5] Ragıp reunites with his father at his deathbed and whilst seeking for the answer to why his father left them when he was young, he finds himself in the middle of an adventure, fighting a female monster in the form of a snake. Having met the monster, he learns that the girl did not die with the bites and that the continuous biting of the snakes turned her into the monster, the "Damned Princess of the Snakes". Such references to the mysterious or the fantastical underline an exotic romanticism in the perception of the city. For both the outsider and the native, Istanbul often instigates such imagination, with its history already embellished with many stories, literary or otherwise.

Reciprocally, this sense of romanticism is also one of the main reasons for the narratives of Istanbul to travel through time. Whether it is the Orientalist representations of the city or the natives' own romanticisation of it, Istanbul has always carried intense sentiments such as melancholy, passion and alienation in the literary perception. Since there is a wide range of primary and secondary material on the Orientalist gaze, a discussion on self-perception is more apposite at this stage, as some of the poets preferred a similarly Orientalist self-image and expressed romantic sentiments.

Istanbul, for the Romantic poets, is a city that is to be loved with great passion. It is never fully graspable, always beyond the power and the perception of the poet, always stronger than him. It is personified, sublimated and interacted with through literature. For instance, Yahya Kemal Beyatlı calls out to Istanbul, as he gazes at the city from a hilltop:

> Sana dün bir tepeden baktım aziz İstanbul!
> Görmedim gezmediğim, sevmediğim hiçbir yer.
> Ömrüm oldukça gönül tahtına keyfince kurul!
> Sade bir semtini sevmek bile bir ömre değer.[6]

Beyatlı says, "no part of you I have not loved, you shall remain in my heart till the end of my days." Another poet from about the same period, but with essentially a different style, Orhan Veli shares the romantic experience[7]:

> İstanbul'u dinliyorum gözlerim kapalı;
> Kuşlar geçiyor derken
> Yükseklerden, sürü sürü, çığlık çığlık;
> Ağlar çekiliyor dalyanlarda;
> Bir kadının suya değiyor ayakları;
> İstanbul'u dinliyorum, gözlerim kapalı.

As the persona listens to Istanbul, "his eyes closed," he hears the birds flying above, the fishermen are pulling the nets from the traps, and the feet of a woman touch the water.

However, the picture is not always so benign for the poetic persona. When it is unrequited, chaotic or troubling, the love drives the lover to despair and fury. Tevfik Fikret's Istanbul is dark, as a veil of fog covers the city. The persona blames the city, in a kind of a pathetic fallacy, for all the misery that is experienced within its boundaries. Istanbul then becomes a land of tyranny. Once again, the city is personified and the Romantic personification is a very masculine one:

> Ey köhne Bizans, ey koca fertût-i musahhir,

ey bin kocadan artakalan bîve-i bakir;
hüsnünde henüz tazeliğin sihri hüveydâ,
hâlâ titirer üstüne enzâr-ı temâşâ,
Hâriçten, uzaktan açılan gözlere süzgün
çeşmân-ı kebûdunla ne mûnis görünürsün![8]

Istanbul is a bewitching old woman, a widow of many husbands, yet with her enchantment of youthful beauty, she can still allure people. She is friendly like a "dirty woman". Still, the dark, the forbidden, the dirty is attractive.

Attilâ İlhan is a poet from a later generation. As his persona protests with anger to the unfaithfulness of the city, another form of sublimation can be sensed. The feeling of unfaithfulness in the poem is a personified version of the persona's longing for the city[9]:

peki İstanbul ya ben
ya mısralarını dört renkli duvar afişleri gibi boy boy
gümrük duvarlarına yapıştıran yolcu abbas
ya benim kahrım
ya senin ağrın
ağır kabaralarınla uykularımı ezerek deliksiz yaşattığın
çaresiz zehirle kusan çılgın bir yılan gibi
burgu burgu içime boşalttığın
o senin ağrın

İlhan's Istanbul is chaotic, dark, dirty, miserable, yet, it is still worshipped. The persona, with the vivid imagery of blood coming out of his ears, exclaims that the city has won and that he is under its command: "ulan yine sen kazandın İstanbul/ sen kazandın ben yenildim/ kulaklarımdan kan fışkırıncaya kadar/ yine emrindeyim."[10] (...)

Another dominant, equally intense sentiment in the portrayal of Romantic Istanbul is melancholy, which tends to be manifest often in prose. Orhan Pamuk's memoir is constructed upon this sentiment. Pamuk is very careful in differentiating melancholy from what he calls *hüzün*, through comparisons of the Islamic definitions of the word, such as that of El Kindi and the European ones of melancholy, such as in the works of Levi-Strauss. He writes:[11]

> *Hüzün* in İstanbul is both an important feeling of local music, an essential word for poetry, and a perspective on life, a spiritual condition, as well as the product of what makes the city what it is. And because it carries all these features at the same time, *hüzün* is a state of mind that the city embraces, or appears to embrace with, pride. Therefore, it is considered both a constructive and an adverse sentiment.

The examples Pamuk gives for where *hüzün* can be found, such as the old ferries at empty docks, fathers coming home with their shopping after work, the unemployed sitting about at coffeehouses, and women waiting at unfrequented bus stops blend, once again, the geography and the history of the city. What is prominent in his examples, however, is the silence, or at least the fragmented sounds of an aging soul. For Pamuk, this aging soul, in a way, is the glory of the past, the decaying traces of a once powerful empire silently existing and doing so too close to the people, discomforting them with the reminisces of things that are irretrievably lost.

There are strong connections between the *hüzün* of Istanbul and Pamuk's own romanticism that seeks sympathy and affection from the readers, which create a sense of belonging. This sense of belonging – or lack thereof – is another prevalent leitmotif in the narratives of the city. Belonging becomes a particularly complicated and intricate issue when the so-called minority writers, most of whom are more rooted in the history of Istanbul than the not-so-minority residents of the city, are considered. One of these writers is Mario Levi, who begins his novel, *İstanbul Bir Masaldı* with this very issue of belonging.

Seeing Istanbul as a narrative in itself and linking his personal narrative to that of the city, Levi is preoccupied with the issue of language. In his own words, as a member of a nation without a country, he lacks a language in the conventional sense. Yet, the language he has as "the other" is his "home". As such, that language is his tool for a self-search. Yet, this problematic kind of self-search is also what enriches his narrative world. He is both "inside" and "outside" his own narratives, he claims the "walls" as his own. His words are among those whereby the city and its narratives become one without the necessity of further search for connections:[12]

> But it wasn't my fault to be born as a foreigner in Istanbul's westernmost peninsula. Living Istanbul like a fairytale wasn't my fault either; or sometimes, wanting to be similar to characters of plays, to other people in books, in the stories that shaped my life. It wasn't my fault to use, with an old illusion, the words of others without being aware, and considering them a new journey, a hope for salvation… After all, my Istanbul was a fairytale… My Istanbul was a fairytale… This fairytale was my story… This fairytale was their story… This fairytale was our story… This fairytale was your story… This fairytale was the story of those who felt themselves like strangers in their own city… This fairytale was the story of wanting to see the waters of the Bosphorus as a mother's womb… This fairytale was the story of being afraid of being swallowed or taken to a totally different sea by the currents with a wrong stroke… This fairytale was, just that, a fairytale…

In this example, in a modern novel, narrative traditions from old times are resurrected with a sense of romanticism. In some ways, this constant resurrection is not just common, but also rather befitting to a city that has so much baggage and so many stories to tell.

Contemporary Narratives of the City: A Different Form of Popularisation

Although Istanbul has changed immensely in 2500 years, the old narratives coexist with the new ones. Due to the city's dynamic nature, fresh stories will always emerge. Yet, the myths will be told and retold and different ones will be invented. Moreover, some kind of romanticism will be there even in the most unromantic of times. Such a trend can be seen in contemporary Turkish literature, as a form of popularisation with darker undertones or mystery and thriller elements has emerged in the relatively recent narratives of Istanbul.

Ahmet Ümit's detective fiction is widely read among the younger generations. Different from the works of Agatha Christie and Barbara Nadel, both of whom are linked with the city, Ümit's narratives are embellished with many historical details that, for better or worse, push the works beyond simple detective fiction. The rich texture of Istanbul has also enabled a branching out of underground literature that feeds on the dark, narrow streets of districts such as Beyoğlu and its vicinity, where nightlife, with both its lights and shadows, shape the narratives. Metin Kaçan's *Ağır Roman* is probably one of the most renowned ones of these works.

Kaçan's Kolera street has a life of its own as the Romany music rises to the sky. Transvestites, thieves, prostitutes and perverts people the streets. The blood on the streets is washed away without much shock or fear. The kids get high on thinner. An unconventional moral code based on communion and acceptance rules the population. Istanbul is not just a setting in this picaresque novel, but a character that shares the miseries, poverty, dreams, passions and perversions of its inhabitants. The speed of the narrative as the plot unfolds normalises everything as even the most dramatic of incidents are followed by either an equally dramatic incident or something that is utterly trivial. There is not much chance or time to moan over or ponder about anything in such a fast-paced life depicted through a fast-paced narration. As Barber Ali tells his son: "Look, son, this is the city. You'll also kick the one who falls. You'll eat if you find food, you'll run away if you see beating up coming. You will not laugh like a sissy in front of everyone."[13] Similar to other underground works, *Ağır Roman*'s world is a very masculine one, whereby being tough and rough is the only way to survive.

A New York Publisher has caught the great potential of the dark side of such an exciting city as Istanbul and put together a set of stories, under the title *Istanbul Noir*.[14] This collection, which is a part of a series of noir stories set in different cities, brings together both Turkish and non-Turkish writers.

Each story is set in a different district of Istanbul and their themes range from lust and vengeance to grief and grievances. The darkness of the stories range from bloody and gory to somewhat funny, but they are all dark in a way that reveals a glimmer of what Istanbul can breed.

This type of darkness parallels the darkness depicted by the Romantics earlier. The main difference between the two approaches is the attitude that such imagination entails. For the Romantics, the dark side of Istanbul is dirty; it is to be avoided, or at best, it is criticised and complained about. However, the darkness of Istanbul in contemporary depictions is seen as a natural aspect of the city, as natural as its rich history and geographical beauty, and even by some more desirable. Orhan Pamuk, for instance, mentions that he has often felt more comfortable in the half-lit backstreets of his beloved city.[15]

It is not an easy task to encompass the tremendously rich narrative world of Istanbul, but a glimpse at it serves the purpose of highlighting the potential it bears. As the city continues to fascinate writers, poets and visitors with its history and geography, its liveliness and dynamism, as well as its problems, which all big metropolises are prone to have, it will inspire many narratives to come. Moreover, it will do so in different media as well, for its signals can be seen in films, television programmes and even computer games that try to grasp its ungraspable spirit. To sum up, narrating the narratives of Istanbul is indeed an attempt at constructing a literary paradigm of a lost image, as Kuban notes, but even more than that, an image that keeps taking on more layers: a living, continually growing palimpsest.

NOTES

[1] There are many works on the history of Istanbul. One of the more recent ones in English, Peter Clark's *Istanbul: A Cultural History* (Northampton, MA: Interlink Books, 2011) is the main point of reference in this essay.

[2] *Doğan Kuban,* "An Ode to Istanbul", *Dünya Kenti İstanbul/ Istanbul – World City* (Habitat II) (Istanbul: Tarih Vakfı Yay., 1996), p. 6.

[3] Walter Benjamin, "The Storyteller", *Illuminations* (New York: Schocken Books, 1969), p. 84.

[4] *Ibid*, pp. 86-87.

[5] Alberto Jiménez Alburquerque, "Kuledeki Miras", *Çiztanbul* (Istanbul: Rodeo, 2012), pp. 59-66.

[6] The poem was published posthumously in 1964. Yahya Kemal Beyatlı, "Bir Başka Tepeden", *Bizans'tan Günümüze İstanbul Şiirleri*, Istanbul: Alfa, 2002, p. 68.

[7] Orhan Veli, *Bütün Şiirleri*, Istanbul: Adam, 101-102. Poem originally published in 1947.

[8] Tevfik Fikret, "Sis", *Bizans'tan Günümüze İstanbul Şiirleri*, Istanbul: Alfa, 2002, pp. 59-65.

[9] Attilâ İlhan, *Ben Sana Mecburum*, Istanbul: Ataç Kitabevi, 1963, pp. 8-10. First published in 1960.

[10] Ibid.

[11] All translations are my own. Orhan Pamuk, *İstanbul: Hatıralar ve Şehir* (Istanbul: İletişim, 2010), p. 91.

[12] Mario Levi, *İstanbul Bir Masaldı* (Istanbul: Remzi, 1999), p. 13.

[13] Metin Kaçan, *Ağır Roman* (Istanbul: Metis, 1990), p. 38.

[14] Mustafa Ziyalan and Amy Spangler, eds., *Istanbul Noir* (New York: Akashic, 2008).

[15] Pamuk, *İstanbul*, p. 342.

Reflecting on the City in Turkish Literature – A Comparative Approach to the Apartment and the Issue of Urban Change

Lisa Maria Teichmann

University of Leiden, Leiden/ The Netherlands
l.m.teichmann@umail.leidenuniv.nl

Abstract

How are representations of Turkish society in fiction of the Republican period and the 1930s connected to urban space? This article wants to seek the traces of the apartment building in terms of a constructed social space and its relation to the society in Turkish fiction of the early Republican Period (*Kiralık Konak* by Yakup Kadri Karaosmanoğlu) by comparing it with a later example of Turkish literature (*Ayaşlı ile Kiracılar* by Memduh Şevket Esendal). Thereby the author hopes to generate a discussion on how literature is involved in the process of urban change.

Wie sind die Darstellungen der türkischen Gesellschaft in der Literatur der Zeit der Republik-Gründung und der 1930er Jahre mit dem städtischen Raum verknüpft? Dieser Artikel untersucht die Rolle des Apartments (des Mehrfamilienhauses) im Sinne eines konstruierten sozialen Raums und seiner Beziehung zur Gesellschaft in der türkischen Literatur der frühen Jahre der Republik (*Kiralık Konak* von Yakup Kadri Karaosmanoğlu), indem er Texte dieser Zeit mit Werken der neueren türkischen Literatur vergleicht (*Ayaşlı ile Kiracılar* von Memduh Sevket Esendal). Die Autorin hofft, so die Diskussion darüber befördern zu können, wie Literatur am Prozess urbaner Veränderung teilhat.

When we look at representative Turkish novels written during the first half of the twentieth century, it is striking that many texts specifically deal with the issue of urban change and the image of the city. In this regard literature can both represent the changing order of things and at the same time it can be instrumentalized in order to impose certain ideas or to perpetuate an existing social, political or cultural order. As a result of urban development processes and a recurring literary image, the apartment building serves as a field for a discussion on urban space in literature. The selection of literary works analysed in this article follows the premise that space[1] (the apartment) is the organizing force, the narrative architecture that shapes the plot development throughout the text. While questioning whether there is a change or continuity in the representation, function and imagination of the apartment in fiction, I would like to induce a discussion on how the study of Turkish literature can contribute to major research dealing with urban space. Furthermore, by comparing *Kiralık Konak* (1922), which is situated in Istanbul, and *Ayaşlı ile Kiracıları* (1934), which takes place in Ankara, regional differences in the representation of urban change in the form of the apartment building and social life can be revealed.

The establishment of apartment buildings (*apartman*) in certain districts of Istanbul (e. g. Nişantaşı, Şişli) at the beginning of the twentieth century also found expression shortly afterwards in novels and short stories written during the Republican period, which can be termed as "National Literature"[2]. Social life in the private sphere and its shift from older housing traditions (like the Ottoman wooden house called *konak*) to a lifestyle in modernized areas of the city became an important theme, where urban space dominated the plot development. The apartment serves the author to construct a moral landscape in which he is able to introduce his ideas of a national society where men and women are both present in the public sphere. The dominant theme in the novel *Kiralık Konak* is the break with the past, which supports the idea of discarding traditional housing forms linked to the Ottoman past (wooden house). As the *konak*'s ultimate opposite, the apartment is a space of the future, distinguished by modernity and a Western lifestyle, but not necessarily a favourable alternative to the traditional lifestyle. Because of the authors' idealistic approach and interpretation of social life in Istanbul, the novels do not offer a realistic depiction of the apartment life, but rather serve to portray a social order for the Turkish nation. Furthermore, the function of the apartment changes when the juxtaposition to the *konak* fades, while its moral function stays present. Accordingly, the Republican period is an important moment in the depiction of urban developments in Turkish literature because meanings ascribed to the apartment building will subsist throughout the 1930s representing the shift of attention in urban housing areas from Istanbul to Ankara.

Kiralık Konak (Mansion for Rent)

> *Two eras took place in Istanbul: The stambouline and the redingote era ...*
> *The Ottomans were never as elegant,*
> *decent and polite as the people in this stambouline era.*[3]

Kiralık Konak begins in one of the old wooden houses in Istanbul with Naim Efendi, a former minister with Abdülhamid II., who lives together with his family, his son-in-law Servet Bey and Servet's daughter Seniha. The first part of the book describes the life in the *konak*. At that point Seniha deepens her relationship to Faik Bey, a dandy snob (*züppe*) and the poet Hakkı Celis, who comes to visit the *konak* often to see his beloved Seniha. When the financial situation of the family starts to deteriorate, Naim Efendi has to let the mansion for rent. With financial support from Naim Efendi, Servet Bey moves to an apartment in the district of Şişli. From then onwards Seniha starts living a life of entertainment while Naim Efendi stays alone in the konak. Hakkı Celis is constantly travelling between these two places, in search of Seniha. After coming back from a time in Trieste, Seniha finally rejects Hakkı Çelis by announcing that she is engaged. Naim Efendi is lying on his deathbed in the *konak*, while Seniha is moving back to her father's apartment in Şişli. In the end Hakkı Celis dies in the battle of Gallipoli and Naim Efendi spends the rest of his days alone in the *konak* waiting for Seniha, who appears at a party in the apartment in the last scene.

As several literary critics suggest[4], the characters become metaphors and symbols for a historical era. In the end Seniha represents the empire, empty and corrupt, and Naim Efendi stands for the mortality of the empire. The novel ends with Hakkı Celis, who symbolizes the impossibility of being saved from the decline of the empire without breaking with the past and turning to a hopeful future. The *konak* symbolizes the old form of upper-class social life (a household, *hâne*) in the Ottoman Empire: a place in the neighbourhood (*mahalle*) shared by many, related people.[5] Here narrative and architectural space is the main device through which temporal metaphors are transmitted. Foucault views space as "the most obsessive of metaphors", where the introduction of an "empty space" encompasses "views that are not decided upon, but under option, and which, between the things that are no longer and the film that is yet to be, form with language the weaving point of the book."[6]. Accordingly, "it is in space that it transports itself, that its very being 'metaphorizes' itself"[7]. The "weaving point" of this book is without any doubt the play between past, present and future in confrontation with an "empty space". The "metaphorized space" of the apartment building is detached from both, the notion of a space attributed to a Westernized lifestyle and the *konak* which represents the past and the inability to connect with it, and points at an undefined social order in the private and public sphere; a "screenplay" that has yet to be introduced. With Hakkı Celis' death the former oppositions of apartment and *konak* are suddenly being dissolved. What has been the space of the past, the *konak*, seems just as meaningless as the degenerative apartment-life. Hakkı Celis' death shows the impossibility of a future in these two worlds and the need for the past to become a foreign country.[8] Accordingly, we can see the mansion for rent as the empty space left behind by the inhabitants of the past, not yet occupied by the future, and therefore an attempt to leave it open for the "views that are not decided upon" and the indefinite inhabitants of the future nation. Each space, the *konak* personalized in Naim Efendi, the *apartman* embodied in Servet Bey and Seniha as well as the empty space in between, with the actor of the present Hakkı Celis, is referring to the "film that is yet to be".

> Hakkı Celis was now thinking like this and for him the world left behind was a mixed up, unfermented and rotten world, composed of Senihas, Faik Beys, Naim Efendis, Sekine Hanıms. Nevertheless, a feeling like a bit of clemency and a bit of hatred still kept him attached to the world; In his ways to Naim Efendi, his visits to Seniha, there was something beyond these two feelings.[9]

These juxtaposed urban images can be seen as metaphors shaping the city and at the same time representing and symbolizing the whole empire. In *Kiralık Konak*, Istanbul is conceived as a dirty, depleted place, a hopeless place, a space between past and future. This image is emphasized even more in Karaosmanoğlu's next novel *Sodom ve Gomore* (1928), where he describes the decadent social life of the Istanbul upper-class society during the occupation by foreign forces during the First World War. In his next novel the author devotes himself entirely to the new capital of the Republic. In *Ankara* (1934), Karaosmanoğlu depicts the city as a utopia. This shift in the interest from the urban area of Istanbul to Ankara after the Turkish War of Independence (May 19, 1919 – July 24, 1923) can also be observed in the novels by Memduh Şevket Esendal. But what new attribute does the Ankara apartment carry? How is it constructed in order to represent Turkish society in the new capital?

Ayaşlı ile Kiracıları (Ayaşlı and His Tenants)

We are living in a nine-room section of a newly built, big apartment. Someone called Ayaşlı Ibrahim Efendi rented this section, he sublets it room by room to whoever wants.[10]

The same year the Turkish Republic was proclaimed on October 29, 1923, Ankara became the capital of the republic. The Ankara apartment not only can be understood as the symbol of the new capital, but it represents a place where the private and public sphere blur, where people living in the same building have almost free access to any place in the house. In a time of economic recession, the apartment became an attractive income source to landlords subletting it to tenants. In other sources, such as architecture journals from the years 1931 – 1950, the term "rental house" (*kira evi*) is more fashionable than the *apartman*.[11] The *kira evi* is owned by a single person who sublets it to several tenants. Changes in society's internal structures such as the family (from an extended family to a nuclear family) are also reflected in exterior structures and consequently the transition from the *konak* (extended family) to the apartment (nuclear family) was an interconnected process. In that way Esendal profits from the given spatial conditions. In his novel it is possible to follow social changes through the narrative architecture of the apartment and how it becomes a representative microcosm as well as a symbol of Ankara.[12]

The novel *Ayaşlı and His Tenants* follows a strict pattern in which each room and its inhabitant(s) is ascribed to one chapter. This room-by-room organization is the dominating organizing principle throughout the first half of the novel. Chapter one starts in the narrator's room then moves to the kitchen making the apartment's architecture the plot's structure, playing with the privacy of rooms and common areas, like kitchen, corridor or hallway. In thirty-five chapters firstly all characters are introduced according to their place in the apartment. In *Ayaşlı ile Kiracıları* the reader is invited to investigate private space and its different characters through the eyes of the narrator, whose moral position and decisions the reader observes. The apartment life dominates the plot at first, which is defined by gambling, entertainment and immoral relationships. The narrator clearly expresses the necessity of an urban lifestyle and social structures up to the point where living together with different people becomes an unavoidable reality although it may not be a preferable one.

> However, who knows if it will be more comfortable to move out from here and lock oneself up in a house all alone! It is right that they are awkward people. One day they might affect me harmfully, but what can one do? One wants to

> meet, to talk. It's not as if we have the power to create the people how we please …[13]

The last sentence is significant, for it expresses a change in the perception of urban social norms and manifestations. If we interpret the apartment as a microcosm representing the macrocosm of the nation's social strata during that time, this sentence carries the message that in any case people with diverse backgrounds and social status have to accept living together, sharing the same space. When the narrator formulates the wish to get married and find a place appropriate for his moral standards, he breaks out of the former confining apartment's structures. The reorientation and gradual moral degeneration of the apartment inhabitants take place synchronically. The story line is constituted by the narrator's moral journey and his position in society, whereby the apartment is the carrier of moral values and social realities which evolved due to urbanization, questioning the immorality of society.

By placing his novel *Ayaşlı ile Kiracıları* in Ankara Esendal brings about a change in construction and representation of the apartment. Most importantly, the binary opposites *konak – apartman* are now dissolved, for the former architectural referential point, the *konak*, was lacking in the newly proclaimed capital. The author isolates an entity assigned with specific meanings, defined by contemporary moral values of society, and implants it into a new social context. The red line which makes the continuing story of the apartment and its inhabitants concise in a new setting is precisely the representation of a morally charged space. Additionally, the apartment evolves to be a closed, defined entity. It can be deconstructed room by room, floor by floor. The former abstract figure in *Kiralık Konak* unfolds in a socially organized and specialized space. It represents a microcosm purporting a picture of the contemporary social strata. The apartment becomes a more sophisticated, exposed space and from the interiority of its inhabitants, it transgresses the temporal binaries that dominated Karaosmanoğlu's writings.

Conclusion

The apartment resembles a most profane, common and normal place as the product of urban development. Accordingly, apartment literature defined by the most ordinary space where daily life takes place in a repeating routine, did not lead to a utopian dream for the future. The *konak* or traditional 'Turkish House'[14] was not the answer to the desire of belonging somewhere (in *Ayaşlı ile Kiracıları* the apartment appears as the only dominant, plot-generating force, while the *konak* is not referred to in any way). When the apartment turned out as the successor to earlier housing types, in literature it became a closed and defined entity which had the ability to carry the city and its inhabitants in a nutshell, representing a social microcosm. Consequently, the apartment became a translatable, exchangeable structure which could serve to portray a specific, composed image of society at large. As the former temporal binaries were dissolved, the spatial narrative structure became more specialized (e. g. room by room like in *Ayaşlı ile Kiracıları*). The very first break with the former opposites was only possible in a new setting, like Ankara, where these old categories were not valid. New categories were drawn from the nation's current social situation: class differences, social grievances, poverty, and gender relations. The Ankara apartment is, therefore, giving account of the society of a whole new capital while generating a certain image of the city.

The fictional apartment clearly constitutes a structure that relates to social realities outside the work insofar as the architectural features displayed are derived from a material equivalent in urban reality. The relationship between the material and the narrative apartment on the verge of literary representability of social realities, touching the boundaries between real and fictional is an important issue and ought to be questioned. I tried to show that purposefully represented social realities of apartments are aligned with similar connotations throughout different works. This led me to the conclusion that narrative space cannot only be perceived as something abstract and constructed or representative, simply reflecting urban reality, but that it is first and foremost something imagined. I argue that literary imagination is mainly triggered in spatial terms. The literary theorist Bart Keunen speaks of the major concept of narrative imagination in his book *Time and Imagination*[15] and criticizes the former emphasis on time, arguing that the narrative world is imagined through places, or coordinates prior to time[16]. He contends that defining the implicity of space is essential for the understanding of writing. As a consequence, the way in which society is imagined and takes shape is also defined in spatial terms, and changes in society and urban life can be reflected and imagined in space. The literary image can, therefore, also be perceived and analysed as a product and generating or driving force in the process of urban change.

NOTES

[1] The term *space* in this context refers to various physical environments in which novels are situated.

[2] A term firstly introduced by Ali Canip in the magazin "Genç Kalemler" (Young Pens), which was founded in 1910. Many of the members were important writers, including Yakup Kadri Karaosmanoğlu, Ömer Seyfettin, and Ziya Gökalp. It was one of the main instruments in the nation building process, promoting a simple and primal Turkish language. See: Muharrem Dayanç, "Millî Edebiyat Dönemi, Milliyetçi Edebiyat ve Millî Edebiyat Kavramı Üzerine Düşünceler", *Eskişehir Osman Gazi Üniversitesi Sosyal Bilimler Dergisi.* 13/1 (2012), 91-103.

[3] "Istanbul'da iki devir oldu: Biri İstanbulin; diğeri redingot devri ... Osmanlılar hiçbir zaman bu İstanbulin devrindeki kadar zarif, temiz ve kibar olmadılar", Yakup Kadri Karaosmanoğlu, *Kiralık Konak.* 47th ed. (İstanbul: İletişim Yayınevi, 2012, 1922), 10.

[4] See: Berna Moran, *Türk Romanına Eleştirel Bir Bakış I. Ahmet Mithat'tan A. H. Tanpınar'a.* 3rd ed. (İstanbul: İletişim Yayınları, 1990) and Erol Köroğlu, "Mahzendeki Geçmiş. Yakup Kadri Karaosmanoğlu'nun Romanlarında Birinci Dünya Savaşı". In *Victoria R. Holbrook'a Armağan.* Ed. Özgen Felek, Walter G. Andrews (İstanbul: Kanat Kitap, 2006).

[5] See: Alan Duben, Cem Behar, *Istanbul Households: Marriage, Family and Fertility, 1880-1940* (Cambridge: Cambridge University Press, 1991).

[6] Michel Foucault, *The Language of Space.* trans. Gerald Moore from *Le langage de l'espace. Dits et écrits.* Vol I, 407-412, firstly published in *Critique*, 1964. In *Space, Knowledge and Power. Foucault and Geography.* Ed. Jeremy W. Crampton and Stuart Elden (Burlington: Ashgate, 2009), 166.

[7] Michel Foucault, *The Language of Space,* 163.

[8] Referring to the famous phrase "*The past is a foreign country: they do things differently there*" by Leslie Poles Hartley, *The go-between* (London: Hamish Hamilton, 1953), 9.

[9] "Hakkı Celis, şimdi böyle düşünüyordu ve onun için şimdi, geride kalan âlem, Senihalardan, Faik Beylerden, Naim Efendilerden, Sekine Hanımlardan müteşekkil olan karışık, mayasız ve çürümüş âlemdi. Bununla beraber, biraz merhamete, biraz da nefrete benzeyen bir his onu hâlâ âleme bağlı tutuyordu; Naim Efendi'ye gidişlerinde, Seniha'ya uğrayışlarında, işte, bu iki zıt histen bir şey vardı". Yakup Kadri Karaosmanoğlu, *Kiralık Konak,* 168.

[10] "Yeni yapılmış büyük bir apartımanın dokuz odalı bir bölüğünde oturuyoruz. Bu bölüğü, Ayaşlı İbrahim Efendi adında biri tutmuş, isteyenlere oda oda kiraya veriyor". Memduh Sevket Esendal, *Ayaşlı ile Kiracıları.* 3rd ed. (Ankara: Bilgi Yayınları, 1983[3]), 9.

[11] Murat Balamir, "Kira Evi'nden 'Kat Evleri'ne Apartmanlaşma: Bir Zihniyet Dönüşümü Tarihçesinden Kesitler". *Mimarlık.* Chamber of Architects Pub. No: 260: 29-33.

[12] Çetişli İsmail, "Memduh Şevket Esendal'ın eserlerinde toplumsal değişmenin 'ev'e yansımaları". *Bizim Külliye*, no. 11 (2010), 43.

[13] "Yalnız buradan çıkmak, tek başına bir eve kapanmak daha rahat olacağını kim bilir! Bunlar, doğrudur, biçimsiz insanlardır. Bir gün bana zararları dokunabilir, ancak ne yapmalı? Görüşmek, konuşmak da ister. İstediğimiz gibi insanlar yaratmak da elimizde değil ki..." Memduh Sevket Esendal, *Ayaşlı ile Kiracıları,* 133.

[14] See: Carel Bertram, *Imagining the Turkish House: Collective Visions of Home* (Austin: University of Texas Press, 2008).

[15] Bart Keunen, *Time and Imagination: Chronotopes in Western Narrative Culture* (Evanston: Northwestern University Press, 2011).

[16] "It is hard to see how anyone can ignore the fact that narratives are stored in memory by means of spatial images". Bart Keunen, *Time and Imagination,* 16.

From Reality to Myth – the City of Alexandria in Lawrence Durrell's *Justine* (1957)

Souad Baghli Berbar

University of Tlemcen, Tlemcen/Algeria
berbar.souad@gmail.com

Abstract

Lawrence Durrell's *Justine* offers an impressive image of the city of Alexandria. It is a place where reality borders on myth, where the sense of mystery goes hand in hand with the commonplace, and where emotional ecstasy and physical rapture accompany mental exertion and highbrow investigation. This article purports to explore the image of Alexandria in *Justine* by following its progression from reality to myth and trying to trace the gradual transfiguration of the city from a convincingly realistic oriental place to a mythical feminine entity merging the eroticism of a Cleopatra with the mysticism of a Jewess.

Lawrence Durrells *Justine* bietet ein eindrucksvolles Bild der Stadt Alexandria. Es ist ein Ort, an dem Realität in Mythos übergeht, wo der Sinn für das Geheime Hand in Hand geht mit dem Alltäglichen und wo emotionale Ekstase und physische Verzückung begleitet werden von mentaler Anstrengung und intellektueller Nachforschung. Der Artikel untersucht das Bild Alexandrias in *Justine*, indem er seine Entwicklung von der Realität zum Mythos verfolgt und versucht, die allmähliche Transfiguration der Stadt von einem überzeugend realistischen orientalischen Ort zu einem mythischen weiblichen Wesen nachzuzeichnen, das den Erotik einer Kleopatra und die Mystik einer Jüdin in sich vereint.

The *Alexandria Quartet*, and more particularly its first component *Justine*, offers an interesting instance of Lawrence Durrell's manipulation of form and content which sets him apart from his contemporary novelists in drawing an impressive image of the city of Alexandria. In this tetralogy Durrell has endeavoured to create "a four-dimensional dance, a relativity poem" (Durrell 279) largely diverging from the mainstream of English fiction, as he said in the *Paris Review* interview with Mitchell and Andrewsky.

Even after a first reading of the novel, one is left with the impression that Alexandria is the connecting thread that unites the whole work, and that themes and characters all melt into the Alexandria world displayed in *Justine*; a place where reality borders on myth, where the sense of mystery goes hand in hand with the commonplace, and where emotional ecstasy and physical rapture accompany mental exertion and highbrow investigation.

Owing to its prominent role in the novel, Alexandria is present in the various stages of artistic creation. It constitutes the novel's background as a setting; it serves as its backbone, as the controlling structure which prevents the novel from falling into disconnected episodes and loosely-related psychological comments. It is all in one: the subject-matter, the main character, and the pervading theme, combining sensuality with reflection.

Exploring Lawrence Durrell's city of Alexandria in *Justine* involves following its progression from reality to myth and trying to trace the gradual transfiguration of the city from a convincingly realistic oriental place to a mythical feminine entity merging the eroticism of a Cleopatra with the mysticism of a Jewess.

Alexandria as a Realistic Setting

In his note to *Justine*, Lawrence Durrell warns the reader that "the characters in this story, the first of group, are all inventions together with the personality of the narrator, and bear no resemblance to living persons. *Only the city is real*" [my emphasis] (7). The picture of Alexandria that he draws in *Justine* is of considerable local effectiveness as it relies on first-hand knowledge of the place. Indeed, Durrell served in the British Information offices in Cairo and Alexandria during WWII and wrote topographical studies of Mediterranean subjects which prove that he possesses a powerfully photographic memory, enabling him not only to record places and sites but also to convey their characteristic atmosphere and ambience.

The "peculiar sensitivity to light and landscape" (Fraser 294) which distinguishes his poetry is at work in *Justine* where Alexandria is reproduced with variety and richness – its streets, cafés, brothels, carnivals, funerals and other teeming activities and places. Durrell manages to provide an apprehension of the city through the five senses as he offers, scattered all along the novel, a perception that is at once visual:

> the shuffling of white-robed figures from the station yards. The shops filling and emptying like lungs in the Rue des Soeurs. The pale lengthening rays of the afternoon sun smear the long curves of the Esplanade, and the dazzled pigeons, like rings of scattered paper, climb above the minarets to take the last rays of the waning light on their wings (16),

as well as auditory: "ringing of silver on the money-changers' counters (16), Clip-clop of horse-drawn carriages" (16), tactile: "the iron grille outside the bank still too hot to touch" (16), olfactory: "an air full of brick-dust – sweat-smelling brick-dust and the odour of hot pavement slaked with water" (12), and even gustatory with the taste of *Arak*, lemons and watermelons.

He is equally able to capture the changing climate of Alexandria in the succession of the seasons: "In summer the sea-damp lightly varnished the air, everything lay under a coat of gum. And then in autumn the dry, palpitant air harsh with static electricity" (12) while in spring the Khamseen wind invades everything and "the hard sobbing air dries the membranes of throats and noses (131) and chokes fountain pens" (131).

Durrell's depiction of Alexandria is carried even further to naturalistic description of poor quarters:

> Shuttered balconies swarming with rats, and old women whose hair is full of the blood of ticks. Peeling walls leaning drunkenly to east and west of their true centre of gravity. The black ribbon of flies attaching itself to the lips and eyes of the children – the moist beads of summer flies everywhere; the weight of their bodies snapping off ancient flypapers hanging in the violet doors of booths and cafés (21).

Durrell does not refrain from projecting vivid images of the dark alleys of downtown Alexandria and its narrow streets "lined with booths of prostitutes sitting on stools in front of their dolls' houses" (166). Such impressive passages establish his proximity to Naguib Mahfuz's drab images of Cairo in *The Cairo Trilogy* (1956-57).

Alexandria as an Artistic Entity

Lawrence Durrell's Alexandria retains such a considerable importance in the novel that it outgrows characters and imposes on events, to the extent of becoming the main living persona in *Justine* as well as constituting its dynamic structure, ordering otherwise disconnected occurrences.

Indeed, the *Quartet* as a whole and *Justine* in particular is intended by Durrell as "a challenge to the time-saturated novel of the day" as he claims in the preface to the fifth edition. He has deliberately eliminated overt references to dates or contemporary events save in oblique hints such as Scobie's remark "there is going to be a war" (138), and has introduced in its stead a new sort of time particular to Alexandria introduced by Balthazar: "today is Saturday in Alexandria. He spoke as if a different time obtained here, and he was not wrong" (84). So that in *Justine* the spatial dimension not only undermines the temporal one but replaces it.

Actions in the novel are determined and controlled by the city as if to suggest that the seemingly dispersed and fragmentary episodes only make sense because they occur in Alexandria. It is the city which can contain the "stereoscopic narrative" (Mitchell & Andrewski 278) obtained by the superposition of the teacher's voice on that of Arnauti – Justine's former husband – and host the jungle of impressions, scenes and comments, of free associations and brutal shifts of tone.

Beyond this unifying role, the city performs another aesthetic function as the protagonist of the novel.

Alexandria as a Character

Although the novel is titled *Justine*, she, as well as the main "protagonists, remain flat surfaces upon which are inscribed, in ornamental profusion, all kinds of gestures, habits and sayings but they never become three-dimensional creations" (Phelps 427). Indeed, the novel imparts the impression of a pervasive personification of Alexandria which – together with the deliberate flattening out of the human characters – contributes to the idea that it is Alexandria itself which is the main character.

Durrell himself admits that "in the *Quartet* my people tend, as some people complained, to be dummies" (Mitchell & Andrewski 278), so that the narrator, Justine, Melissa, Nessim and Balthazar turn out to be mere mimics of the city they live in. As Justine observes: "We have been trapped in the projection of a will too powerful and too deliberate to be human – the gravitational field which Alexandria threw down about those it had chosen as its exemplars" (16).

Alexandria is initially portrayed as a loving woman to whom the narrator returns after a short absence in Upper Egypt, finding that "never before had the city looked so entrancing in that soft morning air. [He] took the light wind from the harbour on [his] stubbed cheek like the kiss of an old friend" (207). Yet, the city soon grows harder, "smiling with a heart-breaking indifference" (209) and reaches the state it has retained throughout the novel, namely that of an oppressive, stifling entity, maintaining its tenuous grasp on its inhabitants who are described as its "flora" and its "children".

That the city exercises a pervasive influence on all those within its reach is made clear in Justine's confession to her lover "You talk as if there was a choice. We are not strong enough or evil enough to exercise choice. All this is part of an experiment arranged by someone else, the city perhaps" (23). This is a hint at the image of Alexandria as a monstrous chess player, tossing human pawns to and fro on its huge chess board – the physical city – and arranging combinations, meetings and partings according to its all-powerful whim.

Hence, the only way to eschew this compelling will is to flee from the city, either to a deserted island like the narrator or to a Kibbutz in Palestine like Justine. The novel actually opens with the narrator stating that he has "*escaped* to this island" (11) though not unscathed since he is "a sick man" (11), having "come here to heal [him]self" (11) from the destructive power of Alexandria. In the same way as the narrator and Justine have been able to recover some peace of mind so far away from the city, Nessim and Melissa have reached self-discovery and a shared sympathy in the summerhouse that Nessim had built some miles away from Alexandria. However, as they drive back towards the city they are "reluctant to surrender each other to the life which awaited them, they lagged, the car lagged, their silence lagged" (181) knowing that their brief happiness will not survive the crushing influence of Alexandria.

Moreover, Nessim's pleading to his wife, "Why don't we leave this city, Justine, and seek an atmosphere less impregnated with the sense of deracination and failure?" (160), and Pombal's advice to the narrator, "You should get out, back to Europe. The city will undermine your will" (202), emphasize the evil domination that Alexandria seems to wield in the novel.

Alexandria as a Mythical Entity

The stylistic manipulation which allows the realistic image of Alexandria to dissolve into the mythical one created by Durrell and which permits to highlight "the spiritual city underlying the temporal one" (84) reveals the attributes of this city through those of its "children" or "exemplars" as he labels them. More than a metaphor, Alexandria is "a living organism" (Sobhy 32) and "the unknown mysterious power that subtly governs the behaviour and the life of the *Quartet*'s main characters" (Sobhy 32).

Durrell's treatment of Alexandria as the main protagonist of the novel is so complex as not to consist simply in an independent entity wielding its domination on characters and events from above, but more significantly as part and parcel of these people and their actions; the cumulative outcome of characters, especially the female ones.

Being typical Alexandrian women, Justine and Melissa are the medium through which the author builds the mythical Alexandria whose attributes are those of its women as their depiction amounts to a symbolic representation of Alexandria itself. These women are sheer allegories of Alexandria rather than true characters; they form the different facets of a single mythical entity taking shape out of the juxtaposition of opposite, yet, complementary features in its representatives.

In *Justine* Durrell emphasises the idea that "as an Alexandrian, one has to reconcile two extremes of habit and behaviour which are not due to the intellectual disposition of the inhabitants but to their soil, air, landscape. I mean extreme sensuality and intellectual ascetism" (87). The Alexandria myth he creates is made up of a seductive Cleopatra and a meditative Jewess.

Alexandria as Cleopatra

One of the facets of Alexandria that Lawrence Durrell presents in *Justine*, though it can be traced in the whole *Quartet*, is that of the conventional oriental woman; the fatally attractive promiscuous sorceress, largely inspired by the mythical Cleopatra that has pervaded the Western mind since Shakespeare's play, and superposed with the more recent image of the dancing girl, selling cheap sex to the Western man.

Such a perception, essentially based on physical attraction, is embodied in the novel by the title character Justine and by Melissa, the narrator's girl before he met Justine, who is literally unrolled from a carpet "like Cleopatra" (50). Melissa is the typical eastern prostitute, part of "the sexual provender which lies to hand, staggering in its variety and profusion" (12). She dances in one of the city's night-clubs and does not mind satisfying the customers' exigencies after her performance, wallowing in the licence natural to the readily permissive Alexandrian environment, where sexual inhibitions are dispensed with. She even pays off her lover's debts by having sex with his creditors; believing that it is "the least of sacrifices" as she says (31).

Justine, on the other hand, is "reputed to have had many lovers" (26) and is "a shallow twentieth-century reproduction of the great hetaerae of the past" (67). Though a more refined courtesan than Melissa, she contributes to the image of Alexandria as a compliant woman, displaying a "pliancy which was Oriental – a passion to serve" (46) since "in her as an Alexandrian, licence was in a way a form of self-abnegation, a travesty of freedom" (35).

However, the unbridled physical indulgence welcome in Alexandria is not synonymous with pleasure and satisfaction but rather with suffering and distress, for the city "decrees that its women shall be voluptuaries not of pleasure but of pain, doomed to hunt for what they lest dared to find" (41). The Alexandria-woman is thus a target for the forces of destruction at the same time as she is an unnerving and a destructive power herself. She is, like Melissa, the epitome of loneliness – "Monsieur, je suis devenue la solitude même" (41) – and like Justine who is "marked down for self-destruction" (118) – the living evidence of Durrell's statement that "the Orient cannot rejoice in the sweet anarchy of the body for it has outstripped the body" (12).

Besides being harmful to herself, she constitutes a danger for the men who fall in her net, western and Levantine alike. The intertwining of woman and danger in the Alexandria myth is not confined to physical danger; like the narrator who is threatened by Melissa's lover, the old furrier following him with "a pistol sagging in the pocket of his overcoat" (20), or by Justine's husband Nessim at the duck-shooting party. It is extended to the spiritual danger of experiencing disintegration and madness like Nessim or undergoing moral undoing like the narrator who ends up emotionally strung on a deserted island.

Although they do not die like Mark Antony, the men that are possessed by Durrell's Cleopatra continue to endure the surreptitiously effect of attrition caused by Alexandria, typifying the poet's words: "Just as you've ruined your life in this/ One spot of ground you've ruined its worth/ Everywhere now – over the whole earth" (221).

Alexandria as a Jewess

Intimately interwoven with the myth of the *femme fatale* ascribed to Alexandria is that of the meditative intellectual, since they are both epitomized in the same character Justine besides being interspersed in the novel. The city of Alexandria itself is seen as the site of scholarship and erudition as well as the centre of occult activities and metaphysical speculation. These characteristics are represented in the Cabbala study group including Justine.

The group's leader Doctor Balthazar is the epitome of the professed "ratiocinative faculties" of the Jews (83) while being closely related to the physical aspect of the city as a specialist in venereal diseases, living "in the heart of the city's life – its genito-urinary system" (81). He also lives at the heart of Alexandria's spiritual life as the guide to the mysterious universe of the Cabbala, the "unpredicated ground of that Gnosis" of which no definition can be attempted, consisting of mysteries and "raw experiences that only the initiates can share" (87).

Justine and the narrator have been brought to share a mystical experience before being entangled in a love-affair. Justine confesses that they are closer to each other because of their intellectual communion than because of their actual copulation. As a Jewess herself, and therefore prone to meditative contemplation and possessed with "a Judeo-Coptic mania for dissecting and analysing the subject" (19), Justine considers that their intimacy was "of a strange mental order". "It was if you like, the flirtation of minds prematurely exhausted by experience which seemed so much more dangerous than a love founded in sexual attraction" (23). Her former husband Arnauti also admits that it was "not in the lover that [he] met her but in the writer" (63).

She represents Alexandria's contemplative aspect as well as its unsubstantial and mystical quality for "Justine and her city are alike in that they both have a strong flavour, without any real character" (123). Any attempt to explain her, justify or excuse her "takes away all her mythical substance – the only thing she really is" (68).

Like Alexandria, Justine seems to ally reflection and inquiry with superstition and mystery, "moving in a world of books and ideas" (148), and fascinates by the hidden and the unknown "with her Tarot cards kept on the shelf among the books" (160).

However, neither she nor the Alexandria she embodies is able to find answers to her perpetual questioning, and she continues to dwell in a mind-racking anxiety. "The whole universe of her city, of the world, was formed out of her agony and remorse. The tragic seed from which her thoughts and actions grew was the seed of a pessimistic Gnosticism" (35), so that the meditative mysticism of Alexandria produces in her a feeling of tormenting anguish similar to that which results from unrestrained eroticism.

Ultimately, Alexandria emerges forcefully in the novel as an entity made up of body and soul, "a hybrid, a joint" (24), being as prone to get involved in physical gratification as to engage in disturbing mental speculations.

With its polyglot cosmopolitan nature, Lawrence Durrell's Alexandria is essentially an open city, where any permutation of relationship, any indulgence in the senses, any variety of religion and any trend of speculation is not only permitted but almost enjoined. That it is "an anarchy of flesh and fever, of money-love and mysticism" (*Balthazar* 152) does not preclude its actual existence as the second most important city in Egypt.

Durrell's originality in drawing this polymorphic representation of the city rests in his kaleidoscopic reflection of Alexandria which develops it from a real, tangible place into a fantastic mythical entity.

WORKS CITED

Durrell, Lawrence. *Justine*. London: Faber, 1957.

Durrell, Lawrence. *Balthazar*. London: Faber, 1958.

Fraser, G. S. "English Poetry 1930-1960". *History of Literature in the English Language Vol. 7: The Twentieth Century*. London: Barrie and Jenkins, 1970. pp. 277-309.

Mahfuz, Naguib. *The Cairo Trilogy* (1956-57). Trans. William Hutchins et al. NY & London: Knopf, 2001.

Mitchell, Julian and Gene Andrewski. "Lawrence Durrell". *Writers at Work: The Paris Review Interviews*. Ed. Van Wick Brooks. NY: Viking Press: 1963.

Phelps Gilbert. "The Post-War English Novel", in: *The New Pelican Guide to English Literature*, Vol. 8. Ed. Boris Ford. Harmondsworth: Penguin, 1984. pp. 427-28.

Sobhy, Soad Hussein. "Alexandria as Groddeck's It". Cited by Linda Stump Rashidi in "Durrell's City as Interior Space: 'The city begins and ends in us'", in *Durrell and the City: Collected Essays on Place*. Ed. Donald P. Kaczvinsky. Lanham: Rowman & Littlefield, 2012. Pp. 31-42.

Images of the City/ Urbanity in Feature Films

Film as a Map – Cinema, City and Spatial Practices

Massimiliano Gaudiosi

University Suor Orsola Benincasa, Naples/ Italy
gaudiosi@gmail.com

Abstract

In some contemporary movies the narrative creates a cartography crossing the screen borders, in an attempt to open it to the globe's curvature and to a reconfiguration of the city. The spectator is led through a journey inside locations: aerial views allow taking a turn around the earth at the speed of a glance, sliding from one end of a planisphere to another. Like in the modern locative media, the classical cinematic map dissolves in a coming and going among places, similarly to the experience of surfing the Net.

In einigen zeitgenössischen Kinofilmen schafft der Erzählstrang eine Kartografie, die die Grenzen des Bildschirms (der Leinwand) überschreitet, und sie öffnet für die Krümmung des Globus und für eine Re-Konfiguration der Stadt. Der Zuschauer wird auf eine Reise durch das Innere der Schauplätze geschickt: Luftaufnahmen erlauben es, mit der Geschwindigkeit eines Augenaufschlags Abstecher ans andere Ende des Globus zu machen und von einem Ort zum anderen zu springen. Wie in den modernen ortsgebundenen Medien löst sich die klassische kinematische Landkarte auf in ein Kommen und Gehen von Orten, ähnlich der Erfahrung beim Surfen im Internet.

One of the key points characterizing some contemporary American movies is probably related to an increasing importance of the film as a quite dynamic *map*: a bird's eye/ zenithal view seems to prevail assuming an aesthetic eminence in the representation of the city, transformed in a grid of blocks scanned by aircrafts, satellites or computer monitors. This phenomenon is evident in a range of heterogeneous recent productions such as disaster films (*2012*, R. Emmerich, 2009), computer-animated adventures (*WALL-E*, A. Stanton, 2008), action thrillers (*The International*, T. Tykwer, 2009), science fiction movies (*District 9*, N. Blomkamp, 2009), and war thrillers (*Zero Dark Thirty*, K. Bigelow, 2012). If, akin to a satellite survey system, in the aforementioned titles the camera frequently controls landscapes from an aerial point of view, at the same time the spectator is drawn into a surrogate journey through urban locations. The audience is immersed in a virtual tour of cities mixing viewpoint of characters in flight with "on-the-ground" explorations filtered by sophisticated screens, digital displays and Geographic Information Systems (GIS).

This article intends to analyse this stylistic propensity focusing the attention on two case studies – *Premium Rush* (D. Koepp, 2012) and *Inception* (C. Nolan, 2010) – in which the classical map, based on the fixed Cartesian coordinate-system, dissolves in an incessant tour into different places, similarly to the experience of internet and the digital navigation in videogame fictional worlds. The aim is to question the role of the cinematic city as a result of the "crisis of the cartographic reason" in the age of globalization (Farinelli, 2009): behind the prominent function of the film as a map it is, in fact, possible to recognize the transformation of the traditional map-making and map-reading in the field of cartography. Nowadays everything in the media world can get mapped:

> Cell phones have become location-aware, computer games have moved outside, the Web is tagged with geospatial information, and geobrowsers like Google Earth are regarded as an entirely new genre of media. Spatial representations have been inflected by electronic technologies (radar, sonar, gps, Wi-Fi, Bluetooth, rfid, etc.) traditionally used in mapping, navigation, wayfinding, or location and proximity sensing. We are seeing the rise of a new, location-aware generation. [...] The unusual location-based nature of communication in the electronic media, in particular, is currently leading to a renaissance of cartographic representations, as maps are often indispensable to "locative media" in producing an index for the illustration of spatial relationships. (Thielmann 2010: 2)

Within such a relocation process concerning cinema as well as old and new media in the "convergence culture" era (Jenkins, 2006), the value of maps has increased considerably, and urban screens, videogame displays, and smartphones involve a performative cartography – a challenge to the common and logic experience of space and time in navigation: "the city becomes a clickable screenspace, a terrain of pop-ups that are triggered by real-life avatars in the physical world whose movements are tracked on-screen by GPS. In contrast to two-dimensional maps, [...] the digital tour-map is dynamic, layered, expandable, mutable, and flexible" (Verhoeff 2012: 154).

In the last years, the relation between maps, cartographies and cinema has also been at the centre of a number of discussions and publications, with the contagious spread of multiple metaphors of mapping across social and cultural areas of study. As a symptom of the spatial turn in humanities resulting from the recent surge of scholarly interest in space, *maps* and *mapping* practices function "as a means to explore new approaches and understandings of film and spatiality" (Roberts and Hallam 2013: 3). One of the chief purposes of this article is to analyse these cartographic properties reframing film practices as *spatial practices* (Roberts and Hallam 2013: 9). Particularly, attention will be paid to the affinities and the differences between cinema and digital maps, using the categories proposed by Michel De Certeau in *The Practice of Everyday Life*. In this famous work, the French author describes the interesting effects of a sight from the top of the Twin Towers:

> To be lifted to the summit of the World Trade Center is to be lifted out of the city's grasp. One's body is no longer clasped by the streets that turn and return it according to an anonymous law; nor is it possessed, whether as player or played, by the rumble of so many differences and by the nervousness of New York traffic. When one goes up there, he leaves behind the mass that carries off and mixes up in itself any identity of authors or spectators. [...] His elevation transfigures him into a voyeur. It puts him at a distance. It transforms the bewitching world by which one was "possessed" into a text that lies before one's eyes. It allows one to read it, to be a solar Eye, looking down like a god. The exaltation of a scopic and gnostic drive: the fiction of knowledge is related to this lust to be a viewpoint and nothing more. (De Certeau 1984: 92)

The author outlines how such a peculiar position transforms the spectator into a celestial eye contemplating a panorama-city, a picture whose features can cause a misunderstanding of the everyday practices of the urban space. In fact, the voyeur-god, observing and reading the landscape from the top, perceives space in a very different way compared to ordinary pedestrians living "down below", which cannot read the city because they experience it by walking.

According to De Certeau, the basis of the everyday narrations concerns the relationship and the oscillation between both the poles of space practice mentioned above: the "map", the privileged and unusual perception from a distant and elevated point of view, "a plane projection totalizing observations", a *tableau* working as an act of *seeing* (the knowledge of an order of places); and the "tour", the action of the ordinary walking users, a discursive series of operations organizing *movements*, an itinerary and a form of *going* (spatializing actions). If maps are abstracted accounts of spatial relations, tours are told from the point of view of the traveller; if maps document places, tours describe movements through spaces (De Certeau 1984: 118-122). This suggestive distinction can offer valid instruments for the analysis of the city as resulting from the convergence between digital maps and cinema. De Certeau's thinking about spatial practices has been discussed by scholars interested in new narrative platforms like, for instance, videogames (Fuller and

Jenkins 1995; Lammes 2009). Nevertheless, De Certeau focused his categories on a traditional understanding of spatial relations, and a readjustment will be necessary if one considers the theoretical challenge arising from the revolutionary conversion to interactive digital maps or satellite views. An example of the complex intersection of narrative "maps" and "tours" in recent productions is offered by *Premium Rush* (D. Koepp, 2012), an action film set in the streets of Manhattan and following Wilee (Joseph Gordon-Levitt), a bicycle messenger chased by a corrupt and gambling-addicted police officer (Robert Shannon) who tries to prevent the delivery of an envelope. The movie is quite evidently an in-depth exploration of the streets of New York, and the camera flies parallel with the fast bicycle of the protagonist, who skilfully avoids taxis, buses and pedestrians. But even though the repeated spatial movements and the multiple itineraries could be described in terms of *operations*, with an overwhelming presence of tour practices, *Premium Rush* transforms the city into a visual abstraction of space, into an interactive digital map. In some sequences, Wilee's uncontrolled rush is marked by interstitial Google-map-style sections that zoom out for an aerial view of the route, and zoom in showing the street view of the destination. Sometimes described with a smartphone display, the itineraries mirror the everyday internet experience of millions of Google Maps users. During the film, it is possible to watch a satellite 3D view of the city with a dynamic arrow showing the trajectory, for instance, from the corner between 54th Street and 3rd Avenue to the corner between 28th Street and 11th Avenue. The narrative takes the form of a geobrowser, manipulating space as well as time: flashbacks break the chronological order focusing on different aspects of each individual character, with an overlaid digital clock showing the time advancing rapidly forward and backward in the story. Moreover, in some dangerous traffic situations time is slowed down, and a point of view shot demonstrates Wilee's particular sixth sense, namely his ability to prevent accidents predicting the consequences of a wrong choice. In such an "interactive" structure, the city of New York moves in a flux of information and topographical connections, sharing many features of a digital navigation, where it is the movement that establishes the map, and where space and time unfold during the journey. In the performative cartography of the locative media, the map becomes in fact a procedural form not measurable in predetermined lines, that causes a time-space collapse involving the practices of making and viewing images (Verhoeff 2012: 144-153).

Premium Rush is a good example of the way in which recent popular feature films absorb technological advancements in cartography, with visible impacts on the representation of the city. The characters of contemporary action and thriller movies live the urban space shown through a constant interface with technology. The use of computer and broadcast devices frequently reveals a veritable screen city (Cameron and Cubitt 2009: 153). A dimension melts distinct spatial categories like maps and tours and sheds a light on the complex relationship between city and cinema. If on the one hand the latter comes out from the former, on the other hand the cinematic image incorporates the urban experience in an aesthetic movement where instability becomes a structural principle: "it is exactly the instability of the cinematic image that allows it to evoke the city in all its errancy in ways that stable images cannot" (Abbas 2003: 144-145).

As Thomas Elsaesser assumes, the complex storytelling visible in many "puzzle films" and "mind-game films" – a cycle of productions in the last thirty years that repudiate classical storytelling – is partly connected to the impact of new technologies, which engender new forms of narrative:

> The hotspots and network nodes that now link the web are clearly breaks with narrative linearity, and the literate community has adapted surprisingly quickly to the labyrinth pathways and navigational principles behind such architectures. [...] The consequence is that narrative (as the traditionally most efficient organizing principle of connecting disparate information to a user) has to contend and rival with the archive and the database and their forms of organization and user-contact. (Elsaesser 2009: 23-24)

Cinema has progressively lost its role as a privileged form of narrative and exploration of fictional spaces, and, challenged by the widespread emergence of digital media (3-D effects, augmented reality, smartphones, GIS, etc.), has turned towards multiple directions, such as the rhizomatic structure of hypertext architectures and towards a full immersivity of the audience in a virtual space, clearly visible in *Premium Rush*, as well as in titles like *The Matrix* (Wachowski Brothers, 1999), *eXistenZ* (D. Cronenberg, 1999), and *Inception* (C. Nolan, 2010).

This last title provides another example of the reconfiguration of the spatial practices of the city. *Inception* is an unusual spy movie set in a world in which powerful corporations manipulate politics and economy penetrating human dreams with sophisticated psychic espionage techniques. The protagonist Dom Cobb (Leonardo Di Caprio) is a talented extractor of information secretly hidden into thoughts and dreams, which uses a dream-within-a-dream strategy. This narrative structure creates a complex *mise-en-abîme* of worlds within worlds, similar to the immersion in imaginary lands of videogames and virtual reality. Every dreamer in the film, in fact, "is situated immobile in a chair and wired to a computer which generates the dream programmed with architectural mazes to be filled out by the 'subject', the unsuspecting target unaware of being in a dream, and who is drugged into ever deeper dream levels" (Taylor, 2012). The characters become a sort of players of a videogame, like the heroes of *The Matrix*. *Inception* creates first of all a worldwide journey, in line with the James Bond movies tradition and the trend of recent action-thrillers like *The International*. During the film, the spectator continuously travels along places covering huge distances: the film starts in Japan; next Cobb will fly to Paris, where he will find Ariadne, a new "architect" for dreams; next to Mombasa, Sidney, New York and finally to Los Angeles. Secondly, a central figure in *Inception* is the architect, the person employed by Cobb. His task it is to engineer the "location" of a dream. As Cobb declares, he offers architects "the chance to build cathedrals, entire cities, things that have never existed, things that couldn't exist in the real world". In the sequence at the Parisian Café, during Ariadne's first lesson in shared dreaming, a dialogue discloses an important reference to the architectural construction of the world in a dream:

> Cobb: Imagine you're designing a building, right? You consciously create each aspect. But sometimes, it feels like it's almost creating itself. If you know what I mean.
>
> Ariadne: Yeah, like I'm discovering it.
>
> Cobb: Exactly. Genuine inspiration, right? Now, in a dream, our mind continuously does this. We create and perceive our world simultaneously, and our mind does this so well that we don't even know it's happening. That allows us to get right in the middle of that process.

In the last lines of this dialogue an idea of a mental world planned (the map) and perceived (the tour) is included at the same moment, just in line with the logic of the spatial exploration seen in *Premium Rush*. This coexistence of the act of reading the city together with the act of moving inside it is epitomised in the surprising scene that follows the dialogue between Cobb and Ariadne. When Ariadne realizes that the conversation at the Parisian Café is only a dream, she concentrates on the street creating herself the world and upsetting the laws of physics: the street starts to bend in half, with the buildings on either side folding in until they form the inside of a cube of a city, and the gravity functioning independently on each plane; a clear evidence of a performative cartography disentangled by the constraints of the two dimensions.

Both *Premium Rush* and *Inception* indicate the signs of a crisis in the classical representation of the city and its spatial practices, a collapse that is affected by the revolution of the cartographic systems. The mainstream cinema of the last years seems to investigate the new frontiers of the *overexposed city* in multiple (and also contradictory) directions. As Paul Virilio points out (Virilio 2002: 440-448), the overexposed city is deprived of objective boundaries, and the screen interface of computers erases any distinctions between *here* and *there*, *near* and *far*, *micro* and *macro*. In this context, Hollywood merits the attention of urbanists and geographers, because there, more than anywhere else, advanced technologies form a synthetic space-time continuum; an experience that can reveal hidden urban aspects, showing the modern city in all its complexity.

WORKS CITED

Abbas, A. (2003), "Cinema, the City, and the Cinematic", in Krause, L. and Petro, P. (Eds) *Global Cities: Cinema, Architecture, and Urbanism in a Digital Age*, New Brunswick, N. J.: Rutgers University Press, pp. 142-156.

Cameron, A. and Cubitt, S. (2009), "*Infernal Affairs* and the Ethics of Complex Narrative", in W. Buckland (Ed.), *Puzzle Films. Complex Storytelling in Contemporary Cinema*, Malden; Oxford; Chichester: Wiley-Blackwell, pp. 151-166.

De Certeau, M. (1984), *The Practice of Everyday Life*, trans. S. Rendall, Berkeley; Los Angeles; London: University of California Press.

Elsaesser, T. (2009), "The Mind-Game Film", in W. Buckland (Ed.), *Puzzle Films. Complex Storytelling in Contemporary Cinema*, Malden; Oxford; Chichester: Wiley-Blackwell, pp. 13-41.

Farinelli, F. (2009), *La crisi della ragione cartografica*, Torino, Einaudi.

Fuller M., and Jenkins, H. (1995), "Nintendo® and New World Travel Writing: A Dialogue", in S. G. Jones (Ed.) *Cybersociety: Computer-Mediated Communication and Community*, Thousand Oaks: Sage Publications, pp. 57-72.

Hallam, J. and Roberts, L. (2013), "Film and Spatiality: Outline for a New Empiricism", in J. Hallam and L. Roberts (Eds), *Locating the Moving Image. New Approaches to Film and Place*, Bloomington; Indianapolis: Indiana University Press, pp. 1-30.

Jenkins, H. (2006), *Convergence Culture: Where Old and New Media Collide*, New York: New York University Press.

Lammes, S. (2009), "Terra Incognita. Computer Games, Cartography and Spatial Stories", in M. van den Boomen, S. Lammes, A. Lehmann, J. Raessens, and M. T. Schäfer (Eds), *Digital Material. Tracing New Media in Everyday Life and Technology*, Amsterdam: Amsterdam University Press, pp. 223-235.

Taylor, H. M. (2012), "The Junkies of Plato's Cave: *Inception*, Mindbending, and Complex Narration in the Shadow of Philip K. Dick", *CineAction*, 86. http://cineaction.ca/issue86sample.htm. Accessed 15 December 2013.

Thielmann, T. (2010), "Locative Media and Media Localities: an Introduction to Media Geography", *Aether. The Journal of Media Geography*, vol. 5a, pp. 1-17. http://130.166.124.2/~aether/volume_05a.html. Accessed 15 December 2013.

Verhoeff, N. (2012), *Mobile Screens. The Visual Regime of Navigation*, Amsterdam: Amsterdam University Press.

Virilio, P. (2002), "The Overexposed City", in G. Bridge and S. Watson (Eds), *The Blackwell City Reader*, Malden; Oxford; Chichester: Wiley-Blackwell, pp. 440-448.

The Impact of the Arts and the Media on the Perception of Urbanity

The Magic Line in Matteo Pericoli's *Unfurled Cities*

Anna Notaro

University of Dundee, Dundee/ UK
A.Z.Notaro@dundee.ac.uk

Abstract

The article discusses *Manhattan Unfurled* (2001) and *London Unfurled* (2011) by architect/ illustrator Matteo Pericoli (www.matteopericoli.com/), two beautiful books in accordion format, containing a collection of pen and ink drawings of the two cities' skylines. Pericoli's line is silent and yet it tells a lot, it becomes a simple but effective device; in order to capture "the image(s)" of the city, to narrate its story; a story that no illustrated book, even the most accomplished one can fully comprise between its covers.

Der Artikel behandelt die beiden Werke *Manhattan Unfurled* (2001) und *London Unfurled* (2011) des Architekten und Illustrators Matteo Pericoli (www.matteopericoli.com/). Die Bücher im Akkordeon-Format enthalten eine Sammlung von Bleistift- und Federzeichnungen der Panoramen *(Skylines)* der jeweiligen Städte. Pericolis Strich ist ruhig, und doch erzählt er eine Menge; er wird zum einfachen, aber wirksamen, Werkzeug, um das „Bild" der Stadt in den „Bildern" der Stadt einzufangen und ihre Geschichte zu erzählen – eine Geschichte, die kein Bildband, selbst das gelungenste nicht, in ihrer Gänze zwischen Einbänden zusammenfassen kann.

Nulla dies sine linea (Apelles)

Q. Why is London like Budapest?
A. Because it is two cities divided by a river. (Angela Carter)

Briefly, a few words on the two epigraphs above: The first which literally means 'no day without drawing a line' refers to Apelles of Kos the greatest painter of antiquity[1], about whom very little is known except his extraordinary skill in drawing the finest and steadiest of lines. The second one is from Angela Carter's last novel *Wise Children* (1991). A passion for drawing outlines, and rivers' roles as dividers (but also uniters), are crucial elements in the appreciation of *London Unfurled* (2011) and *Manhattan Unfurled* (2001) by architect/ artist Matteo Pericoli.

London Unfurled (2011) and *Manhattan Unfurled* (2001) are two beautiful books in accordion format containing a collection of pen and ink drawings of the two cities' skylines.

Fig.1: Pericoli, Sketches (reproduced with permission of the author)

The circumstances surrounding the conception of *Manhattan Unfurled* are worth dwelling upon: in 1995 Pericoli took a job as a liaison architect at Richard Meier & Partners Architects in New York City. During his daily bicycle commute along the Hudson Pericoli developed a keen interest in the riverfront skyline to the point of getting himself a motorcycle in order to observe the buildings from the New Jersey shore. He also took many trips on the Circle Line, the cruise line which offers magnificent views of the Manhattan skyline. Pericoli began drawing in his free time, mostly at night until a 1-foot-wide, 37-foot-long black and white drawing showing the entire West Side of Manhattan as seen from the water was completed. Friends encouraged him to show his drawing to several art book publishers, but no one could imagine how to turn it into a book until, in late 1999, a small mock-up of the drawing caught the attention of Mr Menaker, senior editor at the Random House Publishing Group. Pericoli completed a matching drawing of the East Side skyline, and the publishing house turned the two drawings into the double-sided fold-out book *Manhattan Unfurled* in 2001. In the following extract Pericoli admits that, like most Europeans, his view of New York was:

> informed mostly by movies, commercials, magazines, things like that. When I moved here I was expecting to feel detachment, massive buildings pushing me away. But in reality this place is very different from what anyone can see from far away. I found it to be […] very liveable and humane. And it's antiquated in a way I didn't expect. Going into the subway was like going into the ruins of an ancient city. So, I felt a sense of injustice that much of what I'd been led to believe about New York […] was not true […] That's why I began the first drawing – to understand New York, and to appreciate it (Snoonian 2001).

So behind the *Manhattan Unfurled*'s project there is what one could define, in almost ethical terms, a desire to remedy injustice, to represent a closer-to-the-truth image of the city, in order to better 'understand' and 'appreciate' it. This task could only be accomplished thanks to the power of the gaze, that is by looking long enough at thousands of photographs until every building acquired a character in its own right. "It is as if I were drawing a face", Pericoli states (Goldberger 2001)[2]. And yet there is a subtle irony which cannot go amiss in thinking about the city as a 'face with a character', as a 'living organism', having previously repudiated any fictional representation. I shall return to the fictional quality of urban representation later on.

As the Pulitzer Prize-winning, architecture critic Paul Goldberger (2001) accurately notes in his "Delicacy and Grandeur", the introduction to *Manhattan Unfurled*, there is an egalitarian spirit that permeates Pericoli's representation of New York's skyline, in that every building has its specificity within the whole,

> This is the most obvious urban lesson of all – that a city is all of a piece – [...] Not that the parts of the city all look the same, or that they should, but that in the idea of the city there is a whole that is more than the sum of its parts, and that every building is a part of something larger than itself. There is no prima donna architecture in Pericoli's graceful lines.

This seems to corroborate Pericoli's view of the city as an 'organic' entity made up of characters all equally worthy of representation. In addition the metaphor of the 'prima donna' creates for the reader obvious connotations of performativity and urban theatricality.

Manhattan Unfurled was published just a few weeks after September 11th, and soon became a best seller, but it also became a document of something that had been lost forever (the New York skyline as it was prior to the tragic events) and, maybe more pertinently, of the futile attempt to fix on paper what is perpetually unstable, the city's skyline. For the 10th anniversary of September 11th *The New Yorker* asked Pericoli to revisit lower Manhattan by drawing that same section of the skyline again. In a very interesting video interview, Pericoli talks about his artistic process and how lower Manhattan had evolved over the past dozen years. Noting the continuous evolution of the city and the cranes on top of several buildings he comments on how the drawing represents "a moment of introspection" for a place "that it is trying to figure out what it is and what it will be like"[3]. In another interview with Blake Eskin (2011) released at the same time Pericoli also rehearses the familiar theme of 'making sense' of the city by looking at it until "a simple looking synthesis of the many possibilities of reality" emerges, and muses about the meaning of the term skyline (a 'strange concept'), to be intended as a living organism, one that, almost counter intuitively "is indifferent to what happens to it". For Pericoli there is a noticeable difference between the idea of the American city, continuously under construction and the Italian one which is fixed, being "either finished or […] a ruin"[4]. And yet, once again, one cannot but note the contradictory irony inherent in a drawing project that, while it praises the 'under construction' status of the American metropolis on the one hand, on the other 'fixes' exactly this on paper in the attempt to make order out of the urban chaos.

In the afore-mentioned introduction to *Manhattan Unfurled* Goldberger (2001) notes another key feature in Pericoli's work:

> By making the riverfront the city's face, Pericoli has performed a subtle, not to say subversive, transformation. Streets [...] the defining element in the urbanism of Manhattan have disappeared 'while the rivers [,..] become the streets, the arteries that matter' [...] And the buildings which [...] have almost never seemed to pay much attention to the river, are now forced to present themselves to the water.

When it comes to the role of the water, the two cities, New York and London, differ dramatically, "Unlike the rivers that encompass Manhattan", Pericoli writes in the "Afterword" to *London Unfurled* (2011) "the Thames is a gap: a uniter and a divider. Like two magnets, the riverbanks have been rejecting and attracting each other forever. And the resulting energy flows between them".

For the twin sisters Chance, the protagonists of Angela Carter's novel *Wise Children* (1991), the river is above all a divider. Here is how Dora Chance emphatically puts it:

> My name is Dora Chance. Welcome to the wrong side of the tracks. Put it another way. If you're from the States, think of Manhattan. Then think of Brooklyn. See what I mean? Or, for a Parisian, it might be a question of rive gauche,

> rive droite. With London, it's the North and South divide. Me and Nora, that's my sister, we've always lived on the left-hand side, the side the tourist rarely sees, the bastard side of Old Father Thames (Carter 1991, 1).

For Carter, as Will Self writes in his "From the wrong side: looking north", the introductory essay to *London Unfurled* (2011), "the Thames was the 'sword' that divided her from money and pleasure. The north bank represented culture, government, law, official memory: old London, the original settlement, as it liked to show itself". And the river is exactly the vantage point from which the complexity of London 'unfurls' in *London Unfurled;* that same river that both divides the city and seals it together, using the city's north and south banks as gateways to its dozen boroughs, hundreds of buildings and countless landmarks. One could argue that the accordion format of the book itself, which allows the reader to trace the river's north bank by opening the book in one direction, and the south by opening in the opposite one, is an apt metaphorical representation of the role performed by the river, as described above. What is a book-page after all but a uniter and a divider?

Differently from New York, Pericoli had no knowledge of London at all when he started drawing it. Over the course of two weeks he walked more than 60 miles, taking some 6,100 photos, which he spent the following two years recreating in his obsessive pen-and-ink drawings. There is also a digital edition of London Unfurled, *London Unfurled for iPad* (2011) which is more than just a 'book-as-app'. As Pericoli notes in the promotion video it "complements and completes the book", by offering a different experience: one can scroll the entire drawing seamlessly, flipping from north to south, from place to place, finding famous landmarks, zooming in on its extraordinary detail and discovering over a hundred points of interest with added facts and background information[5]. *London Unfurled for iPad* is not some sort of late digital appendix to the printed version. In fact, James Long (2011), editorial director at Pan Macmillan, confirms that "the intent to do a digital edition was there from the start of the project", and by the end it was recognized that "this new device would bring the intimate and tactile experience that would make a digital edition feel natural". This is not the time to address the complex dynamics of digital textuality and how 'natural' (or not) it might 'feel' – I have discussed similar themes elsewhere (Notaro 2012) – what I would prefer to do instead is to place Pericoli's work within the long established tradition of the art of urban sketching[6], in the hope that by suggesting similarities and contrapositions, the scale of his earnest creation emerges more clearly. According to Goldberger (2001) Pericoli's "real aesthetic kindred spirit" is the Swiss amateur artist Edward Burckhardt who, between 1842 and 1870, drew a twenty-foot-long New York City Panorama. To do so, he stood in the steeple of the North Dutch Church on the northwest corner of Fulton and William streets in lower Manhattan, and pivoted 360 degrees. The obvious difference with Pericoli is that Burckhardt posits himself at the center of the city drawing all around him whereas Pericoli draws from a distance, in a more detached manner.[7] Yet, as Goldberger (2001) argues "both artists leave you with a sense of New York as a rhythmic agglomeration of forms, sitting on the water – little boxes punctuated by steeples for Burckhardt, towers playing off against one another for Pericoli. For both artists, the city is a play of masses against the river and the sky".

The "combination of jauntiness and authority" makes Goldberger think also of the children's book illustrator Mirolaslav Sasek, author of *This is New York* (1960). The obvious difference in this case is that Pericoli, unlike Sasek, uses no colour. "Color would diminish *Manhattan Unfurled*, pushing it towards illustration", whereas "Pericoli's fine lines, for all their exact replication of the city, come together to create a kind of abstraction […] and it has gravitas". It is worth remembering at this point that Pericoli has published several books for children and young people, *See the City: the Journey of Manhattan Unfurled* (2004), *The True Story of Stellina* (2006) and *Tommaso and the Missing Line* (2008), which share with his unfurled cities the same charm and simplicity of the line. In fact, it is hardly surprising that, in talking about *Manhattan Unfurled*, Pericoli declares that it was his intention "to do something that even a child could understand" (Eskin 2011). A similar child-like quality is to be found also in the work of the Australian illustrator James Gulliver Hancock, who has endeavoured to draw all the buildings in New York and post them on a blog (http://allthebuildingsinnewyork.com/new/). Describing his creative process Hancock suggests that "the interesting thing about drawing is that it makes you look at objects in more detail. Instead of just passing by a building, you realize that there's this weird little sign and it says these funny things about what the deli sells"[8]. Similar to Pericoli, it is an obsessive attention to details what lies behind every Hancock drawing. More about the obsessive quality of Pericoli's unfurled cities later; before then I wish to mention the work of Werner Kruse, a German illustrator going by the single name Robinson, who in 1967 published a collection of pen-and-ink drawings called *New York.* In his foreword to the 2009 reprint *New York Line by Line*[9] Pericoli manifests a great affinity with Robinson when he writes:

> And it's astounding to think that someone has accomplished just that. "Drawing it all" means that out of all the possible billions of lines that one could draw, you have to choose only the right ones. And those that Robinson drew tell us of a New York City at a particular time; they show us how the city is organized and *how it works as an organism; they tell us about its character* and its life, about its people and their habits (emphasis mine) (*Entropy* 2009)

One last name worth recalling in this sketchy history of urban illustration is that of Saul Steinberg (1914-1999), whose covers and drawings appeared in *The New Yorker* for almost sixty years. Steinberg's style is different from Pericoli's and yet, when one reads that for Steinberg drawing was a: "way of reasoning on paper" (*Poster Art*) it is tempting to recognize an ideal connection with Pericoli's own reasoning when asked what he liked about line drawing:

> I think that line drawings show you what one thinks rather than what one sees. Sketching and painting mirror other brain activities. A 'simple' line, a hard line, is, more often than not, the result of a very specific decision process. Reality is messy, and line drawings look for a narrative that can be easily understood (*Foyles* 2011).

As for Steinberg, "[he] […] remained committed to the act of drawing in an era dominated by large-scale painting and sculpture" (*Poster Art*). It seems to me that, in spite of their different backgrounds, what Pericoli and Steinberg share is precisely a 'commitment to drawing', an 'inspector' like quality which is averse to any pretension, disinterested in metaphors, ordered and modest.

I mentioned earlier the aspect of compulsive obsession which characterizes Pericoli's work. This is detectable in the tour de force of lines, in his years long drawing projects, in counting, 'out of curiosity', the thousands of lines that make up some of the buildings or their windows (!). In the case of *London Unfurled* (2011) Pericoli brakes down his epic journey in numbers as follows:

> Length of each of the two originals: 11.50 m
> Height of the each of the two originals: 30 cm
> Number of bridges
> Total: 41 (of which, North: 21, South: 20)
> Number of waves
> Total: 3,262 (of which, North: 1,842, South: 1,420, i.e. bigger waves in the South drawing.)
> Number of cranes
> Total: 58 (of which, North: 29, South: 29 – amazing, same number!)
> Number of buildings
> Total: 1,343 (of which, North: 766, South: 577, Houses of Parliament: 823)
> […] (*Abitare* 2011).

The obsessive accuracy of these numbers is reminiscent of what Umberto Eco calls the 'giddiness of lists' in his illustrated essay *The Infinity of Lists* (2009). Such an obsession is typical of many authors, Rabelais, Cervantes, and Perec among others. "We like lists" Eco explains, "because we don't want to die". I do not wish to speculate whether a similar intent lies behind Pericoli's obsession, whether his lines are 'life-lines' of sorts, I would rather locate Pericoli's work in a wider theoretical debate regarding the representation of urban space, a debate which I have discussed elsewhere (Notaro 2009), by considering the formations and functions of the illusory power of representation. The city is inseparable from its representations, but it is neither identical with nor reducible to them – and so it poses complex questions about how representations traffic between physical and mental space and render the city legible, responsive to our desires to read and see it. Also, one should consider that Pericoli is an architect by training and for an architect pen and ink (before the advent of computerized representation) has traditionally been the most natural way in which to express one's own ideas, the architectural drawing being a sort of manifesto on which the validity of the whole project depends. For an architect there is always a mental creation prior to its representation. In similar terms Pericoli describes in the "Afterword" to *London Unfurled* (2011) the imaginary line that he could "actually see" as his work progressed. This is architectural documentation of an artistic kind.

As Goldberger (2001) writes, "he [Pericoli] gives us a New York that has all of the uncontainable force of the real city and he contains it". I am not sure I share Goldberg's view; to my mind the obsessive character of Pericoli's desire to make sense out of the urban chaos is symptomatic instead of due to the impossibility to contain the 'excessive' force of the real city. I would also add that the simplicity of his lines is misleading, in that they hide a deep emotional entanglement with their subject, an invisible weight of "fear and pleasure", as he admits (Snoonian 2001). The verb 'unfurl' which Pericoli has chosen to describe his cities is revelatory of his intentions, the city is unfurled, made known, unfolded like a story, a narrative. It becomes a form of visual storytelling, and we know that telling stories is the way in which humans make sense of the world. Pericoli's line is silent and yet it tells a lot, and this is because the line has a key role in the history of drawing, art and writing. The line is what all these systems of human communication have in common; it is deeply embedded in our cultural heritage. In his *Natural History* (circa 77-79AD) Pliny the Elder famously narrates how painting originated in tracing lines round the human shadow[10]. We might also be familiar with the legendary contest between the two great painters of antiquity, Apelles and Protogenes, as to which could draw the finest and steadiest line, a contest won by Apelles. The line crosses the boundary between writing and painting thus becoming a sort of universal language, just like a river it can be a divider but also a uniter. According to Giorgio de Chirico, who was not only a celebrated neoclassical painter and graphic artist, but also an influential philosopher of the art of drawing, the line had an immense conceptual value, even some mystical qualities. He identified the 'magic of the line' in the works of masters such as Apelles, Protogenes, and Giotto (Pontiggia 2009). And so, in conclusion, one could justifiably argue that there is more than a touch of magic in the gracefully beautiful lines of Pericoli's drawings.

NOTES

[1]http://www.britannica.com/EBchecked/topic/29427/Apelles

[2] A precious insight into Pericoli's creative process is revealed in this video first broadcasted on the CBS channel on October 28, 2001, "Osgood File" on *Manhattan Unfurled* http://www.facebook.com/video/video.php?v=1071205181480

[3]Video: The Skyline Redrawn. Posted by *The New Yorker* September 5, 2011 http://www.newyorker.com/online/blogs/newsdesk/2011/09/video-matteo-pericoli-manhattan-skyline.html#ixzz2IFIYLc1F

[4] Interview with Blake Eskin, 'A Living Skyline' September 12, 2011 podcast

http://www.newyorker.com/online/2011/09/12/110912on_audio_pericoli#ixzz2CmVVDzMv.

[5] The video of *London Unfurled for iPad* with Matteo Pericoli is available at http://www.youtube.com/watch?v=6YblAELwZ9k 10 October 2011.

[6] *The Art of Urban Sketching* (Campanario 2012) is the title of a book which includes a brief history of the genre while showcasing location drawings by international artists who draw the cities where they live and travel. It is worth also remembering that cityscapes have a long history in art which dates back to the first century A. D. with a fresco at the Baths of Trajan in Rome depicting a bird's eye view of an ancient city.

See: http://www.theartwolf.com/articles/cityscape-painting.htm

[7] Pericoli adopts Bruckhardt's technique in his *Manhattan Within* (2003), a full-color 22-foot-long drawing, in an accordion fold-out format, which provides a 360-degree view of the Manhattan skyline as seen from within Central Park.

[8] The video of the talk is available at http://www.brainpickings.org/index.php/2011/02/16/all-the-buildings-in-new-york-illustrated/

[9] To view some of Robinson's astonishing drawings visit http://www.parkablogs.com/content/book-review-new-york-line-line-broadway-battery

[10] See "The Origin of Painting", a blog entry on projection systems

http://projectionsystems.wordpress.com/2009/09/06/the-origin-of-painting/

REFERENCES

Abitare, 2011. http://www.abitare.it/en/illustration-2/london-unfurled-by-matteo-pericoli/ Accessed January 20, 2013.

Britannica Encyclopaedia: "Apelles". http://www.britannica.com/EBchecked/topic/29427/Apelles Accessed January 15, 2013.

Campanario, Gabriel. 2012. *The Art of Urban Sketching.* Minneapolis: Quarry Books.

Carter, Angela. 1991. *The Wise Children*. London: Chatto.

Eco, Umberto. 2009. *The Infinity of Lists.* Milano: Rizzoli.

Entropy, December 7, 2009 "NEW YORK: LINE BY LINE by Robinson". Foreword by Matteo Pericoli. http://www.entropy.in/manhattan-unfurled/ Accessed January 21, 2013.

Eskin, Blake. 2011. "Audio A Living Skyline". September 12, 2011 podcast http://www.newyorker.com/online/2011/09/12/110912on_audio_pericoli#ixzz2CmVVDzMv Accessed January 15, 2013.

Foyles. 2011. "Matteo Pericoli". http://www.foyles.co.uk/matteo-pericoli Accessed January 15, 2013.

Goldberger, Paul. 2001. "Delicacy and Grandeur". In Pericoli Matteo. *Manhattan Unfurled.* New York: Random House.

Hancock, James Gulliver. "All the Buildings in New York". http://allthebuildingsinnewyork.com/new/ Accessed January 19, 2013.

Long, James. October 17, 2011. *London Unfurled for iPad* http://www.theliteraryplatform.com/2011/10/london-unfurled-for-ipad/ Accessed January 18, 2013.

Notaro, Anna. 2009. "Going Digital: How Technology Is Shaping the Future of Urban Literature" in Eleonora Federici and Marilena Parlati (Eds). *Locating Subjects*. Roma: Aracne. Pp. 377-411.

Notaro, Anna. 2012. "The many futures of the book". In Marijan Dović and Jernej Habjan (Eds), *Primerjalna književnost*, letnik 35, št. 1, Ljubljana, Slovenia, pp .3-19.

"Osgood File" on *Manhattan Unfurled.* CBS broadcast October 28, 2001. http://www.facebook.com/video/video.php?v=1071205181480, accessed January 17, 2013.

Pericoli, Matteo. 2001. *Manhattan Unfurled.* New York: Random House.

Pericoli, Matteo. 2003. *Manhattan Within*. New York: Random House.

Pericoli, Matteo. 2004. *See the City: the journey of Manhattan Unfurled.* New York: Knopf for Young Readers.

Pericoli, Matteo. 2006. *The True Story of Stellina.* New York: Knopf for Young Readers.

Pericoli, Matteo. 2008. *Tommaso and the Missing Line.* New York: Knopf for Young Readers.

Pericoli, Matteo. 2011. *Manhattan Unfurled.* London: Macmillan.

Pontiggia, Elena. 2009. La magia della linea. La magia della forma. De Chirico teorico del disegno. http://www.archimagazine.com/mmagialinea.htm Accessed January 11, 2013.

Popova, Maria. "All the Buildings in New York, Illustrated", http://www.brainpickings.org/index.php/2011/02/16/all-the-buildings-in-new-york-illustrated/, accessed January 24, 2013.

Poster Art. Saul Steinberg". http://www.posterart.com/ourposters/newyorker.html, Accessed January 17, 2013).

Robinson, 2009. *New York Line by Line.* New York: Universe.

Sasek, Mirolaslav. 1960. *This is New York.* New York: Universe.

Self, Will. 2011. "From the Wrong Side: Looking North". In Pericoli Matteo *Manhattan Unfurled.* New York: Random House.

Snoonian, Deborah. 2001. "Matteo Pericoli's drawings pay homage to the city he adopted" *Architectural Record.* http://archrecord.construction.com/people/profiles/archives/0412profile.asp Accessed January 12, 2013.

The New Yorker. September 5, 2011 Video: "The Skyline Redrawn". http://www.newyorker.com/online/blogs/newsdesk/2011/09/video-matteo-pericoli-manhattan-skyline.html#ixzz2IFIYLc1F, accessed January 15, 2013.

THE SATIRICAL LINE. THE IMAGE OF THE CITY IN THE *NEW YORKER'S* CARTOON 1968 – 1978

Daniele Campobenedetto

Université Paris Est – ENSA Paris Belville, Paris/ France and Polytechnic University of Turin, Turin/ Italy

daniele.campobenedetto@gmail.com

ABSTRACT

This article aims to explore how between 1968 and 1978 the *New Yorker's* cartoon was able to influence and at the same time to capture that view of the city of New York which, in the same years investigated by this study, had an important role in the process towards identity setting in the northern American cities.

Dieser Artikel setzt sich zum Ziel, zu untersuchen, wie die Karikaturenreihe des Magazins *The New Yorker* in den Jahren 1968 bis 1978 jene Ansichten der Stadt New York sowohl einfing als auch beeinflusste, die in den in der vorliegenden Studie betrachteten Jahren eine wichtige Rolle im Prozess der Identitätsschaffung der nordamerikanischen Städte spielten.

Since its first issue in 1925, the *New Yorker* magazine is the mirror of the Big Apple's engaging culture: attentive to the political life of the city and at the same time a mirror of the deep processes that were changing the town's characters between the Nineteen-sixties and -seventies. Its pages are more than a cultural guide to the metropolitan most interesting happenings and events. They hosted essays, reports and short stories by Philip Roth, J. D. Salinger and Irwin Shaw, which have often been pervaded by a sharp satire which contributed to the magazine's fame. What is more, the cartoons[1] scattered among the articles and the famous cover drawings, constituted little by little the characterization of a magazine able to extend its influence beyond the city borders which itself is reflected through its name.

Between 1968 and 1978, the city of New York underwent a large transformation made possible by the redefinition of its own image through the effects of housing policies, the increasing population pressure, the city's financial crisis and the struggle for the conservation of many emblematic historical buildings[2]. The coeval press addressed these themes with a high frequency, for example through the articles by Ada Luise Huxstable and by Paul Goldberg on the *New York Times*. In this context the perspective of the *New Yorker*, under the leadership of its second director William Shaw[3], appears original and polyphonic. The magazine's setting, given by the founder Harold Ross and confirmed by Shaw, deals with a wide range of issues which in the cultural and political field is democratic party oriented and which is able to intercept the debates related to the perception of the city, addressing an intellectual public of which it soon became a sort of *Pravda.*

As for the writing dimension, the cartoon panorama shows a plurality of authors and visions, in which we can identify some particularly prolific authors on the urban themes. This is the case with Alan Dunn, already cartoonist for *Architectural Records*, who was an exceptional reporter until his death in 1974, and Saul Stainberg who was able to introduce architecture and space within his social satire drawings.

The perspective in which the architectural themes and the image of the city are treated on the *New Yorker's* pages is the cultural one. The cartoons establish a peculiar image of the city of New York with exhibitions, happenings and episodes of cultural life of that particular slice of the society defined by Tom Wolf as *Radical Chic*[4]. This point of view is also underlined in the cartoons through architectural critics often related to episodes and debates dealing with historical buildings preservation, with the requalification of urban areas and with the protection of the suburbs from the city sprawl.

The cartoons follow these themes and are also able to create new and independent ones, in which the image of the city and its architecture play a fundamental part on the scene as a social identifier related to the characters who populate these drawings. Moreover the importance of the graphic dimension of the *New Yorker* suggests an analysis of the line adopted by the magazine on the city related themes especially through these cartoons which appear with a regular frequency during the decade.

The first theme faced by the *New Yorker* is related to the happenings of the New York cultural life. Between the end of the Nineteen-Sixties and –Seventies a number of articles and cartoons regularly appeared dealing with exhibitions, restoration and preservation of historical buildings in New York and elsewhere[5].

A representative case of the image of the city, shown through satirical cartoons, is related to the activities of the New York Landmark Preservation Commission. This authority was created in 1965 to preserve, through specific conservation and oriented legislation, buildings or entire urban areas from destruction. It first came to prominence in an episode which claimed the attention of public opinion and was largely commented on by the *New Yorker*: the demolition of the old Pennsylvania Station which had to make way for the Madison Square Garden[6].

Starting from 1968 the-dandy-with-monocles magazine paid attention to the Commission's activities. A few weeks after the approval of the New York City Zoning Resolution, which allowed the destruction of buildings already classed as *Landmark*, a cartoon by Donald Reilly appeared denouncing the consequences of such a policy[7].

Furthermore, the same year another episode underlined the growing importance which the *Landmark Commission* was taking: Even before the demolition of the Penn Central Station the Grand Central Terminal was menaced by the high pressure generated from the increasing land value. Starting from 1954 some projects aiming to demolish the train station to give place to business buildings were foreshadowed because of the easy connection with the suburbs provided by the railway.

Several proposals were presented by Pei, Minoru Yamasaki (who pronounced for the demolition) and Marcel Breuer (who promoted the integration of the new project with the historical building). In 1967 the façade of the Grand Central Terminal was classed as a Landmark, and in 1968 the English real estate promoter Morris Saady commissioned Breuer to create a new building on the old station: the project was analysed cautiously by the same Breuer, was reviewed by Huxstable, who defined it as «grotesque»[8]; and Alan Dunn increased the satirical mockery on the *New Yorker* by publishing a cartoon in which Breuer's project is inversed[9]. In a short time the Landmark Commission protection was extended to the entire building and any real estate development was implemented, ratifying one of the most important successes of the Commission, whose influence was underlined again by Dunn some months later[10].

Despite these successes in the late Seventies there were many demolished historical buildings, among them the Metropolitan Opera House, reallocated at the Lincoln Centre, or the Villard Houses. In the light of these demolitions several demonstration groups were created which were active throughout the Seventies[11], till the battle for the conservation of the Radio City Music Hall, classed as a landmark in 1978. It became the subject of the satirical work of

Dana Fradon, describing not only the episode but also the *New Yorker*'s readers' radical chic attitude towards it[12].

Between 1971 and 1973 another series of cartoons underlined the attention given by the New York residents to the conservation of historical buildings: the drawings condemned in a generic way the demolition politics[13] and pointed out landmarks to be the litmus test of the downtown degradation condition, due to oblivion and pollution[14].

The importance of the Landmark Commission in these years was again underlined in 1976 by Everet Opic, who used the already established fame of the authority to describe the working psychosis of the urban middle class, confirming the debate on preservation as part of the common life of the citizens[15].

In these cases the satirical line of the *New Yorker* is a thermometer of the perception of the urban problems by a specific urban society and at the same time a powerful means to influence the same perception of the city among the inhabitants. The image of the city, given through the *New Yorker's* cartoons, show us the importance of urban spaces and the preservation of New York identity as the result of the preservation of specific architecture rather than urban systems. Only a few lines are dedicated to the macro system social problems.

Furthermore, we can also find this conservation perspective we met dealing with historical buildings concerning the new urban development areas in downtown Manhattan during the Seventies. On the *New Yorker's* pages we can find some generic reports about the effects of modern architecture[16], shaping the city in a more and more standardized way, as well as the speculation policies in the city suburbs[17]. However, in this context there is not a lack of critics of specific architecture and town areas: the case of the Twin Towers is an outstanding example.

The World Trade Center was strongly debated at the beginning of the Seventies since the appearance of the propositions by SOM, Adler and, finally, by Mironu Yamasaki for lower Manhattan. The aim of the New York Port Authority (which was the developer) was to re-create the same process of urban regeneration that was produced by the Rockefeller civic center in midtown, producing a wide reaction in public opinion and architectural criticism.

At the beginning even A. L. Huxtable remained fascinated by the Yamasaki project but since the construction started in 1966 she expressed misgiving until she wrote in 1973: "These are big buildings but they are not great architecture"[18].

Between 1971 and 1972, i. e. during the final phase of the construction, on the *New Yorker* some cartoons appeared dealing with this topic. Donald Reilly reported about the critiques expressed by A. L. Huxtable with a drawing in which the reference to the *New York Times* journalist is explicit[19]. A week later the first cartoon referencing the Twin Towers appeared in which the author made fun of the rhetoric built around the highness of the buildings (the highest in the world)[20] when Chicago was constructing the Sears Tower which in 1973 left this record to the Yamasaki skyscrapers.

The highness is the catalyser of the *New Yorker's* irony from Alan Dunn, who suggested there must be a mad site manager because of the uncontrolled increase to many more than the previewed 110 floors of the towers[21]. And in 1972 a laconic commentary on the impact of the towers on the city skyline was committed to a middle class couple imagining the effect of shrubbery on the new towers[22].

The *New Yorker's* cartoons relating to the architectural critics illustrate once again a city in a deep process of transformation, in which the preservation of a previous condition (in this case referring to the skyline) is widespread. The creation of a rhetoric of preservation addressed to the left-winged, engaged society is once again promoted by the *New Yorker* which confirmed its importance in shaping the perception of the city changes among the inhabitants.

Furthermore, the territorial scale does not escape the *New Yorker's* irony which extends its subjects well beyond architectural criticism: the satirical cartoons involve Urban sprawl, infrastructures and, more in general, the territorial-related image of the city. While during the Sixties the population of Manhattan decreased by ten per cent, in the same years the metropolitan area population increased, due to the gradual urbanization and the drop of residential function downtown: consequently the sprawl phenomena become a key theme on the *New Yorker*, most of all between 1969 and 1971.

It is Edward Koren who, during these years, committed a series of cartoons to the *pavillionnaire*[23], to the land consuming[24] and the new logics of land value[25]. At the same time, during the early Seventies, some graphic reflections regarding the mobility infrastructures appear, anticipating what will happen within the articles published in the magazine: It was one year earlier that the explosion of the debate on the renewal of the West Side Elevated Highway, demolished in 1973, appeared as a cartoon and a cover drawing denouncing the great power of the construction lobbies, again by Edward Koren[26]. The high speed in reacting to urban debates proved by means of graphic depiction is amazing in this case: the first article on the topic appeared on the *New Yorker's* pages in 1974[27], and the first alternative design proposals in 1978[28]. Eventually Barney Tobey gave once more space to the mobility infrastructures theme in the urban context drawing a helpless driver, victim of the requalification urban policies[29]: while highways and suburbs development are portrayed as devil, the effects of the urban requalification after the oil shock fall perfectly in line with the magazine's awareness. In the end, even concerning the infrastructural theme, the struggle of preservation against the savage development is confirmed as the *New Yorker's* main line in the representation of the city.

Until now we saw how the *New Yorker's* cartoons acknowledge the events related to architecture and to the urban space portraying New York in a strong preservation oriented way. Nevertheless, during the same decade, the famous drawings confer another important role on the drawn city: the social classifier. In this context, since 1968[30], the architectural element able to show this process in the clearest way is the house, without which it would be difficult to get the sense of the "wisecrack".

A clear example of this role is a series of cartoons by Charles Saxon: in the background architecture appears, which tells us the kind of happening the characters were attending, giving sense to the mockery. Without the house in the background it would be impossible to understand the dialogue, and what is more to socially set the event which is the frame of the cartoon: a white and modern villa on *pilotis* lets us imagine a hip party[31], while the Victorian house is the symbol of the *bourgeoise* boredom leading a wife to be astonished about the *Rolling Stone* quotation by her husband[32]. More than a key for the interpretation of a single series of cartoons, the residential architecture was the central element during the following years in other contributions, especially by Alan Dunn[33].

Also, the interiors play the same role as the exterior of the house: Between 1973 and 1976 Robert Weber published some cartoons in which, for example, a sort of Farnsworth house became the metaphor of an exhausted high society marriage[34]; or an interior full of carpets and pillows is the ironic set for the improbable match of Gregorian chants and cheese, proposed by a hip couple[35].

The great importance of the house within the *New Yorker's* cartoons is definitively affirmed through its role as the main and unique character of the drawing. The New York suburb houses became the only element giving the interpretation key to themes such as demolitions[36], or American middle class lifestyle[37]. Furthermore, this last theme is deepened by a sort of balcony epic, a long cartoon series by different authors, in which through the multi-storey building balcony the neighbourhood dynamics and the lifestyle in a more and more dense city are described[38].

Eventually, the social classification role assumed by the houses is shared at a minor rate by another type of architectures and urban environments. This is the case with the working spaces (here the window's proximity describe the workers level in the company hierarchy[39]) or of the university buildings (here the problem is the lack of ivy on the wall, metaphor of the top league of American universities[40]).

Going through the *New Yorker's* issues between 1968 and 1978, it becomes clear how the image of the city plays a more important role than one would have expected from this kind of magazine. The cartoons are an attentive pair of eyes staring at the architectural and urban changes of New York city, and often they anticipate the content of the articles by a deep criticism of and a careful consideration on working spaces, houses, streets, and urban landscape, which have a leading role and are not only backgrounds on the ironic scene.

This overview of the *New Yorker's* cartoons, on the one hand, shows the setting of a cultural paradigm through both the struggle for preservation of historical buildings and urban landscape and through the architectural critics outlooks, while on the other hand, the setting of a social classification system which is based above all on the house and dwellings representation becomes evident. The image of the city results in it clearly being oriented from the perspective of the *radical chic* society: The *New Yorker's* cartoons show a polished criticism of the same society to which they are addressed; sophisticated enough to laugh at itself but still imprisoned in a certain self-referential attitude.

NOTES

[1] All cartoons cited are available in R. Mankoff, J-L. Chiflet, *The complete cartoons of the New Yorker*, Black Dog & Leventhal publishers, New York, 2004.

[2] R. Stern, T. Mellins, D.Fishman, *New York 1960: Architecture and Urbanism Between the Second World War and the Bicentennial*, The Monacelli Press, New York, 1995, p. 13.

[3] W. Shaw (1951-1987) succeeded to Harold Ross, who founded the magazine.

[4] T. Wolfe, *Radical Chic & Mau-Mauing the Flak Catchers*, Farrar, Straus and Giroux, New York, 1970.

[5] Some examples are: B. Tobey, in *The New Yorker,* 14 June, 1976, p. 25; J. Stevenson, *The New Yorker,* 16 August 1976, p. 23 [from now on the title of the magazine in notes is shortened in *NY*]

[6] A. Dunn, in *NY*, November 9, 1963, p. 45.

[7] D. Reilly, in *NY*, April 13, 1968, p. 45.

[8] R. Stern, T. Mellins, D. Fishman, *New York 1960: Architecture and Urbanism Between the Second World War and the Bicentennial*, The Monacelli Press, New York, 1995, pp. 1139-1142.

[9] A. Dunn, in *NY*, June 7, 1968, p. 21.

[10] A. Dunn, in *NY*, August 24, 1968, p. 35.

[11] A. Dunn, in *NY*, January 22, 1972, p. 24.

[12] D. Fradon, in *NY*, January 30, 1978.

[13] R. Oldden, in *NY*, December 18, 1971, p. 39

[14] C. Saxon, in *NY*, May 19, 1973, p. 33 and 2 June 2, 1973, p.35.

[15] E. Opic, in *NY*, April 26, 1976, p. 37.

[16] M. Richter, in *NY*, October 19, 1968.

[17] L. Starke, in *NY*, September 30, 1974, p. 37.

[18] A.L. Huxstable in R. Stern, T. Mellins, D. Fishman, *New York 1960: Architecture and Urbanism Between the Second World War and the Bicentennial*, The Monacelli Press, New York, 1995, p. 202.

[19] D. Reilly, in *NY*, April 24, 1971, p.37.

[20] M. Richter, in *NY*, April 17, 1971, p.39.

[21] A. Dunn, in *NY*, July 3, 1971, p. 32.

[22] F. Modell, in *NY*, July 29, 1972, p. 32.

[23] E. Koren, in *NY*, August 16, 1969, p. 27.

[24] E. Koren, in *NY*, October 24, 1970, p. 47.

[25] E. Koren, in *NY*, July 10, 1971, p. 29.

[26] E. Koren, in *NY*, August 12, 1972. On the same theme James Stevenson, in NY July 15, 1972, p. 26.

[27] M. Singer, *Highway*, in *NY*, September 16, 1974.

[28] J. Stevenson, *Whither Highway*, in *NY*, June 5, 1978.

[29] B. Tobey, in *NY*, December 29, 1975, p. 25.

[30] D. Really, in *NY*, May 11, 1968, p. 83.

[31] C. Saxon, in *NY*, August 27, 1973, p. 36.

[32] C. Saxon, in *NY*, November 19, 1973, p. 61.

[33] A. Dunn, in *NY*, July 15, 1974, p. 35.

[34] R.t Weber, in *NY*, September 27, 1976, p. 27.

[35] R. Weber, in *NY*, November 10, 1975, p. 53.

[36] L. Lorenz, in *NY*, June 13, 1977, p. 39.

[37] L. Lorenz, in *NY*, June 10, 1974, p. 36. Also Henry Martin, in *NY*, March 17, 1975, p. 42.

[38] Some examples are: E. Fisher, in *NY*, September 2, 1974, p. 27; E. Arno, in *NY*, June 14, 1976, p. 40; R. Weber, in *NY*, February 7, 1977, p. 33.

[39] E. Arno, in *NY*, April 18, 1977, p. 33.

[40] B. Tobey, in *NY*, September 10, 1978.

BIBLIOGRAPHY

Jacobs, Jane: *The Death and Life of Great American Cities*, Random House, New York, 1961.

Mumford, Lewis: *The Myth of the Machine*, Harcourt Brace Jovanovich, 1967-1970.

Papacchristou, Tician: *Marcel Breuer: New Buildings and Projects*, Praeger, Westport Connecticut, 1970.

Robert Mankoff, Jean-Loup Chiflet: *The complete cartoons of the New Yorker, Black Dog & Leventhal publishers*, New York, 2004.

Rosso, Michela: *New York città caleidoscopio*, in *Domus*, no. 903, March 2007, pp. 134-135.

Stern, Robert; Mellins, Thomas; Fishman, David: *New York 1960: Architecture and Urbanism Between the Second World War and the Bicentennial*, The Monacelli Perss, New York, 1995.

The New Yorker 1955 – 1965 Album, Fortieth Anniversary, Harper & Row Publishers, New York, 1965.

The New Yorker Album of Drawings, 1922-1975, Penguin Books, New York, 1987.

Wojtowicz, Robert (Ed): *Sidewalk Critic. Lewis Mumford's Writings on New York*, Princeton architectural press, New York, 1998.

Wolfe, Tom: *Radical Chic & Mau-Mauing the Flak Catchers*, Farrar, Straus and Giroux, New York, 1970.

NEW METROPOLITANS AND THEIR POPULAR PRESS IN *FIN DE SIÈCLE* PRAGUE

Jakub Machek

Charles University in Prague and Metropolitan University Prague, Prague/ Czech Republic

jakub.m@post.cz

ABSTRACT

The author of this article presents the relation between sensational pictorial press, its readers and their collective memory creating the shared image of the emerging metropolis. He demonstrates the role of popular culture in forming a collective memory using the example of the *Pražský Illustrovaný Kurýr* [*Prague Illustrated Courier*] in the period of the rapid urbanisation of Czech lands at the turn of the 20th century. In the emerging urban environment the traditional oral method of transmitting information was no longer sufficient and popular newspapers assisted urban newcomers in developing a shared sense of urban self-identification.

Der Autor dieses Artikels präsentiert die Beziehung zwischen der illustrierten Sensationspresse, ihren Lesern und deren kollektivem Gedächtnis, die gemeinsam die Bilder der aufstrebenden Metropole erschaffen. Er zeigt am Beispiel des *Prager Illustrierten Kuriers* [*Pražský Illustrovaný Kurýr*], welche Rolle die Populär-Kultur in der Bildung eines kollektiven Gedächtnisses während der raschen Urbanisierung der tschechischen Länder an der Wende zum 20. Jahrhundert spielte. In einem sich entwickelnden urbanen Umfeld erwiesen sich die traditionell mündlichen Methoden der Informationsvermittlung als unzureichend, und die Massenpresse unterstützte die urbanen Neuankömmlinge in der Schaffung einer gemeinsamen städtischen Identität.

Introduction

The processes of modernisation, of the rapid economic and technical changes, have led to an increased differentiation of society. The awareness of this differentiation was distinctly present in Central Europe, where the old cultural memory passed from generation to generation by means of repetition and drilling, and was gradually replaced by regional and interregional identities (Csáky 8, 9). Popular mass-press created a new urban space for communication used by readers from a non-elite stratum. According to Pierre Nora, the disappearance of peasant culture, the quintessential repository of collective memory, caused a fundamental collapse of the real environments of the memory. A sense of historical continuity persists in certain sites – the *lieux de mémoire* (the sites of memory) – instead of the no longer existing *milieux de mémoire* (the real environments of memory) (Nora 7). These sites of memory where memory crystallizes were formed by a new urban-democratized and mediatized mass society.

Fin de Siècle Urbanisation and Pictorial Press

At the turn of the 20th century the main feature of central European urban popular culture was the sensational pictorial press. Its emergence was related to the formation of the urban areas, especially the metropolitan ones. During the period of the most rapid urbanisation (related to the process of industrialisation) an enormous stream of newcomers from rural areas came to the cities to find better places to live in – with a sufficient amount of job opportunities, higher wages, and more entertainment opportunities. During the period from 1870 to 1910 metropolises like Vienna or Berlin grew by nearly 150 per cent, and in the same period the population of Prague more than doubled while Budapest almost quadrupled its population. Throughout the region, cities numbering more than 100,000 inhabitants nearly doubled from 1870 to 1910 (Wood 13; Boháč 14).

In this article, I will concentrate on the experience of the Prague metropolitan area dwellers (mostly newcomers) mediated by *Pražský Illustrovaný Kurýr (Prague Illustrated Courier)*, the first successful illustrated sensational daily, published between 1893 and 1918 by *Staročeská strana* (Czech National Conservative Party).

According to Ian Chambers, popular culture played a central role in the formation of urban culture. The development of popular culture was accompanied by a complex visual and acoustic response of the urban environment from which it is impossible to separate (Chambers 17, 18). For the migrants the move from the countryside to the suburbs of Prague meant the need to replace the traditionally oral method of spreading information; to find entertainment, and to search for a new culture and identity different from their rural origins. Sensational illustrated newspapers became not only a guide to life in the new environment but they also assisted readers in developing a shared sense of urban self-identification. During the period even the members of the urban lower social classes broadened their economic and cultural potency, and thus their capacity to absorb the development of a new common culture generated by the rapid industrialisation and urbanisation.

The publisher of the *Prague Illustrated Courier* adapted global patterns of successful mass daily press to address the Czech audience, its specific local beliefs, values and desires. In the case of the *Courier*, the need to accommodate readers' habits resulted in the newspaper's stream of information and entertainment remaining half way between the rural and the metropolitan, between the traditional and the modern. The collective of its readers (and those who just overlooked headers and title illustrations at newsstands) used it as one of the important sources of information about their surroundings, about the life in the metropolis. It became some kind of a guide to Prague and its urban environment. The common experience of its reception – reading, overlooking of its pages, and discussing its contents and lurid illustrations – created in the process of negotiating of meanings kind of a collective notion about life in Prague related to their collective memory.

Prague Dwellers and the *Illustrated Courier*

The *Prague Illustrated Courier* helped readers to create a shared idea about life in Prague and to form its collective memory. On the one hand, the image consists of detailed reports of local and sensational events from small injuries, street accidents, misfortunes, and petit crimes to reports about associations and cultural life (popular theatres, music halls) including lists of funerals, bankruptcies and voluntary contributions. On the other hand, news about 'serious' events from Prague and the rest of world that – not graphically separated – created a kind of counterpoint to the urban everyday routine entering into the collective imagination from the same pages. Nevertheless, political news was often depicted as spectacle too, the same way as bloody crimes, disasters and riots. As a consequence of the regularity of their occurrence on the newspaper they fitted into the mosaic of the urban daily routine.

According to Jiří Štaif, Prague residents are found at the heart of the conflict between traditional mentality related to the rural and small town life (the origin about half of Prague inhabitants) and the trends of modernisation brought by recent developments at the turn of the twentieth century (Štaif 18, 19). The example of popular press, closely related to the urban environment, can help us to observe this dialogue of tradition and modernisation. Compared to the sensational press of other Central European cities, the *Courier* and other Prague press did not offer their readers intense images of metropolitan life from all over the world. To the contrary, editors of the *Courier* specialised in local events. Its everyday summary of even smallest accidents including full name, occupation and address of people involved can be seen as a remnant of oral spreading of news and gossips. This was a feature of the provincial press that reported about persons known to most of readers situated in small areas – a significant contrast to the anonymous life in real metropolises.

The Autumn of 1908 on the *Courier's* Pages

The following case study is meant to show the nexus of the *Courier*, its readers and their perception of Prague. The autumn of 1908 was chosen as a nice example of the blend of 'great history' with everyday urban bustle on the pages of the *Courier*.

First I will introduce the political development in the Czech lands (more strictly Bohemia as a main part of the so called Czech lands) which were a part of the Austrian Monarchy during this period. At the end of September the Bohemian Diet (regional parliament) session culminated in the obstruction of German deputies, who protested against the appointment of only Czech parliamentary clerks by singing *Wacht am Rhein* [*Watch on the Rhine*], the unofficial anthem of the Pan-German movement. This led to skirmishes between Czech and German deputies. A similar situation occurred after the Austrian annexation of Bosnia-Herzegovina, when anti-annexation protests led not only to the prorogation of the session, but also to the demission of the Cisleithanian government (government of the Austrian part of the Habsburg Monarchy) and the nomination of a new caretaker government. The turbulent political atmosphere developed into fierce and violent national disturbances all over Austria and especially in the nationally divided Czech lands including the expulsion of minorities from towns, attacks against minority associations' buildings and schools, and affrays between students of different nationalities and with the police. The turbulent situation in Prague resulted in the imposition of Martial law on December 2, on the day of the Emperor's jubilee of 60 years on the throne – ergo, it mostly spoiled long planned celebrations (the annexation used to be described as a jubilee gift).

The research into memory follows works by Maurice Halbwachs, which are based on the idea that recalling is a group phenomenon. Membership in the group offers the source for memory and invites certain events to be recalled and others to be forgotten. The group cannot only help individuals to reconstitute memories, but even to evoke memories never experienced by individuals. The memory is a product of publicly accessible symbols and narratives as well as the possession of individuals. But the individual memory is shaped socially as the memory is a matter of how minds cooperate in society. Individuals cannot continually and coherently remember outside of their group context. (Olick 334, 335)

In the case of the *Illustrated Courier* the mediated memory had a strong national character. Its publishers addressed Czech readers, who perceived Prague as a primarily Czech town, so they interpreted local as well as international events from the Czech national point of view. Especially during the period of national clashes, both in parliament and on the streets, the division of good and bad, of heroes and villains was strictly national. De Certeau uses the term *region* as a space formed by certain interaction. There can be as many regions in a particular place as interactions or conflicting programs can be found there. Texts of competing groups constantly form borders, and their members not only separate space, but also styles and movements (Certeau 91). As a consequence, Czech and German national memories clashed (not only in a symbolic way) inside Prague city space. The *Courier* was instrumental by its emphasis on detailed descriptions of national hassles, national inequities and national alignments of businesses and spots. German counterparts were regularly characterised by a set of demeaning adjectives and verbs, used to describe their physical appearance, behaviour and negative attributes. The epitome of German nationalism was the figure of the deputy and protagonist of the Pan-German movement, Karl Hermann Wolf. He was not missed from any parliament disorder just like the positively perceived Czech nationalists Václav Březnovský and Jan Vašatý (ironically all of them were not only radical nationalists but radical anti-Semites too).

"Deputy Wolf [...] finally roared in his razor nasty and repulsive voice. The others guffawed in the face of the Prince of Lobkowicz with a cheeky ridicule. German deputies stood in a huddle knot, barracked, and behaved forsooth as scamps" (Pražský Illustrovaný Kurýr, 15/ 01/ 1898, p. 2).

During the autumn of 1908, the pages of the *Courier* were filled with tense happenings. Reports of personal and associational life shrank in number with rising tensions, and they were replaced by sensational news about national riots, rumbustious parliamentary sessions and about the threat of a possible war conflict. The new popular motif of illustrations was aggression against Czech minorities in predominantly German borderlands. But pictorial reports from riots and national clashes were regularly supplemented with murders, suicides, court cases and natural disasters from all over the world to keep the reader's attention. Even some odd photographs kept their place as "'*Consul Peter' Ape-Human in Varieté Theatre"* (Pražský Illustrovaný Kurýr, 18/ 09/ 1908, p. 2) or "*Curious Hare with 8 legs*" (Pražský Illustrovaný Kurýr, 03/ 11/ 1908, p. 2).

Reports of the national aggression were constructed the same way as the crime reports. Expressive phrases, direct speeches, and verbal expressions of empathy with victims were used. The reports in the following issues of the *Courier* were successively supplemented by additional pictures and articles to maintain the excitement.

"We just received pictures from Carlsbad showing a part of the biggest damages – the work of a furious rabble, which perfectly characterises the quality of German nationalist propagators of Prussian culture. It does not need more words" (Pražský Illustrovaný Kurýr, 15/ 10/ 1908, p. 17).

During November, the number of title illustrations (the main attraction of the issue) depicting crimes and disasters were equipollent to those depicting national violence, demonstrations, and to political cartoons. Because of the popularity of the *Courier* we can assume that this spectrum of news topics created the ideal spectacle, the inseparable blend of infotainment that the readers demanded and were looking for. The editors' idea of the importance of different kinds of news for readers can be demonstrated on the issue of November 12, when news and illustrations about the suicide of the chief editor of the German Prague daily *Bohemia* were given preference to be on the title page to the picture of the nomination of the new Prime Minister Bienerath.

Both types of events – political news and human misfortunes – were reported in the same manner as the same kind of deviation from everyday reality with the same emotional charge. We can assume they were perceived by the resembling way too. The pictorial presentation of the most popular urban events formed the readers' notion of the space of the metropolis. Thus it had the chance to be strengthened both in collective as in individual memory of Prague dwellers. The stories reported on in the *Courier* and in the sensational sections of other dailies can be found both in written memories and in fiction written by contemporary authors years and decades later. The best repository of these remembered stories is the famous Jaroslav Hašek comedy novel *Osudy dobrého vojáka Švejka za světové války* [*The Good Soldier Švejk*] published in the 1920s, where characters prefer to spend leisure time by narrating these stories the same way, with the name and addresses of their unfortunate heroes, as they were reported in the period's newspapers, and probably as they were told on Prague streets, in pubs and other public places for years.

At the time of the annexation of Bosnia-Herzegovina and the impending Balkans conflict genre pictures from the countries involved were published regularly. In this way regions considered as far as exotic in the Prague readers' notion of the world and in their mental space became closer and more actual under the influence of imminent war. Another nice example of the period's infotainment is the news about the imprisonment of a Slovak national activist in Szeged supplemented with several views of the city and a description of town's landmarks and places of interest.

The important events of the political life of the Habsburg monarchy were according to the *Courier* as humorous, breath-taking or moving as the usual local sensational events of the politically quieter periods. During the autumn of 1908 both on pages of the *Courier* as probably on the minds of its readers the dark world of politics intermingled with the dark world of criminals, the touching misfortunes with the touching violence against Czech minorities, the fear of impending natural disasters with the fear of possible war conflict, and the weirdness of a strange hare with eight legs with the weirdness of throwing sugar lumps.

"Deputy Iro: Let's call Prášek. – Deputy Wolf: Let Prášek give the oration speech! – Deputy Kubr: Shut up! Do not yell all the time! – (Loud voices: Go to hell, hell, hell!) – Deputy Wolf: I have suggested deputy Prášek would be invited to give the oration speech. (Yelling and barracking: Sugar, sugar, sugar!)" (Pražský Illustrovaný Kurýr, 2/ 10/ 1908).

The issue of December 2 is very telling, too. On the day of the Emperor's jubilee, six photographs depicting various moments of the monarch's life are supplemented by photographs of a bus accident in Bohdaneč and drawings of a Burschenschaft fraternities' riot in Prague. The following issues mostly focus on riots which completely erased the celebration of jubilee set for a month from the interest of readers. This manifests the prevalent interest of the *Courier* readers in the Prague area. It also shows which kinds of events were significant for them (Prague riots) and which kind of events could be omitted (Emperor's jubilee celebration).

Sites of Memory

Prague places, highlighted by the touch of the great history, remained in the public awareness. Readers, informed by the *Courier* about a notable event, decided to come and take a look close up and newspapers subsequently published pictures of people gathering on the place of the event. Even readers from the province made trips to Prague and enjoyed guided tours around places known from newspapers. The bond between the place and a past event deepened this. Thanks to the personal visit, the mediated memory related to the place intermingled with the own experience into an indistinguishable conglomerate. According to Wulf Kansteiner, collective memory is always medialised, even in the case of some members of the group being eyewitnesses, because the memory is structured, represented, used and passed on in a social environment (Kansteiner 190). The connection between the event and the site of readers' memory could be utilised commercially too: The report about the damage caused by yesterday's clashes on *Příkopy* street was supplemented by an illustration of the clothes shop situated there with an announcement to the public about a patriotic business that as „first Czech stronghold [...] has to face alien competition" (*Pražský Illustrovaný Kurýr*, 7/ 11/ 1908, p. 3), as *Příkopy* street was known to all readers as a German high street. So readers who wanted to observe the place of yesterday's clashes could add patriotic shopping to their pleasure of participating in the event.

The editors' selection of notable and memorable information formed the image of the contemporary world for the readers. It was supplemented by the comparison with the biggest world metropolises to create a notion of how metropolises should be like. But editors also participated in the escalation of the further events by their images of metropolitan happenings. For example, the pictorial information about a parliament skirmish caused an anti-German gathering of Prague dwellers, which caused a police intervention. The information (with a picture on the title page) led to another gathering of rubbernecks (with possible new police intervention in the case of martial law) as well as a parliamentary debate about the incident. The report about this debate in troubled times easily elicited another gathering of Prague dwellers.

The *Courier*, as a popular source of information for ordinary Prague dwellers, marked a Czech map of the city – a map of places undistinguishably linked to both the national and the sensational memories (as we can see in Hašek's novel). As this source of collective images of Prague was used not only by readers from Prague but from the provincial areas as well, the *Courier* focused on local events offered as components of collective memory related to particular places to a group of readers defined temporally, spatially and partly socially, i. e. broadly the non-elite Czech inhabitants of Prague.

The images of non-Prague localities could access to urban memory as well. Noticeable events in Bosnia-Herzegovina or in Viennese parliament as well as in the Czech borderlands elicited a strong reaction by Prague dwellers (both Czech and German). Mainly people from lower strata took to the streets and gathered on sites variously related to Prague Czech or German national memory. Symbolical or real fights of national domination took place on these sites. The memory mediated by the *Prague Illustrated Courier* related varied sites of the Prague urban area to diverse meanings and events, and thus influenced the image of the city on its readers' minds. The selection of the events depicted was done by the editors, but they tried to meet the expectations and needs of readers.

BILIOGRAPHY

Boháč, Antonín. *Hlavní město Praha: Studie o obyvatelstvu.* Praha: Státní úřad statistický, 1923.

Certeau, Michel de. "Vynalézání každodennosti." *Cahiers du CeFReS* 10 (1996): 77-96.

Csáky, Moritz. "Úvod." *Kolektívne identity v strednej Európe v období moderny.* Ed. Moritz Csáky, and Elena Mannová. Bratislava: Academic Electronic Press, 1999. 7-20.

Kansteiner, Wulf. "Finding Meaning in Memory: A Methodological Critique of Collective Memory Studies", *History and Theory* 41.2 (2002): 179-197. *JSTOR*. Web. 23 Dec 2008.

Nora, Pierre. "Between Memory and History: Les Lieux de Mémoire [1984]". *Representations* 26, Spring (1989): 7-25. *JSTOR*. Web. 06 Aug 2008.

Olick, Jeffrey K. "Collective Memory. The Two Cultures", *Sociological Theory* 17.3 (1999): 333–348. *JSTOR*. Web. 03 Jan 2007.

Štaif, Jiří. "Peníze a společnost: Několik sond do vztahů mezi tradiční mentalitou a společenskou modernizací v české národní společnosti 19. století." *Finanční elity v českých zemích (Československu) 19. a 20. století.* Ed. Eduard Kubů, and Jiří Šouša. Praha: Dokořán, 2008. 18-55.

Wood, Nathaniel D. "Urban self-identification in East Central Europe before the Great War: Cracow's Popular Press and the Case of Cracow". *East Central Europe/ L'Europe du Centre* 33.1-2 (2006): 1-31.

This study was supported by the project *The Emergence of Popular Culture in the Czech Lands* (GP13-39799P) of the Czech Science Foundation (GAČR).

WHEN ARCHITECTURE WAS THE WORLD

Nicole De Togni

Polytechnic University of Turin, Turin/ Italy
nicole.detogni@gmail.com

ABSTRACT

This article explores the role of specialized magazines in theoretically and critically shaping the architectural discourse about Milan, Italy, during the Nineteen-fifties and -sixties. As the economic and productive capital of the country, and during a time of great urbanization and intense disciplinary debate, the city was expected to demonstrate the potential of brand new planning instruments. At the end of the Nineteen-fifties, following the controversial General Plan of 1953, Milan was instead generally described as polarized between a few knowledgeable professionals giving shape to responsible Italian architecture and consciously misused planning instruments together with real estate speculation.

Dieser Artikel erforscht die Rolle der auf Architektur-Diskurs spezialisierten Magazinen in der theoretischen und kritischen Konturierung Mailands während der 1950er- und -60er-Jahre. Als Wirtschaftsmetropole des Landes erwartete man von der Stadt, dass sie das Potential der brandneuen Planungsinstrumente demonstrierte, und das zu einem Zeitpunkt starker Urbanisierung und intensiver Diskussion zwischen den Disziplinen. Zu Ende der Fünfzigerjahre, im Gefolge des kontrovers aufgenommenen General-Plans von 1953, stellte sich Mailand aber stattdessen als polarisiert dar zwischen einigen wenigen bekannten Fachleuten, die die Attribute verantwortungsbewusster italienischer Architektur verkörperten, und dem bewusst missbräuchlichen Einsatz von Planungsinstrumenten und einer blühenden Immobilienspekulation.

In Italy the second postwar period was characterized by an intense debate about the tasks, limits and tools of architecture and planning, which shaped the reconstruction and expansion of cities, and influenced their representation and perception at a period of much urbanization and change in the concept of urbanity.

Between 1945 and the Mid-Fifties Italy underwent a process of reconstruction that played a very significant role in the post-war affirmation of ideologies, practices and models in architecture and town planning. With over three million rooms lost during the conflict, the housing sector and the real estate market became fundamental in national development, responding to the demand of both housing a growing urban population and employment for unqualified workers.[1]

During the post-war shortage of investments and resources, professional desire for a reconstruction based on quality was strong, and references to transforming "ideal" architecture into realities were not infrequent.[2] Unfortunately, high expectations meant that after a few years there was disappointment with the lack of results.[3]

In the first decade after the end of the war Milan grew by thirty per cent and 150,000 to 200,000 rooms[4] were rebuilt. As the Italian economic and industrial capital it was the first major city to approve a General Plan according to the new National Planning Law[5] of 1942: "a historic occasion, not only for the planning of Milan but for the entirety of Italian planning"[6].

Eight years passed from the first competition organized in 1945 by CLN (the National Liberation Committee) to the final approval, along with the outstanding proposal of "Piano AR"[7], the Reconstruction Plan of 1948, and over 700 remarks on the publication of the General Plan; mostly oriented towards restoring pre-war conditions for public duties and private rights. A progressive differentiation arose between the initial enthusiastic programmatic positions of a combative group of Milanese architects and municipal incubation, final proposals and everyday management[8]. In this polarization the idea of a missed opportunity and of failed reconstruction gained critical popularity, becoming the consolidated historiographical framework of post-war Milan.

Architecture and planning magazines had a key role in defining, strengthening and diffusing this critical disciplinary approach during the Fifties and Sixties, shaping the long-lasting historiographical perspective which was evoked in the main essays published in the Seventies and Eighties. They cross-referenced arguments on planning instruments with the debate on the role and qualities of professionals, building up a complex picture and becoming the signature style of the city.

In 1955 "Urbanistica"[9] briefly introduced the new General Plan of Milan to promote its critical discussion in the light of its significance in the evolution of Italian planning during the proceedings of the fifth National Congress of Planning dedicated to municipal plans [10]. Piero Bottoni discusses the fundamental criteria of the plan, the phases of its conception and actuation, the relation with new normative and planning instruments, and its originality from both a technical and juridical point of view in his report[11]. Although clearly acknowledging its value he underlines the role of private interests and lack in legislation in the Plan, opening a crucial debate on the role and relevance of politics, economy and bureaucracy.

The following year a double monographic issue[12] was dedicated to the cause in collaboration with municipal administrators, providing an introduction on the urban development of the city from the Nineteenth century and a core part about the gestation of the Plan and its realization between 1953 and 1956, with the related cartography and legislation as attachments. The opening contributions by Giovanni Astengo and Luigi Piccinato[13] highlight the positive aspects of active and continuous planning, made possible through executive and detailed plans to compensate the punitive results of the complex elaboration.

On the pages of "Casabella"[14] post-war Milanese urban planning is at first discussed in relation with architectural language and single buildings. In "Alcuni problemi di linguaggio nella recente edilizia Milanese"[15] [Some recent problems of language in the construction industry in Milan] Silvano Tintori selects some works for their ideological and demonstrative aspects, introducing the idea of a small group of enlightened professionals with ethical intentions facing the pressure of real estate speculation. To strengthen the concept he uses very short profiles of the buildings, providing a long series of significant cases over a few pages, in opposition with the traditional presentation of projects through a complete set of pictures, sections and plans.

In the Sixties the debate on the problems of architectural language gave place to wider urban and planning topics. In 1961 Virgilio Vercelloni gave a complete overview of Milanese planning with his twenty-page-long article "Milano 1861-1961: un secolo di occasioni mancate nello sviluppo della città"[16] [Milan 1861-1961: a century of missed opportunities in the development of the city], as in the previous monographic issue of "Urbanistica". In this case, however, the focus was on all the ignored chances to promote the progress of the city, with particular attention to the positive qualities of the preliminary proposals for the post-war General Plan, which were clearly betrayed by speculation on land value and conscious misuse of planning instruments.

A few years later "Controspazio"[17] proposed a series of articles summarizing this thematic and consolidating the historiographical point of view.

In "L'occhio vuole la sua parte: l'edilizia milanese fra la quantità e la qualità"[18] [Appearance matters: Milanese buildings between quantity and quality], and in particular in its first part "Per una critica della condizione architettonica" [For a critique of the condition of architecture] Paolo Portoghesi suggested that quality architecture is likely to be localized in the periphery because of the lower municipal control, while speculation is changing the appearance of the historical centre with the excuse of reconstruction. It is also said that rare good professionals are used as instruments to increase the value of land, being at the same time killers and victims of the market-led renewal. In the second part of the article "L'autoritratto di una classe dirigente: Milano 1860-1970" [Self-portrayal of the ruling class: Milan 1860-1970] Vercelloni frames the negative results of reconstruction as logical consequences of a series of missed opportunities in public planning and private commissions, and of an uncultured and socially irresponsible ruling class. A set of profiles of quality buildings is then provided, together with general comments on their authors, as alternatives to the resulting desolation of misused planning instruments, speculation and incompetence.

In the following issue of the magazine Vercelloni completes the picture with his article "In attesa della città dei servizi, alla ricerca del manufatto credibile"[19] [Waiting for the city of services, searching for a plausible product]. Drawing attention to the periphery, also in the selection of case studies presented through profiles, the author underlines how young architects excluded from projects in the city centre can express their qualities there. Unfortunately, they are forced into very small areas, limiting the impact of their work on the general urban fabric, which is compromised of speculation and blind public policies, regardless of their use for the renewal of the urban scene.

In 1973 Luciano Patetta summarized the discourse again on the pages of "Controspazio". "Alcune opere recenti del professionismo milanese"[20] [Recent works of Milanese professionals] proposes more than twenty projects by enlightened architects sharing handcraft accuracy and civil commitment in a discouraging milieu of speculation and blind planning; much worse than the one discussed more than ten years before by Vercelloni in "Casabella"[21]; when at least quality in the urban fabric was still seen possible.

Patetta and Vercelloni also wrote in the monographic issue[22] of "Casabella" dedicated to plans and projects for Milan for the occasion of the "Variante Generale" in 1979. The first[23] defends the architectural and planning culture of the Thirties against the common opinion of cultural underdevelopment in comparison with the European context, highlighting the original contribution of Italian rationalism in architectural language and the conception of planning instruments. The latter[24] discusses the transition from the General

Plan of 1953 and the Seventies' Inter-Municipal Plan, and underlines the distance between ideal projects and realities which seem to be a permanent part of the story of Milanese planning.

Just after the end of the Second World War Milan was expected to show and realize the potential of the brand new planning instruments, hosting talented professionals in the different fields related to reconstruction (architects, planners, designers, engineers, constructors, and technicians), and to be open to modern influences and progressive social forces. In actual fact, already by the Mid-Fifties, the main features of Milanese architecture and urbanization seemed to be the misuse of planning instruments and the constraints of the profession under the pressure of real estate speculation and private interests.

Architecture and planning magazines had a significant role in determining such a reception. They were theoretically and critically shaping the discourse; emphasizing single valuable creations facing a discouraging milieu, and embodying the geographic specificity of Milan in a polarized situation in which buildings by a small number of knowledgeable professionals materialized the features of the responsible Italian architecture. This was in sharp contrast to the clear failures both in the conception and application of the new General Plan, sacrificing historical heritage and modern influences to speculation.

In this case some of the most representative and influential Italian specialized magazines were fundamental instruments not only in the diffusion but also in the very organisation of architectural culture, being able to build a persuasive and long lasting historiographical framework during two decades. In a sociopolitical and disciplinary situation that was increasingly sensitive to the power of communication. They shaped a picture mirrored in specialized texts of the Nineteen-Seventies and -Eighties which have their roots in these articles and in general public perception.

NOTES

[1] Among others, Piccinato G., *A Brief History of Italian Town Planning after 1945*, in "The Town Planning Review" 3, 2010, pp. 237-259.

[2] See for example Rogers E. N., *Casa reale e casa ideale*, in "Domus" 209, 1946, p. 2: "Casa reale e casa ideale debbono essere, nei programmi della ricostruzione, due momenti dello stesso problema: proprio perché siamo poveri non possiamo sprecare neppure un mattone e quel poco che facciamo bisogna che contribuisca a trasformare l'ideale in realtà".

[3] See for example Bottoni P., *Il punto sull'architettura*, in "Comunità" 3, 1949, p. 35: "Il punto sull'architettura ci dice che le speranze riposte della ricostruzione del dopoguerra sono mi-

seramente fallite [...] la ricostruzione, basata su scopi speculativi, ha ripetuto, ingigantendoli, tutti gli errori delle architetture precedenti".

4 The oscillation, shared by many sources, is due to the difficulties in distinguishing interventions of reconstruction, modifications and new buildings, also in relation to municipal surveys on war damage, as clarified in Tortoreto E., *La mancata "difesa di Milano" dal 1945 al 1950: considerazioni sulle linee politiche della ricostruzione edilizia*, in "Storia urbana" 1, 1977, pp. 97-99.

5 Law n. 1150, 17 August 1942. Published on "Gazzetta Ufficiale" 244, 16 October 1942. In line with international culture, it extended the master plan to the entire municipal territory, considering the use of more detailed plans to punctually define development of inter-municipal plans to connect the city with its surroundings, proposing a sequence of plans at different scales to coherently manage the land use.

6 "Il 30 maggio 1953 segna una data storica, non solo per l'urbanistica milanese, ma anche per tutta l'urbanistica italiana. È stato approvato in quel giorno il primo piano regolatore di una grande città italiana in forza della legge del 1942": Bottoni P., *I concetti fondamentali del nuovo Piano regolatore*, in "Urbanistica" 15-16, 1955, p. 197. All translations from Italian are by the author.

7 The plan "Architetti Riuniti" is considered the most interesting submission for the competition of 1945, gathering the main rationalist architects operating in Milan. Albini F., Belgiojoso L., Bottoni P., Cerutti E., Gardella I., Mucchi G., Palanti G., Peressutti E., Pucci M., Rogers E. N., *La descrizione del piano*, in "Costruzioni-Casabella" 194, 1946, pp. 4-18.

8 Zucconi G., *Strategie urbane, tra impulsi ideali e necessità amministrative: il caso di Milano dopo il 1945,* in Bonifazio P., Pace S., Rosso M., Scrivano P. (Eds.), *Tra guerra e pace. Società, cultura e architettura nel secondo dopoguerra*, Franco Angeli, Milano 1998, pp. 262-272.

9 Founded in 1932 by the regional Piedmont Section of the National Institute of Urban Planning, "Urbanistica" became the national official Journal of the Institute in 1934. In the post-war period, it housed the process of disciplinary definition, proposing a coherent setting of strategies, planning techniques and graphic codes. Under the direction of Giovanni Astengo, from 1953 to 1976, it strongly criticized immediate post-war urban planning because of the poor cultural, practical and scientific results.

10 *Milano: il nuovo Piano regolatore*, in "Urbanistica" 15-16, 1955, pp. 196-206. Reports by Ludovico Barbiano di Belgiojoso, Piero Bottoni, Amos Edallo and Domenico Rodella.

11 Bottoni P., *I concetti fondamentali del nuovo Piano regolatore*, in "Urbanistica" 15-16, 1955, pp. 200-201.

12 "Urbanistica" 18-19, 1956. Monographic issue dedicated to the General Plan of Milan.

13 Astengo G., *Presentazione*, p. 3 and Piccinato L., *Guardare Milano*, pp. 5-8, in "Urbanistica" 18-19, 1956.

14 "Casabella" is an architecture magazine founded in Milan in 1928. Several adjustments of the name, up to the mid Sixties, highlighted its shifting focus. Under the direction of Ernesto Nathan Rogers, from 1954 to 1965, it was named "Casabella Continuità", with reference to the symbolic value in the cultural and professional fields of the rebirth of the magazine after the interruption of the war. Rogers focused on the issues of tradition, architectural language and relation with the urban fabric, to move towards broader topics at urban and territorial scales in the Sixties.

15 Tintori S., *Alcuni problemi di linguaggio nella recente edilizia milanese*, in "Casabella Continuità" 222, 1958, pp. 34-42.

[16] Vercelloni V., *Milano 1861-1961: un secolo di occasioni mancate nello sviluppo della città*, in "Casabella Continuità" 253, 1961, pp. 28-41.

[17] "Controspazio" is a monthly magazine founded in Milan in 1969 by Paolo Portoghesi, who was the dean of the Architecture Faculty of Politecnico at that time and headed the periodical until 1981. At the end of the Sixties it entered the architecture and planning debate with the aim of redefining the profile of the discipline, widening the sphere of interest and documenting both production and research in an intense cultural and theoretical effort.

[18] Portoghesi P., Vercelloni V., *L'occhio vuole la sua parte: l'edilizia milanese fra la quantità e la qualità*, in "Controspazio" 2-3, 1969, pp. 6-21. Including Portoghesi P., *Per una critica della condizione architettonica*", pp. 7-10 and Vercelloni V., *L'autoritratto di una classe dirigente: Milano 1860-1970*, pp. 11-17.

[19] Vercelloni V., *In attesa della città dei servizi, alla ricerca del manufatto credibile*, in "Controspazio" 4-5, 1969, pp. 10-25.

[20] Patetta L., *Alcune opere recenti del professionismo milanese*, in "Controspazio" 1, June 1973, pp. 67-98.

[21] See note 16.

[22] "Casabella" 451-452, 1979. Monographic issue dedicated to "Milan: city plan projects".

[23] Patetta L., *Cultura urbanistica e architettonica nella Milano degli anni '30*, in "Casabella" 451-452, 1979, pp. 45-50.

[24] Vercelloni V., *Dal Piano del '53 al Piano intercomunale*, in "Casabella" 451-452, 1979, pp. 52-55.

Rear Matter

THE EDITORS

Veronika Bernard (PhD) is an Associate Professor (Privatdozentin) with the Department of German language and literature at the University of Innsbruck/ Austria and a member of the research area Cultural Encounters – Cultural Conflicts and the research platform CenT (Cultural Encounters and Transfer). She has been the director of the project *Breaking the Stereotype. Oriental and Occidental Stereotypes in the Course of Time* (www.breaking-the-stereotype2009-2010.over-blog.org) and is one of the two directors of the IMAGES project (www.images-1.over-blog.org). Veronika Bernard is a member of the advisory board of the online journal *CINEJ Cinema Journal* (http://cinej.pitt.edu).

She has earned her postdoctoral qualification (Habilitation) in German literature by her postdoctoral thesis *Das emotionale Moment der Veränderung. Stadt als Dichtung* (The Emotional Momentum of Change – The Fictionalized City). Her PhD thesis is about the Orient in 19th century Austrian travel writings.

Her research interests are: cultural encounters in movies; migrant literature (German-Turkish authors); European views and stereotyping of the Orient; the city in literature.

She is one of the editors of the book *IMAGES (II) – Images of the Poor* (Münster/ Vienna/ Berlin/ New York: LIT Verlag 2013), the online and print publication *IMAGES (I) – Films as Spaces of Cultural Encounters* (online: *CINEJ Special Issue 1/* 2011, Pittsburgh 2011; print: Innsbruck 2011), and of *Breaking the Stereotype. From Orient and Occident to a Mutual Understanding of Images* (Innsbruck: iup 2011). For further publications see www.v-b-publikationen.over-blog.de.

Hatice Övgü Tüzün (PhD) is Assistant Professor at the Department of American Culture and Literature at Bahçeşehir University, Istanbul/ Turkey. She received her BA in English Language and Literature from Istanbul University, and her MA and PhD from the University of Kent (UK). She has published articles on multiculturalism, modern literature, travel writing and the political novel. Her recent interests include posthumanism and emotions in literature.

THE CONTRIBUTORS

Burcu Alkan (PHD) is a staff member at the Department of American Culture and Literature at Bahçeşehir University, Istanbul/ Turkey. She received her PhD from the University of Manchester in 2009. Her research interests include “City and Literature,” “Urban Cultural Studies,” and “The City as an Artistic and Intellectual Sphere” examined in comparative perspective.

Fulya Anılır is an Undergraduate student at Yeni Yüzyıl University (Istanbul/ Turkey), Department of Anthropology. She has worked with Z. Nilüfer Nahya.

Farzaneh Bahrami is a PhD candidate in Architecture and Sciences of the City at the Swiss Federal Institute of Technology (EPFL). She holds a Master degree from *Domus* Academy, Milan/ Italy, Urban Design Institute, and from the Department of Fine arts at the University of Tehran.

Gönül Bakay is an Associate Professor at Bahçeşehir University, Istanbul/ Turkey, holding a PhD in 18th century English novel. She has published many articles both in Turkey and abroad.

Souad Baghli-Berbar is Assistant lecturer at the Department of Foreign Languages, University of Tlemcen/ Algeria. She is writing a Doctoral dissertation provisionally titled “Outward Voyages, Inner Journeys: Exploring the Anglo-American Travel Novel to 1950”. Her interests include Orientalism and travel literature.

Daniele Campobenedetto is an architect and a PhD student of the history of architecture at Paris Est University and Polytechnic University of Turin, where he is a teaching assistant. His research interests: relationship between architectural and planning theories, and between images and real urban transformations. He works as a designer with different architectural studios in Turin and Paris.

Giovanni Comoglio is a Turin-Paris based architect and PhD student in History of Architecture and Urbanism at the Polytechnic University of Turin. He has been doing research on the interaction between space and society, focusing on Paris and Shanghai.

Nerma Cridge currently teaches in the History and Theory department at the Architectural Association in London, where she completed her PhD in 2011. Her research interests are: relationship between architectural drawing, image and building, and 'post-socialist' urban constructs.

Nicole De Togni is a MArch and a PhD student of the History of Architecture and Town Planning at the Polytechnic University of Turin (Italy). She is a teaching assistant at the Polytechnic University of Milan. She is co-founder and member of the architectural collective WABI (www.wabiweb.it). Her research focuses on the reconstruction of Milan in the 1940s-1960s.

Massimiliano Gaudiosi (PhD) is a Lecturer of Film Induced Tourism at the University Suor Orsola Benincasa (Naples). He got the PhD in Comparative Studies with a thesis on the image of Naples in film. His research interests include: theory and film analysis, film/ memory relations and the cinematic representation of the landscape. He is an associate editor of the online independent Film Journal "Cinemascope. Independent Film Journal" (www.cinemascope.it).

Shaida Ghomashchi is a Tehran based artist and researcher, and a Post-graduate in Urban Studies (Bauhaus Dessau, Germany 2011). She holds an M. A. in photography and visual design (NABA – Nuova Accademia Di Belle Arti, Milano/ Italy 2008) and a B.A. in photography (Art University of Tehran 2005).

Magdalena Łukasiuk (PhD) is Assistant Professor at the Institute of Applied Social Sciences, University of Warsaw (Poland). She is the author of many scientific articles and two books. Her research fields include sociology of architecture and the city, sociology of dwelling and processes of internal migration.

Jakub Machek completed his PhD thesis in social history at the Charles University in Prague. He is a researcher and lecturer at Charles University in Prague and the Metropolitan University Prague. He is interested in Czech popular culture between the 19th century and current. He is a founding member of the Centre for the Study of Popular Culture.

Nicolas Marqué is a PhD candidate at the University of Toulouse II. His research interests include: urban history, geo-history, history of Toulouse, and geographical information systems.

Sandra C. S. Marques (PhD) is a Post-doctoral researcher at the Centre for Research in Anthropology at the University of Lisbon, Portugal. She works on images, representations and identities in West Bengal, India, since 2004. Her recent publications are: "Depicting 'the Other' in Award-winning Movies: A Perspective on the Motion Pictures *Slumdog Millionaire* and *The Hurt Locker*", and *Popular & Visual Culture: Design, Circulation and Consumption,* Cambridge Scholars Publ. (Forthcoming 2013).

Z. Nilüfer Nahya (PhD) is an Assistant Professor at Erciyes University (Kayseri/ Turkey). She received her M.A. and her PhD in Ethnology from Ankara University; the latter with her dissertation "Image and Othering in the Context of European Union: In a Group of Ankara University and Middle East Technical University Students". She has conducted several social anthropological research projects on religion, food culture, and tourism.

Anna Notaro (PhD) is Programme Leader and Lecturer in Contemporary Media Theory at Duncan of Jordanstone College of Art & Design, University of Dundee (UK). Her publications include numerous articles in the field of urban/ visual culture, the blogosphere, issues of authorship, storytelling, cinema and new technology and the Electronic Book City Sites: Chicago and New York, 1870s to 1930s (available at http://artsweb.bham.ac.uk/citysites/). For more about her research and teaching interests visit her personal home page: www.notarofam.com/annawork

Mladen Stilinovic is a Brussels-based independent researcher and architect. He graduated as an engineer-architect at the UKIM in Skopje and as a Master of Human Settlements at the KU Leuven. His research interests are in Military Urbanism and Cartographic Exploration.

Lisa Maria Teichmann is currently an MA student in Leiden University´s program of Middle Eastern Studies/ Turkish Studies track. She holds a BA degree in Oriental Studies (specialization in Turkish Studies) from the University of Vienna (Austria).

Peter Volgger (PhD) has studied Philosophy, Architecture and Art History at the University of Innsbruck (Innsbruck/ Austria). Since 2003 he has been working as a freelance architect. He finished his dissertation in 2012 and recently joined the Institute of Architectural Theory at the University of Innsbruck as a teacher and researcher. His research focuses on trans-urban phenomena. Volgger works independently and collectively with the ‘Asmara-Group’ on the preparation and developing of the World Heritage in Eritrea.